WALTHER RATHENAU
AND THE
WEIMAR REPUBLIC

DAVID FELIX

WALTHER RATHENAU AND THE WEIMAR REPUBLIC

THE POLITICS OF REPARATIONS

The Johns Hopkins Press
Baltimore and London

To Georgette

The Johns Hopkins Press, Baltimore, Maryland 21218
The Johns Hopkins Press Ltd., London

Library of Congress Catalog Card Number 76-132338   *7- //- 77*
ISBN 0-8018-1175-9

Frontispiece from Harry Kessler, *Walther Rathenau: Sein Leben und sein Werk* (Berlin: Klemm, 1928), p. 128.

Contents

070874

Acknowledgments

I have had important help from the beginning. Rudolph Binion communicated a spirit of humane scholarship and provided the early direction for this project. Jacques Barzun and Lionel Trilling subjected my first expressions to a testing, and fixed standards of taste and clarity that I shall never forget. Jacques Barzun also assisted me substantially in other ways. Fritz Stern and Istvan Deak gave valuable information and research suggestions, and Fritz Stern later let me increase my debt by advising on the organization of my findings. Peter Gay counseled me, and Christoph M. Kimmich joined in helping me through the final stages. Both men have contributed hard work and professional judgment of the highest order. I have been received as a member of the community of scholars.

Peter B. Kenen, Gerhard Bry, and Karl Erich Born have read the chapter on the economics of reparations and corrected errors and disproportions. Gerald Freund suggested extremely useful materials and ideas for my account of the Genoa Conference. I have also received advice personally and by letter from Sir John Wheeler-Bennett and A. J. Nicholls, Gerald D. Feldman, Klemens von Klemperer, Hans W. Gatzke, Henry Cord Meyer, Peter Loewenberg, and Hans W. Rathenau.

My research in Europe was helped by Veronica Andreae Schnewlin and Ursula von Mangoldt, Margarete and Gert von Eynern, Ernst Laubach, Hermann Wiesler, Fritz Dickmann, Kurt Sontheimer, Hans Rothfels, Edwin Redslob, Günter Milich, and Étienne Weill-Raynal.

I am grateful to all these archives and other institutions and their staffs for the research assistance they gave me: New York Public Library, Butler Library of Columbia University, and Leo Baeck Institute, New York City; National Archives, Washington, D.C.; Hauptarchiv, Landesarchiv, Historische Kommission zu Berlin, and the libraries of the Free University of Berlin, the Otto-Suhr-Institut, and the Allgemeine Elektricitäts-Gesellschaft, all in West Berlin; the library of Humboldt-Universität, East Berlin; Bundesarchiv, Coblenz; Politisches Archiv, Auswärtiges Amt, Bonn; Deutsches Industrie-Institut, Frankfurt; Institut für Zeitgeschichte, Munich; Deutsches Zentralarchiv, Potsdam; Bibliothèque nationale, Paris; and the Public Record Office, Beaverbrook Library, and Wiener Library, London. Wolfgang Mommsen of the Bundesarchiv, Gerhart Enders of the Deutsches Zentralarchiv, and Monika Richarz of the Historische Kommission have been especially kind.

Frederick Burckhardt of the American Council of Learned Societies, supporting my research project with a grant, demonstrated a faith in it that provided a maximum of encouragement. Previously, a Ford Foundation fellowship had been most helpful.

An undertaking of this kind, whatever objective realities it refers to, is personal before and after everything else. My friends, Harry Kressing and Marilyn Gayes, studied me as well as my project and contributed counsel of every dimension. I cannot do justice to all that my wife, Georgette, gave to me and my work. She also labored with me on a professional level as an editor. That she typed the manuscript as well suggests how inadequate any expression of recognition can be.

Abbreviations

Major Archives

BA   Bundesarchiv (Federal Archives), Coblenz, West Germany

PA,AA Politisches Archiv, Auswärtiges Amt (Political Archives, Foreign Ministry), Bonn, West Germany

DZA   Deutsches Zentralarchiv (German Central Archives), Potsdam, East Germany

NA   National Archives, Washington, D.C.

PRO   Public Record Office, London, England

Important Archival Series

Ausführung   Reichskanzlei: Ausführung des Friedensvertrags (Federal Chancellery: Implementation of the Peace Treaty), Bundesarchiv

Kabinettsprotokolle   Reichskanzlei: Kabinettsprotokolle (Federal Chancellery: Cabinet Minutes), Bundesarchiv

Cabinet Conclusions Cabinet: Conclusions of the Meetings of the Cabinet, Public Record Office

Important Document Series

Stenographische Berichte Germany. *Reichstag: Stenographische Berichte* (*Reichstag: Minutes*)

Annales   France. *Assemblée nationale. Annales. Chambre des députés* (*Minutes: Chamber of Deputies*)

Documents on BFP   *Documents on British Foreign Policy 1919–1939,* 1st ser.

A Reparation Chronology

1918

February 11   Speech of President Woodrow Wilson calling for a peace with "no annexations, no contributions, no punitive damages."

November 7   Pre-Armistice Agreement: Germans accept American definition of reparations as "compensation . . . for all damage done to civilian population of the Allies . . . ."

1919

January 18–
June 28   Paris Peace Conference; Versailles Treaty.

1920

January 10   Versailles Treaty goes into effect; Reparation Commission begins operations.

July 5–16   Spa Conference: decisions on reparation coal deliveries and German military forces.

1921

January 24–29   Paris Conference: under Paris Proposals, Allied leaders order Germany to pay cash reparations in series of specified rising payments—or make an acceptable counter-offer.

March 1–7	(First) London Conference: Allies reject German payments plan, occupy Düsseldorf and other Rhine localities.
March 21	Plebiscite in Upper Silesia.
April 30– May 5	Second London Conference; London Ultimatum-London Payments Plan: Allies order Germany to pay reparations at an annual rate of 3 billion gold marks.
May 10	Joseph Wirth's new government, carrying out policy of fulfillment, accepts London Ultimatum.
May 29	Walther Rathenau named Reconstruction Minister.
June 12–13	Rathenau and Loucheur begin negotiations on Wiesbaden Agreement.
October 6	Wiesbaden Agreement signed.
October 20	Partition of Upper Silesia announced.
October 22	Resignation of Wirth government.
October 26	Reconstitution of Wirth government—without Rathenau.
November 28	Rathenau in London to negotiate reparation relief.

1922

January 6–12	Cannes Conference; fall of Briand.
January 13	Germany granted temporary reparation relief.
January 31	Rathenau named Foreign Minister.
March 31	Germany granted provisional moratorium in reparation debt.
April 10– May 19	Genoa Conference.
April 16	Rapallo Treaty signed.
May 31	Confirmation of provisional moratorium.
June 1–10	Meeting of Loan Committee in Paris.
June 24	The assassination.
August 31	Germany granted disguised moratorium on all cash payments.
November 14	Fall of Wirth government.

AFTERWARD

1923

January 11	Beginning of Ruhr occupation.
November 15	End of German inflation.

1924

August 16	Dawes Plan in force.

1930

May 17   Young Plan in force.

1931

July 1   Reparation and war debt payments suspended under Hoover
              Moratorium.

1932

June 16–   Lausanne Conference permits permanent disappearance of
July 9   reparations.

WALTER RATHENAU
AND THE
WEIMAR REPUBLIC

Introduction:
The Background of Reparations

The idea of reparations was one of several new ideas which Wood-row Wilson was introducing to the Old World. Reparations would be appropriate to international justice under the League of Nations. Germany was not to be compelled to pay an indemnity, as defeated nations had conventionally done. On February 11, 1918, the American President had demanded a peace with "no annexations, no contributions, no punitive damages."[1] This followed logically from the Fourteen Points, the war aims he had announced in his important address to Congress a month earlier, on January 8. Germany would simply provide restitution for the damage done to the civilian population—reparations.

It took more than three years to determine the character and magnitude of reparations. The Germans were not told what they would have to pay until May 5, 1921.

In 1918 the Allies had immediately begun to resist Wilson's ideas. On the surface the issue was simple: a generous peace that would break the endless chain of nationalistic rancor or a severe

---

[1] Quoted in Philip M. Burnett, *Reparation at the Paris Peace Conference* (1940), 1: 359. The two-volume work is a carefully edited collection of all the important documents relating to reparations.

1

peace that would force the enemy to provide full compensation for all the war costs.

Allied resistance took the form of efforts to restore the older conception of an indemnity. The United States proceeded to define reparations more precisely in a note to Germany on November 5, 1918: "Compensation will be made by Germany for all damage done to the civilian population of the Allies and their property by the aggression of Germany by land, by sea, and from the air."[2] The note, with the German reply accepting this definition, constituted the Pre-Armistice Agreement. Premier Georges Clemenceau of France at first tried to work with the American idea, only stipulating that compensation be mentioned in the armistice terms. At a meeting of the Supreme War Council on November 2 he had said: "All I am asking is simply the addition of three words, '*réparation des dommages*,' without other commentary."[3] That phrase appeared in Article XIX of the Armistice Convention.[4] On December 2–3, Clemenceau and Prime Minister David Lloyd George, meeting in London, tried to advance beyond that point and called for a commission to determine the "reparation and indemnity" to be paid by the enemy. This was communicated to Colonel Edward M. House, Wilson's chief adviser in the peace negotiations, who had been absent from the conference only because of illness. House cabled Wilson on December 5 that he took exception to the word "indemnity,"[5] and Wilson supported him in demanding its exclusion from any agreement among the Allies. Clemenceau and Lloyd George yielded[6] and the word was never used. "Reparations" would have to serve.

The struggle over reparations continued at the Paris Peace Conference, which occupied the first half of 1919. One of the five major committees of the conference, the Committee on the Reparation of Damages, immediately disagreed within itself. At a meeting on February 13, 1919, the young John Foster Dulles, legal adviser to the American delegation, summarized and insisted upon the limits which the 1918 agreements had set to reparations. Over the next

[2] Quoted in Burnett, *Reparation*, 1: 411.
[3] *Ibid.*, p. 399.
[4] *Ibid.*, p. 414.
[5] Cable, with House's summary of the Clemenceau-Lloyd George decision, quoted in Burnett, *Reparation*, 1: 431.
[6] Ferdinand Czernin, *Versailles 1919* (1964), pp. 50–51.

two days, William M. Hughes, the Australian Prime Minister, and Louis-Lucien Klotz, the French Minister of Finances, tried to override such formal considerations by appealing, as they said, to simple justice. Germany, they argued, stood condemned for having started the war and should pay for all the war costs. It was the indemnity redivivus.

Behind the Allied demands were four years of war suffering. The speculator Bernard M. Baruch, who was one of the financial experts of the American delegation, wrote a book, *The Making of the Reparation and Economic Sections of the Treaty*, in which he tried to defend the decisions taken. "The aroused primitive passions of nations and of men had only in a small measure subsided," he wrote. "Within a few hours' travel from the Peace Conference were the battlefields upon which lay 900,000 dead Englishmen and colonials [and] 1,300,000 dead Frenchmen. . . ."[7] He did not list the dead Germans. In Versailles, a mob stoned the German delegation when it arrived in May. Back in December, 1918, Lloyd George's wartime coalition had exploited war hatreds and won a great victory in the "khaki election." Lloyd George himself had originally suggested milder treatment of Germany, but his associates got roaring approval from the electorate when they threw off such restraints. A Labor member of the cabinet said, "Hang the Kaiser," and a Conservative, "Squeeze the lemon until you can hear the pips squeak."[8] On December 9, five days before the election, Lloyd George tried to keep a qualification: "If you take the whole of Germany's wealth away . . . —there would not be enough. . . ." But, he went on, "The British Imperial Committee . . . think that the assets of Germany . . . have been underestimated in the past. . . . We have an absolute right to demand the whole cost of the war from Germany. . . ."[9]

The American members of the Committee on the Reparation of Damages were seriously hampered in maintaining their position against the currents of European public opinion. Wilson returned to the United States in mid-February to deal with domestic politics, and he would be gone a full month during the peace conference.

[7] Bernard M. Baruch, *The Making of the Reparation and Economic Sections of the Treaty* (1920), p. 1.

[8] George N. Barnes and Sir Eric Geddes, respectively, quoted in Czernin, *Versailles*, p. 52.

[9] Quoted in Czernin, *Versailles*, p. 52.

Another difficulty was a half-hidden flaw in the American logic. Baruch first lied about it tactfully in his book: "Of course, it was generally recognized that the indebtedness of the Allies to the United States had no relation to Germany's reparation obligations to the Allies."[10] A few pages later he admitted: "To have insisted . . . that creditors of Germany should waive in part their . . . claims . . . might have encouraged the effort to reopen the whole question of Interallied indebtedness. . . ."[11] The Americans, while demanding the repayment of their war loans in full, were telling the Allies to take less than the full amount they could claim as reparation. But if American reasoning was questionable, American power was not.

Wilson communicated firmness by cable. At a meeting of the Supreme Allied Council on March 10 Clemenceau and Lloyd George once again stopped trying to claim compensation for all the war costs. But nothing had been settled.

The disagreement in the Committee on the Reparation of Damages had led to the creation of the ad hoc Special Secret Committee, with a member each from the United States, Great Britain, and France. The French member was Louis Loucheur, Under Secretary of State for Military Production and Industrial Reconstruction, and Clemenceau's chief reparation expert. In its confidential report, delivered to the Allied leaders on March 15, the secret committee recommended that the German liability be set at 120 billion gold marks.[12] Loucheur, who knew his politics as well as his economics, had been publicly demanding as much as 800 billion gold marks, and he told his British and American colleagues that he would deny he had concurred if the report were made known.[13] It was not made known. The Allied leaders kept it secret and rejected it. "Neither Lloyd George nor Clemenceau could afford to think in terms as small as those presented by [the committee]."[14] Wilson, who had

[10] *The Reparation and Economic Sections of the Treaty*, pp. 52–53.

[11] *Ibid.*, p. 71.

[12] Report in Burnett, *Reparation*, 1: 689–92. I.e., $30 billion. It would be appropriate here to note that the official gold mark-dollar rate was 4.2 to 1. The literature on reparations, however, has rounded this off to 4 to 1 for simplicity's sake. From this point the reader might make the mental operation of dividing by four to get the dollar equivalent for the gold-mark figures—remembering that dollars and gold marks at the time had proportional values different from the dollars and marks of today in relation to individual and national income. Chapter II examines the economic and financial questions.

[13] Paul Birdsall, *Versailles Twenty Years After* (1941), pp. 246–47.

[14] Czernin, *Versailles*, p. 291.

landed back in France on March 13, resisted accepting a figure above 120 billion gold marks, while the French wanted 188 billion gold marks, and the British, for the moment, had gone beyond the French and were demanding 220 billion gold marks.[15] The disagreement got worse when reparations became entangled with another issue. On March 28, Clemenceau, having failed to move Wilson on France's conception of a detached Rhineland under her tutelage, called him pro-German and walked out of the conference room.

Now Wilson retreated. In the midst of the quarrel his delegation proposed that a reparation commission be created to fix the amount of the debt. The negotiations over the new agency permitted him to make concessions without humiliating himself too obviously, and he yielded to the principle of compensation for war-service pensions and separation allowances. Specifically favorable to the British interest, since England could claim very little under the heading of actual damage to its civilians, it meant doubling the reparation liability, as the calculations of the Reparation Commission later demonstrated. In effect, it meant restoring the indemnity after all. On April 8 the Allied leaders composed their differences.

The Allies arrived at their compromise through one of the most tortuous sweeps of reasoning in the history of diplomacy. John Foster Dulles, given the prescription by Lloyd George, drafted a double statement that satisfied, if only verbally, both Allied demands and economic realities.[16] The statement became Articles 231 and 232 of the Versailles Treaty, the first asserting Germany's total liability and the second limiting it in practice by referring to her actual resources. But Article 231 contained the famous war-guilt

[15] Document 196 in Burnett, *Reparation*, 1: 718–19. Many other figures were mentioned in the negotiations. The French indicated a willingness to consider less than their maximum demand, and Lloyd George was alternating between those advisers calling for much and those who would be satisfied with a minimum in reparations. The point was that the Allies could not agree on any figure.

[16] Accounts, including a statement Dulles made to Burnett in 1937, in Burnett, *Reparation*, 1: 66–70, and in Birdsall, *Versailles*, pp. 241–63. At one stage Lloyd George said: "We must in some way justify the action of the British and French governments, which find themselves obliged to accept less than full war costs. We must make it thoroughly clear that, if we do not exact it, it is not because it would be unjust to claim it, but because it would be impossible to obtain it" (Birdsall, *Versailles*, p. 253). On this subject Burnett also gives the minutes of two meetings of Clemenceau, Lloyd George, and experts on April 5, 1919, in 1: 825–29 and 831–35.

clause. It said: "The Allied and Associated Governments affirm, and Germany accepts, the responsibility of Germany and her Allies for causing all the loss and damage to which the Allied and Associated Governments and their nationals have been subjected as a consequence of a war imposed upon them by the aggression of Germany and her Allies." Article 232 admitted: "The Allied and Associated Governments recognize that the resources of Germany are not adequate, after taking into account permanent diminutions of such resources which will result from other provisions of the present Treaty, to make complete reparation for all such loss and damage." It was natural for the Germans not to pause until Article 232 might calm their outraged sense of justice and exacerbated apprehensions. Made guilty of all the war horrors, they reacted accordingly. The Germans resisted for several weeks, changing their government in the process, but they were helpless. They signed the Versailles Treaty on June 28, formally countersigning the statement of guilt, the reparation liability, and many other unhappy things as well.

Wilson left Paris on June 28. He went home to fight for his treaty, especially for the League of Nations, trusting that the league would make up for all the defects of the treaty. In September he made thirty-seven speeches in twenty-nine cities in twenty-two days. He collapsed in Pueblo, Colorado, on September 25 and suffered a stroke on October 2. His opponents in the Senate had made so many reservations to the treaty that Wilson opposed ratification in that form, and the treaty arrangements were twice voted down, on November 19 and, in 1920, on March 19. Within all the confusions of its domestic politics, it was clear that the United States had withdrawn from its international responsibilities.

The Allies attempted to reestablish their world as best they could. Their leaders proposed to mollify public opinion and ease their financial situation by getting as much money as possible out of the Germans. A series of conferences followed. The Reparation Commission commenced its work as soon as the Versailles Treaty went into effect on January 10, 1920, but the issue was too important to be left to it. In 1920 the commission's most important work was to calculate Germany's liability, which it fixed at 226.4 billion gold marks ($56.6 billion).[17] At the beginning of 1920 Clemenceau

[17] Étienne Weill-Raynal, *Les réparations allemandes et la France* (1938), 1: 323.

fell permanently from power as a consequence of French disillusion-ment and political intrigue. Alexandre Millerand succeeded him as Premier and met with Lloyd George at San Remo, on the Italian Riviera, from April 18 to 26, 1920. They discussed various uncom-pleted parts of the peace settlement, including the reduction of the German military forces, and Millerand suggested that Germany be-gin paying 3 billion gold marks annually, pending a definitive repa-ration plan. The two leaders recognized, however, that many diffi-culties were in the way of even a provisional agreement—Allied public opinion wanted more and Germany's postwar conditions promised less—and they set their experts to working on various plans and schedules. The leaders continued their talks at Hythe, on the English coast near Dover, on May 15–16 and June 20. On June 21–22, after crossing over to Boulogne, they agreed at least on how they would divide reparations when they got them: 52 per-cent for France and 22 percent for Great Britain. A meeting of experts in Brussels on July 2–3 filled in some of the details. With all of the major questions still unresolved, Millerand and Lloyd George then invited the Germans to Spa, in Belgium. The Spa Conference, meeting from July 5 to 16, 1920, ranged over many matters and regularized a delivery schedule for coal, which Germany was ship-ping to the Allies as part of her reparation payments. Allied public opinion, however, wanted cash, and the leaders and all their experts had still failed to show how they could procure cash. A later meet-ing of experts, beginning in Brussels in December and resuming in Paris in early January, produced another version of Millerand's pro-posal for annual payments of 3 billion gold marks, but nothing came of it. Millerand himself had become President of France, glad to dissociate himself from the political dangers of the reparation issue. His successor as Premier was driven from office on January 12, 1921. The French had become increasingly angry and dissatis-fied about reparations. The British were losing their war hatred, but the reparation matter still irritated them. In 1921 both peoples, whatever the differences between them, demanded action on reparations.

CHAPTER I

To Fulfill:
The Reparation Issue Crystallizes

The German delegation arrived at Victoria Station in London on Monday, February 28, 1921, and an article in *The Times* said that there had been no demonstration, the police having taken the precaution of barring the public from the platform.[1] While the report was conventionally accurate, its emphasis on a routine police action had the effect of an untruth. The British public was annoyed about reparations but not to the point of feeling strongly about the Germans, and a demonstration had not been expected. *The Times*, lately reverting to the old idioms of the war, was nevertheless rolling out expressions of anger at Germany and a corresponding amity for France which pretended to be echoes of the general will. An important purpose of the London Conference, beginning the next day, was to repair the damage in the Anglo-French association. With that accomplished, the Allies might hope to resolve the problem of obtaining reparations and generally enforcing the fulfillment of the Versailles Treaty.

The official purpose of the London Conference was to hear how the Germans themselves proposed to accomplish fulfillment. There were four major subjects under the general heading of fulfillment: trial of German nationals charged with war crimes and punishment

[1] March 1, 1921.

of the guilty, surrender of territory, reduction of German arms, and payment of reparations. The first two, although unpleasant, were more easily contained within the limits of normal politics. The latter two kept the security and solvency of the Weimar Republic under permanent threat. The interaction among all four complicated matters further. The loss of territory (and population), for example, made financial fulfillment more difficult, Germany having given up six and one-half million people and 13 percent of her land area. Ever since they first had seen the Versailles Treaty the Germans found the idea of fulfilling everything demanded in its 440 articles and numerous annexes not only impossible but also incomprehensible.

Of the first two demands, one was in the process of vanishing. The Versailles Treaty had provided for the extradition of persons accused of war crimes, who would be tried by Allied military courts. In early 1920 the Allies transmitted a list of 895 names to Germany. The list included, besides lesser individuals, virtually the whole of the nation's wartime leadership. The Allied governments, however, permitted the German government to refuse the demand,[2] a fact suggesting that they were not serious about it. Instead, they would let Germany try her own nationals for "crimes against the laws of civilized warfare." In 1921, at the London Conference, the Allies were calling for more dispatch in beginning the trials. If the original Allied demand had been neither practical nor credible, the eventual German response was insulting. The first trial, under the compelling force of the London Conference, began within three months, on May 23, 1921. The Allies drew up a number of detailed indictments and sent them to Germany. A total of twelve cases was tried. The only meaningful punishment was ordered when two submarine officers were found guilty of sinking a lifeboat filled with wounded and nurses. The officers were sentenced to four years in prison, but escaped a few weeks after the trial. They were never found. By 1922 the Allies had ceased to send indictments to Germany.[3]

Territorial fulfillment was a straightforward question in most instances. Much of it was already settled. France, Great Britain, and

[2] The Kaiser, in exile in The Netherlands, was also on the list. The Dutch government refused to give him up.
[3] Erich Eyck, *A History of the Weimar Republic* (1962), 1: 187–88.

the other Allies had simply taken Alsace and Lorraine, the German colonies, and other areas. Germany's eastern frontier, however, was another matter. Germany refused to accept the permanence of the loss of Danzig and the Polish Corridor, and she was resisting the threatened loss of much of Upper Silesia. A plebiscite would be held in the province on March 21, three weeks after the beginning of the London Conference. As specified by Article 88 of the Versailles Treaty, the plebiscite would give the Polish inhabitants the opportunity to vote for the union of their communities with Poland.[4] Of course the Germans would try to prevent the provisions of that article from being carried out.

The Versailles Treaty permitted Germany to maintain an army of 100,000 officers and men. Composed of infantry and cavalry, and lacking military aircraft and tanks, it would be confined to the mission of assuring internal security. There would be a small navy and no air force. The early history of the Weimar Republic demonstated to the satisfaction of the Allies, however, that the German military forces, still much greater than foreseen in the treaty, could not keep internal order. Furthermore, they were needed to maintain a power equilibrium in Europe. In 1919 the presence of German irregulars in the Baltic States held back Soviet expansion. Accordingly, the Allies had conspired with Germany to violate the treaty, but she naturally took license to commit more violations than the Allies had in mind. At the Spa Conference of July, 1920, they began to demand more compliance. General Hans von Seeckt, the head of the Reichswehr, innocently came to Spa to request that the limit be raised to 200,000, but Germany was told to bring her forces down to 100,000 by January 1, 1921.[5] Seeckt thereupon made substantial reductions, enough to satisfy the Allies. In London they were complaining of many other violations, the Interallied Military Control Commission, under the direction of an able and energetic French general, having provided strong evidence.[6] In

---

[4] The article provided for a plebiscite to be held by an international commission: "The result of the vote will be determined by communes according to the majority of votes in each commune." Thereupon the commission would recommend "the line which ought to be adopted as the frontier of Germany in Upper Silesia." Article 88 continued: "In this recommendation regard will be paid to the wishes of the inhabitants as shown by the vote, and to the geographical conditions of the locality."

[5] Michael Salewski, *Entwaffnung und Militärkontrolle in Deutschland 1919–1927* (1966), p. 124.

[6] Salewski, *Entwaffnung und Militärkontrolle*, pp. 135–44 and *passim*.

point of fact, the Reichswehr comprised much the lesser part of the nation's military effectives. Germany was making use of the irregular Free Corps (*Freikorps*), Civil Guards (*Einwohnerwehr*), Military Guards (*Zeitfreiwillige*), and Home Defense units (*Selbstschutz*). She could also deploy formations of the federal Security Police (*Sicherheitspolizei*), who were quartered in barracks under military discipline. In mid-1920, according to the data provided by Seeckt himself, Germany had a million men under arms.[7] Shortly after the London Conference opened, a Bavarian government spokesman admitted in the Landtag that there were 320,000 Civil Guards in that province alone.[8] At London the Allies wanted Germany to promise to keep her violations of the treaty within stricter bounds.

Reparations remained the most difficult problem within the general problem of fulfillment. The many conferences since 1919 had only emphasized the difficulties, which were further complicated by the withdrawal of the unhelpful United States and the presence of the baleful Soviet Union. Most governments, moreover, were changing under the wear of time and all the postwar problems. The Reparation Commission, a temporizing substitute for Allied unity in 1919, could not act as long as the disunity persisted. The Allies might claim that the Spa Conference, besides confirming the decision on the German army's size, had made an approach, at least, to a reparation solution. At Spa they had ordered Germany to begin delivering two million tons of coal a month. In order to get the coal the Allies had to lend Germany 360 million gold marks to buy food for her undernourished miners. Germany probably gained more advantage from this part of the Spa Agreement than the Allies did. In any case, except for such special items as coal, they wanted cash and not goods. In early 1921, however, the victorious powers began a new train of logic. At the Paris Conference on January 24–29 they had agreed on a reparation figure and a payments program, and the completion of the logic required a German response in London.

The Paris Agreement had come after a cooperative struggle between the French and English leaders. Aristide Briand had come

---

[7] *Documents on British Foreign Policy 1919–1939* (hereafter cited as *Documents on BFP*), 1st ser. (1958–68), 8: 458. Lloyd George pointed this out at Spa.

[8] John W. Wheeler-Bennett and Hugh Latimer, *Information on the Reparation Settlement* (1930), p. 179.

to power on January 16, succeeding a premier—himself Millerand's successor—who had been unfairly blamed for failing to get anything done on reparations. The British public and Parliament also wanted something of all that had been promised, but they were sensitive, in view of the nation's important trade with Germany, to the dangers of German bankruptcy. Briand had not dared to admit Germany's economic problems. David Lloyd George first had to check a French demand for 12 billion gold marks a year, amounting to a third of the German national income, but the two leaders worked out their differences and, on the last day of the conference, as *The Times* reported, "all went merrily as a wedding bell."[9] The plan, called the Paris Proposals, ordered the Germans to pay 2 billion gold marks for two years, 3 billion for the next three years, 4 billion for three years, 5 billion for three years, and 6 billion for 31 years, plus 12 percent of export revenue. Without the export percentage, this would have totaled 226 billion gold marks over the 42-year payment period. Calculated on an export percentage at the 1921 level of German trade, the present value of the debt would be about 124 billion gold marks.[10] The French, while still insisting upon a large sum, had relented somewhat. The change in the French attitude was more important than the specific payments demanded under the Paris Proposals. No responsible leader took the sums seriously. In the international game they were counters with no financial meaning at all, whatever exegeses the experts might spin out. The figures appeased Allied public opinion for the moment. Meanwhile, the Germans, if they did not like the Paris Proposals, were responsible for suggesting a plan the Allies would find acceptable.

The Germans had discounted the Paris Proposals and were still appalled. Rudolf Havenstein, president of the Reichsbank, said that the maximum payment could not be more than 1 billion gold marks a year, and only under special conditions.[11] The cabinet

9 January 31, 1921.

10 According to the calculation of Étienne Weill-Raynal, a member of the French section of the Reparation Commission, in *Les réparations allemandes et la France*, 1: 607. Weill-Raynal's three-volume work is the most detailed study of reparations, but it concentrates on the French interest. In the case of a sum of payments remitted over time, "present value" is what the total is worth in the present, i.e., stripped of (compound) interest. Thus with interest at an annual rate of 4 percent, $96.15 would be the present value of $100 due a year in the future, while $100 due in two years would have a present value of $92.45.

11 Cabinet meeting of March 6, 1921. Reichskanzlei: Kabinettsprotokolle

council meeting of January 31 began with negation and halted there. Chancellor Konstantin Fehrenbach, an elderly Centrist, said nothing worth recording. President Friedrich Ebert hoped that the United States could be brought into the negotiations. Finance Minister Joseph Wirth vaguely suggested that various international meetings should be called "in order to prepare the atmosphere for London." Foreign Minister Walter Simons offered to resign, but the cabinet majority, lacking an alternative to Simons' lack of hope or ideas, persuaded him to stay.[12] Without hope or new ideas the government then prepared a counterproposal.

Simons was the leader of the German delegation at the London Conference. He was a "good German," although *The Times* made a point of recalling that he had been a member of the Brest-Litovsk delegation which had imposed a ferocious treaty on the Russians. A lawyer by training, Simons had entered the Foreign Ministry as an expert on questions of foreign property. He had been Commissioner General of the German delegation at the Peace Conference. In his letters to his wife from Versailles he showed himself to be a man of classic German sensibility and innocence, persistently suffering shock at Allied harshness and responding like a middle-aged Werther to the songbirds and blossoming fruit trees of the spring of 1919.[13]

On Tuesday morning, March 1, 1921, Walter Simons faced Lloyd George and Aristide Briand in Lancaster House: "The German government . . . is not in the position to accept the Paris Proposals in the form in which they have been transmitted to it."[14] While arguing that the terms were "economically and financially unfulfillable," Simons attempted to appease the Allied leaders: "Germany, however, is prepared to accept the principle of the

---

(hereafter cited as Kabinettsprotokolle), Bundesarchiv, Coblenz, ser. R43I, vol. 1365.

[12] Kabinettsprotokolle, BA, R43I/1363.

[13] Published in Alma Luckau, *The German Delegation at the Paris Peace Conference* (1941), pp. 114–34. Simons was a lay Lutheran leader and would later become President of the German Supreme Court. As head of the Supreme Court he became Acting President of Germany for two months in 1925, from the death of Friedrich Ebert to the accession of Field Marshal Paul von Hindenburg.

[14] The full Simons statement and other German material, minutes, and the like on the London Conference are in a pamphlet published by Reichsdruckerei, *Sammlung von Aktenstücken über die Verhandlungen auf der Konferenz zu London vom 1. März bis 7 März 1921* (1921); a copy is in Reichskanzlei: Ausführung des Friedensvertrags (hereafter cited as Ausführung), BA, R43I/28. The statement is also in *Documents on BFP*, 15: 218–22; British material on the whole conference, pp. 216–32.

Paris Proposals. . . ." Only a German sophist would have seen the connection between the Allied principle and German implementation. Simons first translated the total debt of 226 billion gold marks spread over 42 years into the debt's present value, but he arbitrarily applied an interest rate of 8 percent instead of a normal 5 or 6 percent. Stripped of future compound interest, the reparation debt was thus reduced from 226 to 53 billion gold marks. He rounded this off to 50 billion gold marks. Then he argued that Allied confiscations had already taken 20 billion, although the Reparation Commission later credited Germany with just 8 billion. Whatever the true value, his supporting figures were obviously exaggerated and incredible. He even claimed compensation for the fleet which the Germans themselves had sunk at Scapa Flow so that it could not fall into Allied hands. Simons had arrived at a debt of 30 billion gold marks which Germany was prepared to pay. But he made conditions: Germany would be permitted to obtain a loan of 8 billion gold marks from the Allied money markets, would be able to export freely, and would retain Upper Silesia. Since 1919 the Germans had been astounded at the Allied efforts to make the peace a real victory, Wilsonian idealism to the contrary, and by the magnitude of the claims they were expected to pay as an earnest of that victory. Now the Allies could begin to be surprised at the German refusal to admit defeat, and the mediocrity—the risibility—of the compensation the Germans were willing to make.

The Allied leaders reacted with signs of rising impatience and distress. Stiff and overcorrect, Simons harmed his case even further by the lawyerlike way in which he tried to protect his client, the German nation. He was making a public presentation of many points which usually go into the fine print of contracts.[15] The scene was recalled by Carl Bergmann, State Secretary in the Finance Ministry and Germany's chief day-to-day reparation negotiator, in a book published in 1926. Bergmann, a banker by training, also thought his country could pay no more than the Simons counteroffer, but he was critical about "this way of putting it—a presentation that pounded the wretched 30 billions into the heads of the

---

[15] Otto Gessler, Minister of Defense from 1920–28, in his *Reichswehrpolitik in der Weimarer Zeit* (1958): "[Simons] looked upon foreign policy essentially as a series of cases in law" (p. 395).

delegates and melted down the reparation figure more and more.
. . .">[16] Bergmann, who was also head of Germany's *Kriegslasten-kommission,* the War Payments (literally *Burdens*) Office in Paris,
was functionally more sensitive to the reactions of the Allies than
to those of his own country. At the moment Germany would not
let Simons go further, no matter how he put it. The gap between
Allies and Germans was much too wide. Simons, who had already
spoken in too much detail, proposed to let a Foreign Ministry
official go into even more detail. Lloyd George stopped him. *The
Times* commented on the Simons speech: "It is not easy to speak
with patience of this combination of business cunning, chicane,
and sheer impudence." With his overpowering skill Lloyd George
had put himself at the head of British public opinion. Almost all
of the British press supported him, and the Labor Party *Herald,*
critical but incapable of suggesting an alternative policy, found
the Simons statement a typical expression of "German jingoes."[17]
The reparation problem was too huge and complex to be solved
by any formal arrangement, but the London Conference could at
least provide the materials for a metaphor of a solution. For Lloyd
George the point was to have the Germans admit defeat once
again.

At the next meeting, on Thursday, March 3, Lloyd George told
Simons: "The counterproposals mock the Treaty." He reiterated
the thesis of German guilt, pathetically reviewed the devastation in
France, insisted that "we regard a free, a contented and a prosperous Germany as essential to civilization,"—and showed his power.
If Germany did not either accept the Paris Proposals or produce a
suitable counteroffer by Monday, March 7, the Allies would impose economic sanctions (i.e., retain customs receipts in occupied
German areas) and occupy Düsseldorf, Duisburg, and Duisburg's
riverside suburb, Ruhrort.[18]

For the next four days Simons sought a compromise between
the irreconcilable positions of Allied and German public opinion.
In private talks with Allied leaders he suggested two other payment plans, but these still assumed that a loan would be granted
and all of Upper Silesia would be retained.

[16] Carl Bergmann, *Der Weg der Reparationen* (1926), p. 89.
[17] Issue of March 8, copy in Reichskanzlei: England, BA, R43I/59.
[18] Statement in *Documents on BFP*, 15: 258–65.

In Berlin Chancellor Fehrenbach conferred with the party leaders on Friday, March 4, and was assured of the cooperation of all the important parties, from the Social Democrats to the Nationalists. The Nationalist Karl Helfferich, a bitter enemy of the Weimar Republic, asked how his group could best support the government.[19] On Sunday, March 6, Fehrenbach, after two cabinet meetings and another conference with party leaders, cabled an order to Simons to withdraw his plans in favor of one developed in Berlin[20] by Walther Rathenau, an industrialist and writer on social and economic problems. Rathenau proposed that Germany take over the Allied war debt to the United States—some $11 billion or 44 billion gold marks—in lieu of reparations.[21] The idea mixed a wilful disregard for the facts into its common sense. Common sense begged for a simplification of the world's indebtedness. The leadership of the Allies, however, was not willing to admit that they could get no more out of Germany than the equivalent of what they owed America. As for the United States, no one could mistake its position. Since the Peace Conference the Americans had been repeating that there was no connection between reparations and war debts. Such a connection would only confuse the simple matter of getting their money back. It was bad business to trade off a claim on the economies of the victorious Allies for a mortgage on a defeated and insolvent Germany. Rathenau, who knew America well, knew better, but he was a gourmand of combinations. Sometimes he would forget to use his keen critical sense on his own ideas. Yet the Germans were so desperate that even Helfferich, who was an economist of distinction and a future enemy of Rathenau, supported Rathenau when he explained his idea to Fehrenbach.[22] Had the Chancellor attempted to clear it with the American commissioner in Berlin, he would have gotten a flat rejection. Actually, Rathenau offered the plan himself to the commissioner a month later, and an expert in the State Department called it "politically and financially grotesque."[23] As it was,

---

[19] Minutes of meeting in Ausführung, BA, R43I/18.

[20] Copy of the cable and minutes of the two cabinet meetings and the party-leader conference, Kabinettsprotokolle, BA, R43I/1365.

[21] Copy of proposal, "Vorschlag Rathenau," in Ausführung, BA, R43I/17.

[22] At the conference with party leaders; see n. 20, above.

[23] According to a telegram from the commissioner, Ellis L. Dresel, and the expert's memorandum, both dated April 10, quoted in Dieter B. Gescher, *Die Vereinigten Staaten von Nordamerika und die Reparationen 1920–1924* (1956), pp. 60–61.

Simons told Fehrenbach in a cable on Monday, March 7—the last day of the conference—that the character of the Allied refusal of his own second proposal made it impossible to bring up the Rathenau plan.[24]

The final conference meeting confirmed all the impossibilities. Simons suggested a provisional arrangement of payments of 3 billion gold marks for five years. He did it only for form's sake, since the Allies had already rejected the idea in the course of the negotiations.[25] As uselessly, he tried to attack the great abstraction of the Versailles Treaty—the guilt of Germany—that was justifying the Allied action: "Only history will decide whether a single nation can be taken to be exclusively guilty. . . ."[26] The argument was directed to German domestic opinion and the future wisdom of the Allies, and not to the logic of the London Conference. On March 3 Lloyd George had called attention to the solipsism in the Allied logic with the innocence of a confidence man: "For the Allies, German responsibility for the war is fundamental. . . . It is the basis on which the structure of the Treaty has been erected and if that acknowledgment is repudiated or abandoned, the Treaty is destroyed."[27] Germany was not being punished by the Versailles Treaty because of war guilt; she had to be guilty because she was being punished. In the late afternoon of March 7 Lloyd George was indignant about German presumption and legal-minded about German violations of the treaty. This was the signal for sanctions to go into effect. In the early hours of the next morning Allied occupation troops in the Rhineland traveled the few miles to enter Düsseldorf, Duisburg, and Ruhrort—the Belgians from Crefeld, the British from Cologne, and the French from several other bases. The conference's metaphor of a solution was compounded with a modest amount of force. Afterward, the negotiators could resume discussions on a power basis that had been somewhat altered.

One important result of the London Conference was the strengthening of Briand's position. The French parliamentary process had mysteriously determined that his talents for compromise were best fitted to represent France's extreme demands. At the

[24] Ausführung, BA, R43I/18.
[25] *Ibid.*
[26] German minutes, Ausführung, BA, R43I/18; also in *Documents on BFP*, 15: 320 (full statement, pp. 319–24).
[27] *Documents on BFP*, 15: 258–59.

Paris Conference in January Briand had established the appearance of unity with Great Britain. On February 9 he won a vote of confidence in the Chamber of Deputies, but the figures—363 supporting votes, 104 negative votes, and 102 abstentions—indicated that the Chamber's confidence in the future would require greater success than that represented by the Paris Conference. Lloyd George's management of the London Conference gave Briand that success in March. On March 16 he swept the Chamber with him as he rendered "homage to M. Lloyd George for the beautiful, for the magnificent eloquence with which he associated the cause of justice with the cause of France. . . ."[28] The next day he won 490 affirmative votes against only 69 *nons*. It was a fine but fragile victory and Briand tried to form a hard shell of words around it. As Germany thrashed about following the London Conference Briand told the Senate on April 5 that "a firm hand will grab her by the collar" and he promised to occupy the Ruhr as well if she failed to agree to a satisfactory settlement.[29] On April 12 he repeated the threat before the Chamber of Deputies.[30] But the eloquence did not carry over the Channel.

The limits to Allied severity were traced at the Second London Conference.[31] Briand frankly and almost pitifully exposed the weakness of his position to Lloyd George at the first official meeting on April 30. French opinion was dissatisfied and André Tardieu was accusing him of letting Germany cheat on her obligations. "France proposed to occupy Essen in three days' time, and to proceed immediately with the occupation of the Ruhr," Briand said. He begged his "British friends and Allies [to] give France support in this difficult hour."[32] Lloyd George, while helping the Premier in his weak position, could also take advantage of the weakness: "Mr. Lloyd George said that, as he understood it, M. Briand said that France was prepared to undertake the task alone."[33] Lloyd George knew that that was not the case. On February 4, defending the results of the Paris Conference against Tardieu, Briand had told the Chamber:

[28] France, *Assemblée nationale: Annales: Chambre des députés*, 113: 2nd sect., 1049.
[29] France, *Assemblée nationale: Annales: Sénat*, 94: 1st sect., 636 and 636–37.
[30] *Annales: Chambre des députés*, 113: 2nd sect., 1295.
[31] *Documents on BFP*, 15: 487–587.
[32] *Ibid.*, 15: 492 and 503.
[33] *Ibid.*, 15: 503.

"It would have been a catastrophe for the country, if we had come out of it without the unqualified agreement of our Allies. . . ."[34] At the end of April in London Briand was no less aware of the need for British cooperation, and the minutes of the Second London Conference continue: "Mr. Briand dissented." Lloyd George was gracious: "He was delighted to hear that he had placed a wrong interpretation on M. Briand's words. . . ." At an informal discussion on May 1, Lloyd George set British against French public opinion: "The British government could not contemplate taking action in defiance of British public opinion." He also argued that the occupation of the Ruhr "would throw the whole of the industrial and financial interests of Great Britain into strong opposition to the Government."[35] On May 3 Briand accepted Lloyd George's formula. The Ruhr occupation would be used as a threat only: "His plan was to get immediate cash for reparation purposes rather than the occupation of the Ruhr Valley."[36]

The German government, meanwhile, as it tried to find a new basis for negotiations, had been struggling with other fulfillment and postwar problems. In March and April it was engaged in suppressing Communist risings in central Germany and the Ruhr. It was also trying to meet the situation created by the Upper Silesian plebiscite of March 21. There had been 707,605 votes for remaining with Germany and 479,359 votes for union with Poland. Germany, ignoring the reasonably clear sense of Article 88, claimed that the plebiscite confirmed her moral right to all of Upper Silesia. Poland insisted on her right to large parts of the province and trusted France to help resolve doubtful questions of detail in her favor. Both Germany and Poland were organizing military forces to influence the decision, Germany building up the Home Defense forces in Upper Silesia and drawing upon Free Corps units from Bavaria. On May 3 a Polish rising began in the eastern part of the province, and the Germans reacted vigorously. By May 18 heavy fighting was in progress. This range of problems helped defeat the efforts of the German government to develop a coherent policy on reparations.

On reparations, Simons undertook one more initiative. He tried

[34] *Annales: Chambre des députés*, 113: 1st sect., 228.
[35] *Documents on BFP*, 15: 509–10.
[36] *Ibid.*, 15: 555.

to reverse the American isolationist tendency and persuade the United States to mediate a new offer. Implicitly admitting the sophistry of his London claims, he was willing to go to 50 billion gold marks. Charles Evans Hughes, Secretary of State in Warren G. Harding's new government, discussed the offer informally with the British and French Ambassadors, and got an unequivocally negative response from both on April 28.[37] On May 3 the American Commissioner thereupon informed the Germans: "This government finds itself unable to reach the conclusion that the proposals afford a basis for discussion acceptable to the Allied governments."[38] With the Americans retreating from European problems, no other response could reasonably have been anticipated. The Fehrenbach-Simons government could only await the pleasure of the Allies.

The sense of the situation, as it unrolled from the events of January—Briand's accession to office and the Paris Conference—and March—the (First) London Conference and the economic and military sanctions—required that the Allies keep the initiative on a reparation plan. Germany's domestic politics obviated the possibility—or danger—that she would produce a new offer attractive enough to require an Allied acceptance.

The Allied leaders managed matters to give public opinion in their countries the satisfaction it had been seeking. On April 27, the Reparation Commission, preparing the ground for the Second London Conference, met in London and announced the German reparation debt in a brief communiqué. The commission put the figure at 132 billion gold marks. The total was substantially lower than the 188 billion gold marks the French had demanded in 1919, but the disappointments of the past two years made it look like a victory of French rigor over British mildness. *The Times* of May 2 treated it as such—purchased by Briand's relinquishing of the threatened Ruhr occupation. The 132 billion, as Briand could explain to his country, was really the equivalent of the 226 billion demanded at the Paris Conference. This was because the 132 billion gold marks was the present value of the debt, while the Paris figure was the total of all payments spread over 42 years, including

[37] James McN. Hester, "America and the Weimar Republic" (dissertation, 1955), pp. 279–81.
[38] Copy of note, Reichskanzlei: Vermittlung Amerikas, BA, R43I/461.

compound interest. The communiqué of the Reparation Commission had not, however, gone into detail about payment conditions. A study of the conditions would make the German reparation debt look quite different, but the Allied public, under the guidance of the communiqué, was not encouraged to undertake it. The method of payment was drawn up in the London Payments Plan, which was sent to the German government as a part of the London Ultimatum of May 5. In any case, Germany, at last, was being directed to pay.

In the London Ultimatum, the Allies, meticulously carrying out the whole logic of the Versailles Treaty, addressed themselves to all of the unimplemented aspects of fulfillment. They found Germany "in default in the fulfillment of the obligations . . . under the terms of the Versailles Treaty as regards 1. disarmament, 2. the payment due on May 1st, 1921 . . . [and] 3. the trial of the war criminals. . . ." They perfunctorily ordered compliance on disarmament and war crimes,[39] and went on to their real interest, reparations. The center of gravity of the London Ultimatum rested upon the London Payments Plan.[40]

The plan began with the announced figure of 132 billion gold marks as an evaluation of the war damage caused by Germany.[41] The damage thus evaluated was to be made good by reparations, defined as a debt of 132 billion gold marks. But then the mention of 132 billion gold marks, having done its work of public relations, began to disappear. In Article 4 of the London Payments Plan, after a complex explication of the debt arrangements, Germany was ordered to pay 2 billion gold marks plus 26 percent of her export revenue annually, a total of slightly more than 3 billion at the current export level. This was the only serious part of the London Payments Plan. The 3 billion represented a payment of 6 percent on a debt of 50 billion gold marks. In the mathematics of reparations 132 billion equals 50 billion.

The debt arrangements, drafted in Articles 2 and 3, had accomplished the transformation. The 132 billion gold marks was

---

[39] *Documents on BFP*, 15: 579–80.

[40] *Ibid.*, 15: 566–69.

[41] To which was appended a first-priority obligation for special compensation to Belgium, the great victim of the war. This amounted to 5.6 billion gold marks, the magnitude of the Belgian war debt. Theoretically, Belgium would get the 5.6 billion gold marks before the other Allies would begin to receive their share of the 132 billion gold marks.

divided into three parts, represented by three series of bonds which the German government was to give the Allies. There was no significant difference between Series A, totalling 12 billion, and Series B, 38 billion. The 50 billion gold marks of Series A and B was to carry coupons of 6 percent to cover interest of 5 percent and amortization of 1 percent. This 6 percent would approximate the 3 billion indicated in Article 4 as the annual reparation install-ment: it was impossible to have bond coupons carry a variable like 26 percent of future annual export revenue. (The avowed purpose of the Allies was to sell these bonds on the world money markets— "capitalize the reparation debt"—but the international financial community had its own opinions about their investment attractions. No serious effort was made to buy or sell the bonds.) Thus, Series A and B, comprising 50 billion of the reparation debt. Series C, the greater sum of 82 billion gold marks, was another matter. Series C carried no coupons. The Reparation Commission, as agent for the Allies, said it would issue the coupons when satisfied that Germany could pay more than the installments on the debt of 50 billion. Series C was not a debt but a vague promise of becoming one. With the London Payments Plan the Allies confessed that they had been making unrealistic demands on Germany, and the old dispute between the principles of indemnity and reparation became meaningless.

For a week following the release of the Reparation Commission communiqué, public opinion could indulge itself in fantasies about the 132 billion gold marks. On May 3 *The Times* gave the first details of the London Payments Plan, but its report was false and misleading: the 82 billion of Series C was "understood to be pay-able in one year." The next day *The Times* mentioned that Series C carried no interest, but it avoided explaining what that meant. On May 6 a skillfully confused *Times* editorial said that the no-interest provision was "a valuable concession" to Germany, but again did not explain. The Allied citizen reading his newspapers— the French press was no more helpful—was protected from the realization that the 132 billion had vanished. Retaining that figure, Allied public opinion now lost itself among the labyrinthine de-tails of the London Payments Plan.

The Allied leaders, the opposition as well as those in the govern-ment, joined in a conspiracy to believe in the 132 billion. In the

House of Commons on May 5, according to the *Times'* parliamentary reporter, "Lord Robert Cecil, Mr. Asquith, and Mr. Clynes all fell on the Prime Minister's neck in carefully adjusted embraces." In France, the most uncompromising enemies of Germany refused to see the significance of Series C and confined their criticism to lesser points. In the Chamber on May 19, André Tardieu, speaking long and bitterly, attacked Briand because 132 billion gold marks represented less than 50 percent of French war demands.[42] While this was an accurate statement, it was a remarkable way of attributing reality to the 132 billion. As a leading advocate of the hard line, Tardieu was obliged to attack any payment plan as too mild, but he had been one of the drafters of the Versailles Treaty, and to admit the full truth about the London Payments Plan would have been to admit too much of the truth about the treaty. The speech, like the other hostile comments, was a deliberate act of futility. Briand's rivals let him have another triumph. The consensus in both Allied countries accepted the London Payments Plan with relief.

Germany struggled to understand the London Payments Plan. In his book Bergmann pointed out what the Allied leaders blandly ignored—that the Plan's 50 billion equaled the 50 billion offered by Simons through the agency of the United States. It was true that the 50 billion of Simons was clouded over with unresolved questions, the conditions about export freedom and Upper Silesian integrity which the Foreign Minister dared not give up officially. These issues, however, could have been negotiated. The dramatic construction mounted by Lloyd George required that the Allied leadership retain all the initiatives. To the Allies, furthermore, the present government represented German intransigence. Germany had been given six days from May 5 to accept the London Ultimatum. Only a new government could make the German acceptance credible.

Fehrenbach resigned on May 4, and on May 10 Joseph Wirth presented his cabinet to the Reichstag. Several posts had not been filled, but the Allies did not permit more delay. The Reichstag gave Wirth an affirmative vote, and he promptly accepted the London Ultimatum. As Fehrenbach's Finance Minister, Wirth had been

[42] *Annales: Chambre des députés*, 114: 1st sect., 3–10.

author of a budget with a huge deficit. He had his doubts about Germany's capacity to pay 3 billion gold marks annually, but he also had an appreciation of other factors in Germany's situation. His greatest resource would not be German finances but German good will. The best representative of German good will was Walther Rathenau, who had tentatively articulated the principle of fulfillment at the Spa Conference almost a year before. It was typical of the contradictions of both the time and the man that Rathenau was opposing acceptance of the London Payments Plan in early May of 1921. In a speech to a private group on May 7 he said: "We would be acting dishonestly if we signed the agreement."[43] In the *Berliner Tageblatt* of May 10, the day Wirth formed his government, Rathenau published an article repeating the negative advice. Rathenau, however, had qualifications far outweighing these opinions of the moment. Because of Rathenau's initial reluctance, Wirth was unable to bring him into the government immediately. At last, on May 29, Wirth achieved his purpose. On June 1 Wirth explained the necessity of fulfillment to the Reichstag. On the next day Rathenau, in his first public appearance as Minister of Reconstruction before the Reichstag, spoke about his hopes for Germany and the world—the promise of fulfillment.[44]

[43] Rathenau, *Gesammelte Reden* (1924), p. 222.
[44] See chap. V, n. 1.

CHAPTER II

The Economics
of Reparations

Under the London Payments Plan Germany had to pay reparations at a rate of slightly more than 3 billion gold marks annually. The fulfillment terms of the Versailles Treaty also imposed other charges. Through the Clearing Operation Germany had begun to pay another half-billion gold marks to Allied citizens on claims arising from the war.[1] (Additionally, Germany owed payments on occupation costs that were accumulating at the rate of 1.5 billion gold marks annually, but the Allies, realizing they would have enough difficulty collecting the 3.5 billion gold marks in reparations and clearing payments, found it politic not to press the matter.)[2] Germany's national income was about 35 billion gold marks in 1921.[3] So stated, the problem was a simple exercise in the arith-

[1] Germany was remitting about 40 million gold marks monthly. The payments totaled 615 million gold marks by August, 1922. A reminder: the gold mark-dollar rate was 4 to 1 (see Introduction, n. 12).

[2] Weill-Raynal, *Les réparations allemandes,* 1:528–29. The Reparation Commission said Germany owed 3.6 billion gold marks to May 1, 1921. The Allies also did not insist on payment of the 360 million gold marks lent Germany under the Spa Agreement to buy food for her miners.

[3] John Maynard Keynes gave this estimate for 1922. National income in 1913, according to Karl Helfferich, who was the generally accepted authority for the prewar period, was 43 billion marks. Keynes obtained his figures by assuming a 15 percent production loss from the 1913 level. Working back from the Keynes figure, one might guess at a figure closer to 30 billion gold marks for 1921, and

metic of economics: Germany was being fined 10 percent of her income. The penalty might cause some pain, but many nations—and individuals—have suffered greater privations at some time in the course of their lives. The national income of the United States, for example, fell by nearly half from 1929 to 1933. The economic problem was not that simple. Nor was the problem simply economic.

Still considered as an abstract exercise in economics, the problem becomes more difficult when other relevant economic components are inserted. In the fiscal year just ended when Joseph Wirth took office, April 1, 1920, to March 31, 1921, the German federal budget had a general operating deficit of the equivalent of 6 billion gold marks.[4] The general operating deficit was in the process of being somewhat reduced, but it would still be very large in the period to come. The Wirth government had to deal with a crippling deficit while accepting the additional charge of 10 percent represented by the 3.5 billion gold marks in reparations and clearing payments.

The literature on reparations seldom mentions the general operating deficit. Normally, when a nation has to pay an external charge, the first question would be about the trade balance.[5] A trade surplus, like an individual's excess of income over expenses, is the usual source for such a payment. The situation was grossly abnormal, a fact few persons completely appreciated at the time.

The general operating deficit compounded within itself the

Rathenau himself used 30 billion as his estimate in a speech to the Reparations Committee of the National Economic Council on November 9, 1921. All figures, however, are gross approximations, and I prefer to use the higher estimate in order to avoid any possible exaggeration of German hardship. Keynes and Rathenau may have failed to appreciate the extent of productivity increases resulting from the war.

Most German statistical reviews avoid giving national income and many other important figures for the war and postwar periods—until 1924. The chaotic conditions, accompanied by inflation, made evaluation difficult. Moreover, national income accounting was at an earlier stage of development. I have selected f.gures which, while subject to a large margin of error, should give the approximate proportions of the German economic situation.

[4] Germany, Statistisches Amt, *Wirtschaft und Statistik* (1924), vol. 9 of bound monthly bulletin, p. 276, table. The term *general operating deficit* is mine. The table simply shows the figure of 6 billion (actually 6,053.6 million) gold marks as the difference between government income and expenditures. Income was 3,178.1 million gold marks in taxes and 97 million gold marks in other receipts; expenditures were 9,328.7 million gold marks.

[5] Or *balance of payments*. For this review the *trade balance* should suffice, since the difference between the two was both small and incalculable at this point in German economic history.

nation's various deficits, including the trade deficit. Through its budget the government was making up for all the deficits. Under the extraordinary war and postwar conditions, the German government, like the governments of the Allies, but more totally and baldly, had assumed responsibility for the economy. While the trade statistics are important, the general operating deficit remains the most relevant figure to be set beside the national income in judging Germany's situation.

For the sake of clarity it would be useful to examine the relationship between the general operating deficit and the government's budget. The government started the fiscal year on April 1 with a budget which conventionally provided for anticipated revenues and expenditures. At the end of the fiscal year the general operating deficit showed what had actually happened to revenues and expenditures. In the early postwar years of the Weimar Republic what had actually happened was radically different from what the budget promised. The budget was largely a fiction.

None of the Finance Ministers of the period were able to predict expenditures with any accuracy. Furthermore, none of them dared make realistic provision for many expenditures since this would have required a great increase in taxes. Some of the unexpected items were enormous. In the fiscal year 1920–21 the government had to pay the costs that resulted from right-wing and left-wing risings as well as arbitrary charges under the Versailles Treaty. Moreover, under its general responsibility for the economy, it was financing imports of food and other products defined as vital to the nation, giving subsidies to the states and communities, and compensating private citizens and companies for property and holdings confiscated by the Allies. Through disguised budgetary items it was also providing funds to irregular military units. The result of all this —and the trade deficit—was the global deficit figure of 6 billion gold marks.

The government financed the deficit by borrowing from the Reichsbank, the bank of issue. In effect, it borrowed from itself. It gave the bank treasury notes for the difference between income and expenditures. The Reichsbank discounted the treasury notes and in return gave marks to the government.[6] The security of the

---

[6] The nation's floating debt was represented by these treasury notes. Thus the sum of the treasury notes gave the figure for the total debt at any given time. Since the debt was measured in increasingly inflated paper marks, the figure required

paper marks was only the promise to pay of a deficit-ridden government, and the currency lost value with every new economic difficulty and political crisis. By the end of the war the paper mark had lost half of its face value, going from 4 to 8 to the dollar. A year later it was quoted at 50 to the dollar, and it was at 65 when Wirth took office. The costs of the London Payments Plan and the uncertainties caused by the Upper Silesian problem drove the rate above 300 by November, 1921.

As Finance Minister of the old cabinet, Wirth himself had drawn up the budget for the fiscal year 1921–22. This was the budget with which he had to work as Chancellor and his own Finance Minister. It had failed to close a gap of 1.7 billion gold marks between expenditures of 4.7 billion gold marks and receipts of 3 billion gold marks.[7] It had also failed to make any provision for the reparation and other payments to which Wirth had committed the government of fulfillment. The payments falling within the fiscal year would total about 2.5 billion gold marks of the 3.5 billion gold marks for a full year. Experience strongly suggested, however, that the size of the uncovered deficit was an excessively optimistic calculation.

The trade figures were also discouraging. In the calendar year 1920 there had been a modest deficit of 223.2 million gold marks

---

interpretation to make any sense, a sense that became more tenuous as the debt multiplied. On April 1, 1921, the floating debt totaled 172 billion paper marks, compared with 95 billion paper marks on April 1, 1920. It was 280 billion paper marks on April 1, 1922, and 8,442 billion paper marks on April 1, 1923. When the inflation was officially ended on November 15, 1923, the figure was 191,580,-465,422.1 *billion* paper marks.

The general operating deficit for any financial year was given by the increase in floating debt during that period. This figure, in paper marks, had to be converted to gold marks. Because of the continuing loss in value of the paper mark, the Statistisches Amt calculated the average gold mark value of each month's paper mark debt increase, and then added up the twelve monthly gold mark figures. This is how it arrived at the figure of 6,053.6 million gold marks for the financial year 1920–21. (The increase for the whole year was 77 billion paper marks, but the paper mark had fluctuated from 59 to the dollar on April 4, 1920, to 35 on May 25, to 80 on November 4, and to 63 on March 31, 1921.)

[7] The paper mark figures were 93.5 and 59 billion. Averaging out the fluctuations, financial experts calculated the gold mark equivalent at the dollar rate of 80 (i.e., 1 gold mark equals 20 paper marks). Keynes discussed the budget in his book, *A Revision of the Treaty* (1922), remarking: "Those responsible for the financial policy of Germany have a problem of incomparable difficulty in front of them. Until the reparation liability is settled reasonably, it is scarcely worth the while of any one to trouble his head about a problem which has become insoluble" (p. 105).

on imports of 3,947.2 million gold marks and exports of 3,724 million gold marks. In 1921, although exports were rising, imports were increasing much faster, and Wirth had to struggle with a current trade deficit of more than 1 billion gold marks. The nation finished the year with imports of 5,750 million gold marks against exports of 4,587.4 million gold marks.[8]

Thus the Wirth-Rathenau government, promising to pay 2.5 billion gold marks to the Allies in the fiscal year 1921–22, found deficits where it needed to have income, 1.7 billion gold marks in its budgeted finances and more than 1 billion gold marks in foreign trade.

The character of the government's task could be illustrated by making alternatively false assumptions about the two deficits. Assume, first, that trade was balanced. To eliminate the government deficit and also pay reparations the government would be obliged very nearly to double taxes and halve expenditures. Assume, next, that the budget was balanced. To pay reparations the government would have to transform a trade deficit of 1 billion gold marks into a trade surplus of 2.5 billion gold marks. These considerations are based on more false assumptions, namely *ceteris paribus*. Budget improvements would have negative effects on trade, and a trade improvement could have been purchased only at the price of new deficit items in the budget. In any case the Allies were demanding drastic changes in the German economy, and drastic changes meant unprecedented problems. As John Maynard Keynes remarked about the German trade situation on another occasion: "At a given time the economic structure of a country, in relation to the economic structures of its neighbors, permits of a certain 'natural' level of exports, and . . . arbitrarily to effect a material alteration of this level by deliberate devices is extremely difficult."[9] A comparable alteration of the budget was no easier.

The mechanism of the London Payments Plan, furthermore,

[8] Germany, Statistisches Amt, *Statistik des deutschen Reiches: Der auswärtige Handel in den Jahren 1920, 1921, und 1922* (1924), 310: sect. 1, 2, table. The 1921 export figure, again illustrating the statistical problems, is an estimate by the Statistisches Amt. More precise figures were lacking for the period of May to December because of breakdowns in reporting procedures.

[9] Keynes; Ohlin, Bertil; and Rueff, Jacques, "The German Transfer Problem," *Economic Journal* (1929), 39:6.

would cancel a large part of the positive results from an export increase. According to the plan, Germany, besides remitting the base annual figure of 2 billion gold marks, also had to pay 26 percent of her export revenues to the Allies. In 1922, with exports at 6,206.7 million gold marks, this would have increased the variable part of the reparations total from 1 billion to 1.6 billion gold marks. The penalty came in addition to another factor—normal in this case—that necessarily reduced the advantage from exports. A highly industrialized country, Germany got much of her income by transforming imported raw materials into labor-intensive products. At least a third of her imports went directly back into her exports. Additionally, other imports were necessary to keep the economy operative. These included many items, anything from mining equipment to specialized textbooks, which Germany did not produce because of the international division of labor. (Germany also had to import food; during this period food accounted for 20 percent of total import value.)[10] Thus the 26-percent payment provision and the need to expand imports would cause her to lose a large part of the advantage from an export increase. An economist could set up the problem in this way: He might imagine Wirth holding imports in 1921 to 5 billion gold marks, instead of letting them rise to 5,750 million. According to the export-percentage provision, Wirth would then have had to increase exports to more than double. By raising them above 9 billion gold marks, Wirth could pay reparations of more than 4.3 billion gold marks (2 billion plus 26 percent of 9 billion gold marks) at that export level. This assumes that Wirth could have restricted all the imports necessary to keep the economy operative (and thus indirectly serving exports) to less than 1 billion gold marks; the other import expenditures would have been the 1.25 billion gold marks for food and 3 billion gold marks for raw materials directly serving export production (i.e., one third of 9 billion gold marks). The assumption is false, and the mathematics a fantasy. If the trade situation was bad enough, the London Payments Plan made matters exquisitely more difficult for a responsible German government.

The objection might be made that the possible sources of payment have been limited to current income items. In the analogous case of an individual with a large debt, this would mean that only

[10] Germany, Statistisches Amt, *Statistik des deutschen Reiches*, pp. 5–6, table.

his salary has been taken into account, although he would normally have possessions of considerable value. His house, for instance, could be mortgaged to pay the debt. Similarly, Germany had a large resource, its national wealth of 250 billion gold marks.[11] The Allies had grave problems of their own, and it was conventional politics to make the loser pay the penalty for the war. Could Germany not use her national wealth to pay reparations?

At least three plans tried to exploit Germany's national wealth. On May 19, 1921, Robert Schmidt, the Socialist Economics Minister, submitted a memorandum calling for the confiscation of 20 percent of the value of German private property.[12] Another Schmidt conception, discussed by the cabinet on July 29, would capitalize company taxes for 40 years.[13] Still another plan, drafted later that year in the National Economic Council, proposed to borrow against German property in foreign markets.[14] But the sums promised were small. Schmidt's first idea envisioned a billion, his second, perhaps 3 billion gold marks. The National Economic Council plan anticipated 2 billion. The reason lay in the character of a national economy. Most of the German national wealth was composed of a multiple of tiny units—retail stores, dwellings, peasant holdings, and the like—which were difficult to evaluate and impossible to translate into negotiable values. This left a comparatively small proportion, represented by such choice properties as major industrial firms, that was truly negotiable. As the three plans indicated, a fraction of this fraction produced insufficient returns. Furthermore, the existence and undisturbed operation of these firms was an important present strength—indeed, the best strength of the German economy. Foreign investors, attracted by the reputation of German industry, were presently sending considerable sums into Germany in the hope of future profits. The economy, thus, was receiving returns from its industry over and beyond its current production values. Another alternative would have been to take complete possession of the leading companies. This might have produced 25 or 50 billion gold marks, but here the problem

[11] W. S. Woytinsky, *Die Welt in Zahlen* (1925), 1:198.
[12] Copy of the plan in Julius Hirsch, *Die deutsche Währungsfrage* (1924), pp. 50–69; copy of the memorandum of May 19 and of another memorandum giving more details, this latter dated June 27, both in Ausführung, BA, R43I/20.
[13] Kabinettsprotokolle, BA, R43I/1369.
[14] Copy in Ausführung, BA, R43I/26.

went beyond economics, as in the case of the exercise that would double taxes and halve expenditures, or the exercise that would double exports. The national wealth resisted extraordinary exploitation.

The problem of reparations tended everywhere to break out of the bounds of economics. At the cabinet meeting in July, Rathenau had argued that the second Schmidt plan—the tax capitalization idea—would cause political disunity and reduce the nation's productivity. It was a mildly expressed objection to a modest plan that Rathenau did not take seriously. But a large effort, whether affecting current revenues or the national wealth, would have required profound changes of structure as well as great sacrifices. It would have meant a revolution. The Allies did not want a German revolution.

The word *revolution* is not used lightly. It means violence and repression. The major economic, political, and social groups would have resented the great sacrifices demanded of them. Businessmen and employers would have tried to pass the extra costs on to the consumers and employees. The workers, for their part, would have resisted, and their resistance would have been violent. Many of them were still hungry and cold. The Independent Social Democrats and the Communists would have had the issue they were seeking. There would have been strikes, demonstrations, and other overt action. The government would have had to resort to repression. Only a police state could conceivably have given the Allies the quantities of German wealth they were demanding. The Allies, when they realized it, would find the price too high.

These were the possibilities of payment from the only two sources—current revenues and national wealth.

This view has been restricted to the problem of producing extra values. The consumption of those extra values was no less difficult. The economist R. F. Harrod speculated on what would happen: "Britain and France would be living the life of lotus eaters, with taxation low, hours of work light, their markets gone, enjoying the well-earned fruits of victory over a period of thirty or forty years. Was it not obvious that, if this were actually to happen, at the end of the period France and Britain would be totally at the mercy of Germany?"[15] Harrod might have pointed to the experience of sixteenth-century Spain with silver from the New World.

[15] *The Life of John Maynard Keynes* (1951), p. 271.

Harrod was discussing the transfer problem—the problem of transferring wealth over national frontiers. It was the transfer problem that set the final limits on Germany's efforts to pay reparations.

In Harrod's consideration of the transfer problem he was thinking of an export surplus—current revenues—as the only conceivable possibility for paying reparations. Thus he ignored Germany's national wealth as a potential source. Since this was a real question, it might be looked into before his reasoning is pursued further. The two Schmidt plans and the National Economic Council plan, all trying to exploit the national wealth, envisaged something like mortgage certificates representing that part of the private property confiscated by the German government. These certificates would have been sold on foreign exchanges to produce the money for reparation payments. Any plan would have failed at this point. Foreign businessmen would have resisted the additional competition for the investment money available to their countries. Their opposition would have forced their governments to take prohibitive or restrictive action. In any case, the mortgage certificates could not have attracted investors unless they paid premiums so large as to defeat the sense of the operation. The difficulty could have been overcome by Allied guarantees of the German paper or the solvency of the German economy itself. No Allied government would have been so incautious. On April 27, 1921, the British cabinet discussed accepting shares in German industry. It was objected that such a plan "might lead to speculation and give German industry a preference over Great Britain's" besides also giving "foreign countries an interest in German domestic affairs."[16] The question was never raised again.

Harrod was willing to imagine the Allied populations living upon the comforts provided by free German exports. He imagined it to refute it. He was illustrating the falsity of the assumption that the Allied economies would make the adjustments necessary to receive the import surplus—that is, reduce their production in the articles that Germany manufactured. The Allies would have had to match the German revolution with one of their own. Indeed, the distortions in the German economy of 1921 clearly indicated what would happen. The inflation was enabling German exporters to undersell

[16] Cabinet: Conclusions of the Meetings of the Cabinet (hereafter cited as Cabinet Conclusions), Public Record Office, London (hereafter cited as PRO), CAB 23/25.

foreign producers in their home markets.[17] Great Britain was suffering from unemployment and a trade deficit made worse by the import of cheap German goods, and its businessmen were demanding protection. During 1922 both Great Britain and the United States raised their tariffs. In France the Chamber of Commerce of Nancy, reacting to the threat of German reparation deliveries of goods, protested: "It would be useless to revive our shattered industries, if German competition would simply destroy them all over again."[18] In an interview in April, 1921, John Foster Dulles defended his advocacy of a large reparation sum at the Peace Conference two years before: "A hard-working and intelligent population of sixty million with a magnificent industrial plant can . . . perform wonders." Dulles now recognized a difficulty that transcended his logic: "But the capacity to pay is meaningless when there is no comparable capacity and will to receive."[19] The Allies were demanding reparations while refusing to permit the Germans to earn the revenues with which to pay reparations.

Many persons tried to solve the general problem of reparations with or without regard to its transfer aspect.[20] Nearly all of them used irrelevant or incomplete statistics, or words as substitutes for the ineffable figures. A typical discussion of the German deficit would urge economy but fail to give figures showing how much

[17] Inflation does not necessarily give the advantage to the exporters, but it did in the case of Germany at this time. The point was that the German currency was undervalued on the foreign exchanges. As a result, a foreigner buying cheap marks could get German goods for bargain prices.

[18] Quoted in article of October 29, 1921, issue of trade publication, *L'Usine*. The article was one of a series collected in the pamphlet, *Un danger national* (Paris, 1921), quotation on p. 70. A copy of the pamphlet is in the archives of the Wiederaufbauministerium, BA, R38/159.

[19] Published in *Neue Zürcher Zeitung*, April 27, 1921; copy in Wiederaufbauministerium, BA, R38/157.

[20] The problem-solvers included heads of governments and their experts, businessmen and trade union leaders, French nationalists and Socialists, German internationalists, the leader of a German women's organization and the German manager of an American country club, the Alsatian-Jewish publisher of a French provincial newspaper, a Bordeaux law professor, a Scottish Labor member of Parliament, an American state governor, a Krupp salesman in Budapest, members and former members of the Reparation Commission, and economists. A number of their plans were listed and analyzed in a German government memorandum. An unsigned copy, with no indication of source, is in the Ausführung file, BA, R43I/33. Many other plans are scattered throughout the government's archives as well as the whole literature on reparations. Some persons, like the country club manager and the Krupp salesman, thrust their plans directly upon the Chancellor.

could actually be saved. A typical discussion of foreign trade would demand the forcing of exports but would fail to specify the income reasonably to be expected or to admit the negative effects. An expert once employed in the French section of the Reparation Commission did use figures in a series of tables that produced substantial reparation sums. For the beginning year he got 4.1 billion gold marks by putting exports at 7.5 billion gold marks and imports at 4.4 billion gold marks, and requiring the cession of 1 billion gold marks of capital. For a later year he projected exports of 11 billion gold marks. He did not explain how this would come to pass and he admitted that he had made no provision for protectionist action by recipient countries.[21] Another idea did concede the possibility of Allied resistance to German trade. Its solution was to channel the trade to "third countries," but these were not identified, nor were figures given for their capacity to absorb additional products. In a book published in the United States in 1921, André Tardieu pointed out that Germany in 1913 had a production excess of 8.3 billion gold marks over consumption which it used for reinvestment. A sum of that size, he said, should be made available for reparations.[22] He ignored the fact that a modern economy cannot survive without continuing investment, nor did he inquire how the money would be transferred. But by 1921 most of the plans tended to make reparations disappear at least partially by means of reductions, moratoriums, and loans. Lloyd George soon was giving evidence of doubt about his London Payments Plan. Even a few French opinions indicated a willingness to settle for less, although this was often associated with the idea of compensation in the form of control of German territory or industry. In late 1922 the former president of the Reparation Commission, who was French, saw no alternative but reduction.[23] Some persons, obviously in the hope of easing the conditions, suggested another agency, the League of Nations, an international court, or an international financial commission, to determine and administer reparations. None of the plans could overcome the transfer problem.[24]

[21] Pierre Noël, *L'Allemagne et les réparations* (1924), p. 170, tables.

[22] André Tardieu, *The Truth about the Treaty* (1921), pp. 326–44.

[23] Preface by Louis Dubois to pamphlet by Frédéric Jenny, *La capacité et les moyens de payement de l'Allemagne* (1922).

[24] Actually, as Keynes pointed out, there were two transfer problems. The second one, however, never got the chance to become operative, because the

The best known private effort to solve the reparation problem was the plan given in Keynes's *Economic Consequences of the Peace*.[25] Like Rathenau, Keynes had wanted to see the cancellation of the United States war debts. There was, however, an important distinction in the character of the two proposals. Rathenau's plan was offered for serious political action at the London Conference. Keynes had resigned as British Treasury representative at the Peace Conference because he knew he could not influence immediate political action. Not obliged to suggest what might be acceptable at the moment, he chose instead to write a book that might have its effect by changing public opinion. Nevertheless, he did compromise with the political realities. At the time—he wrote the book in the autumn of 1919, "at the dead season of our fortunes"[26]—he wanted to limit cash reparations to 30 billion gold marks, after crediting Germany with 10 billion gold marks for confiscated material and property. He had little fondness for even that figure. He tried to compensate for it by advocating an international loan fund of $1 billion and also a "guarantee" fund of another billion, to be financed chiefly by the United States and Great Britain, which would directly or indirectly ease Germany's position. He also suggested that payments be adjusted to Germany's capacity to pay, as determined by a reparation commission on which neutrals and the Germans themselves would be represented.[27] The Keynes ideal solution was given two years later in a phrase in his *Revision of the Treaty*:

Allies failed to provide the conditions for solving the first one. The Keynes comments on Germany's export difficulties, quoted earlier in this chapter, were part of a general review of "The German Transfer Problem" (n. 9) at a time when a prosperous but apprehensive Germany was facing the final payments plan under the Versailles Treaty. Keynes wrote: "The expenditure of the German people must be reduced, not only by the amount of the reparation-taxes which they must pay out of their earnings, but also by a reduction in the gold-rate of earnings below what they would otherwise be. That is to say, there are two problems, and not—as those maintain who belittle the difficulties of transfer—one problem" ("German Transfer Problem," p. 4). This could be applied to the situation facing Wirth in the spring of 1921. At the time, the figures showed that he had to increase exports by 5 billion gold marks in order to achieve a trade balance and pay reparations beyond that. Keynes is saying, however, that Germany would have had to sell at a discount to undersell competition and attract new customers. Thus she would have had to deliver perhaps 6 billion gold marks of goods and services for the 5 billion gold marks of revenues she could have hoped to realize.

[25] John Maynard Keynes, *The Economic Consequences of the Peace* (1920).

[26] *Ibid.*, p. 297.

[27] General discussion in *ibid.*, chapter entitled "Remedies," pp. 252–98; loan discussion, pp. 283–88.

"The cancellation, in part or in their entirety, of . . . reparations and inter-Allied debts."[28] He preferred the unqualified cancellation. It would have solved the transfer problem by eliminating it.

Another effort to solve the transfer problem deserves attention because of its ambition and circumstances. It appeared in the book, *The Carthaginian Peace or the Economic Consequences of Mr. Keynes*.[29] The young French author, Étienne Mantoux, wrote the book in the United States during World War II and then died in action while serving with the French forces. Mantoux argued that other international transfers of wealth showed that a reparation transfer had been possible. He gave as examples the transfer of great sums among the Allies in World War I and the American use of the Lend-Lease system in World War II.[30] Both cases, however, disprove his point. The source of both transfers (after the British and French reserves were exhausted) was the American economy, with its great reserves of productive capacity. Most of the inter-Allied debts were not repaid, and the purpose of Lend-Lease was actually to eliminate money payments by Great Britain. A later French student of the problem, who also believed in Germany's capacity to pay, found the Mantoux arguments untenable. He fell back on the compounding of deliveries in kind and gold and stock transfers, but he gave no figures.[31] He had made the full circle and arrived back in 1921 with its arguments.

In view of all the difficulties, why did the Allies expend so much energy in attempting to collect reparations?

[28] P. 183. He had already called for the cancellation of the inter-Allied debts in *Economic Consequences*.

[29] Étienne Mantoux, *The Carthaginian Peace or the Economic Consequences of Mr. Keynes* (1946).

[30] *Ibid.*, pp. 117–32. On p. 132: "The Lease-Lend [*sic*] system is . . . the best possible demonstration of the insignificance of the transfer problem. . . ." Mantoux avoided another example of the transfer process which had been often mentioned. "The Franco-Prussian indemnity of 1871 led economics into a great deal of trouble because it created a precedent for German reparations after World War I when the conditions basic to the payment were altogether different" (Charles P. Kindleberger in his textbook *International Economics* [1963], p. 373). He pointed out that the French government had available to it sufficient foreign exchange to pay the indemnity of 5 billion francs (the gold equivalent of 4 billion gold marks, incomparably smaller than German World War I reparations) without difficulty.

[31] Richard Castillon, *Les réparations allemandes: Deux expériences 1919–1932, 1945–1952* (1953), pp. 71–72 and *passim*. Castillon came also to Harrod's argument: "Would these deliveries have helped the industrial revival of Germany? It is possible and even likely. But any policy requires taking risks" (p. 75).

The ultimate responsibility was American. The United States had forced the reparation policy on the Allies by demanding repayment of $11 billion in war loans. Great Britain, which had loaned out nearly $8 billion to her allies, including $2 billion to France, owed $4.3 billion to the United States; France owed $3.4 billion. The Allied statesmen did not see how they could get the money out of their war-weakened economies, which were burdened also with great internal debts. Their only resource, whether real or imaginary, was the reparation claim on Germany.

The importance of the war debts had not been clear at the opening of the Peace Conference in January, 1919. The simple violence of the feelings of the Allied populations was more important: let the Germans pay. An awareness of the economic data, however, had restrained the conference leaders. It had been politically safer not to resolve the differences, but to pass the reparation problem on to the Reparation Commission. The legal claim might be pressed when time had had a chance to alter the situation.

By 1921 the situation had indeed changed. The American position on war debts had become clearer, if the Europeans were willing to believe their eyes. The Congress, increasingly irritated at the executive's slowness in impelling the Allies to pay, was debating legislation, which it would pass in early 1922, creating a commission under its control to assure payment. The British electorate was beginning to relent on reparations. The London Conference gave its emotions a final release, and it could begin to turn away from such an unproductive issue. Becoming more realistic about reparations, the British remained hopeful about making an arrangement on the war debts. The French, with their devastated areas, had a livelier memory of the war, and a more obvious use for the reparation money. Threatened now by American claims, they had the feeling that they were being swindled and they angrily pressed their government to make the promises real. The contradictions had altered in shape but not in character and depth.

The difficulties had been worsened by a great failure in economic thinking. A world economic revolution, greatly accelerated by the war, had occurred, but few persons could appreciate its extent. The new importance of government in the economy, the development of trusts, the increased economic power of the United States, the Soviet experiment, and the huge debt and deficit figures were all expressions of it. Laymen had no equipment with which to make judgments, but the experts suffered from their training. Denying what they saw, the experts continued to apply the doctrines of classical economics. They went on recommending the expeditious payment of debts and the balancing of budgets, no matter how huge the figures were. They refused to admit the difference in kind between a national debt that was 20 percent of annual national income, compared with one that was 150 percent of income. Yet, if they were optimistic about the speed with which the debts could be reduced or eliminated, they were pessimistic about the capacity of the world to produce new wealth. They had failed to credit the great increase in industrial productivity. They did not see that the world could carry much greater debts for a much longer time without violating sound financial principles. In the name of sound financial principles the experts were recommending self-maiming.

The United States embodied the greater magnitudes of the world economic revolution. It was producing and consuming at least two-fifths of the world's industrial goods.[32] While the war had impoverished Great Britain and France, it had made the United States richer. Nevertheless, America maintained its traditional protectionist policy. With tariffs about 30 percent ad valorem, it had a trade surplus of $4 billion in 1920 and $3 billion in 1921. Great Britain had a trade deficit of $2 billion in 1920 and $1.4 billion in 1921. The German transfer problem was only part of a greater world problem. Due to American policies and the dominant deflationary bias of its economic thinking, Great Britain was enduring a high rate of unemployment, which averaged more than 10 percent from 1921 to 1939. In 1921, while trying to make decisions on reparations, the British cabinet was being increasingly distracted by the need to do something about the unemployment problem.[33] The United States, failing to appreciate its great resources, was unhappy to compare a national debt of $25.5 billion in 1919 with the $1 billion of the prewar years. Great Britain, whose national income was

[32] League of Nations, Secretariat: Economic, Financial and Transit Department, *Industrialization and Foreign Trade* (1945), p. 12, diagram no. 1, "Movement of Manufacturing Production." For 1921 the diagram shows the U.S. with 40–45 percent of world production, compared with Germany, 11 percent; United Kingdom, 10.5 percent; France, 8 percent; and Italy, 3.5 percent.

[33] Cabinet discussions on February 11, 1921, and throughout April and May, at some length on May 26, Cabinet Conclusions, PRO, CAB 23/24 and CAB 23/25. A cabinet committee and a Treasury committee thereupon studied the problem, the cabinet discussing their reports on October 6, and considering a public works plan on October 14, in *ibid.*, CAB 23/27.

a third of America's, had a national debt of $35.6 billion at the war's end. France had a national debt of $22.2 billion. After World War II the United States gave and did not demand money. Only Keynes had imagined such a policy in 1919, and he expressed it in the modest form of international loan and guarantee funds. Thrown back on their resources, the Europeans improvised with expedients and factitious solutions. The French government, for example, had not dared to reduce expenses and increase taxes enough to balance its budget, as the financially more responsible British cabinet had done. The 1921 French budget foresaw revenues of 23.1 billion francs and expenditures of 43.8 billion francs, for a deficit equivalent to $1.6 billion or 6 billion gold marks. The deficit was carried in the budget under the heading, "Recoverable Expenditures," and a League of Nations statistical reporting service explained: "The budget of recoverable expenditures is mainly covered by loans in anticipation of reparations payments."[34] The effect of the American war-debt policy pierced through the Allied economies to strike at the German economy.

The London Payments Plan established the connection. Its announced figure of 132 billion gold marks in reparations was a gesture toward the angry Allied citizen. The Allied statesmen were serious only when they got to the figure of 50 billion gold marks, the principal on which the installments were calculated. This part of the debt was only slightly more than the $11 billion war-debt total.

On January 20, 1921, when Aristide Briand introduced his new cabinet, he told the Chamber of Deputies: "If there is a question of bankruptcy . . . , if someone has to arrive at such an extremity, it would be scandalous if it were not Germany."[35] It was the most reasonable kind of insanity: let the other nation go under first. It was the only policy, even if your country was inextricably bound to the other and its fate. Your country would, at least, have the advantage of some fragments of time over the other nation. The Allies were all agreed on this, although they might quarrel about the details—and about the second bankrupt.

---

[34] League of Nations, *Memorandum on Public Finance 1921–22* (1923), pp. 45–46.

[35] Quoted in Georges Suarez, *Briand: sa vie—son oeuvre*, vol. 5, *L'artisan de la paix 1918–1923* (1941), p. 114.

CHAPTER III

The Minister
of Reconstruction

"What a dish I'll make for the little professor of 1950!"

—Rathenau in his diary, February 18, 1912.[1]

The Ministry of Reconstruction was broadly responsible for administering compensation to the Allies. This suggested reconstructing France's war-damaged areas as a part of the general reparation burden. In giving the ministry its name, the German government had taken the part for the whole because it sounded better. Germany could assume the character of a good neighbor, sacrificially setting to right in peacetime what she had regretfully harmed in the war. French industry and labor objected, however, since they wanted the reconstruction contracts and jobs. During its five years

[1] "Welches Fressen werde ich für den Privatdozenten von 1950 sein!" (*Tagebuch 1907–1922*, edited by Hartmut Pogge-von Strandmann [1967], p. 159). The editor's notes in this recent edition, identifying persons mentioned and explaining the issues, are very helpful. The original edition was published in 1930 by the Reichsdruckerei, the National Printing Office, under the guidance of Edith Andreae, Rathenau's sister. In all likelihood she carefully censored the material, as Pogge-von Strandmann suggests. We know, for example, that Rathenau's published letters were heavily edited, since they show important differences from photographic

of life the Reconstruction Ministry reconstructed nothing in France, its total physical accomplishment having been limited to erecting a score of new wooden sheds. The ministry's true function was vaguer than reconstruction or compensation. The Minister of Reconstruction was equally ambiguous.

The background of Walther Rathenau was rich in accomplishments and problems. Fifty-three years old when he entered the government, he was a member of a prominent Jewish family of Berlin.[2] His father was an unqualified industrial genius and one of the creators of modern Germany.[3] Emil Rathenau had developed a feeling for mass production as a successful manufacturer of small steam engines. He saw Edison's light bulb at a Paris exhibition in 1881 and bought the German patent rights to it. In 1883 he founded the company that became the Allgemeine Elektricitäts-Gesellschaft. By 1919 the AEG was an electrical company of world

---

reproductions of several original pages. In any case, the *Tagebuch*, whatever changes it endured, was more a collection of mnemonic notes than a diary. Most of the entries were impersonal and dealt with a scattering of business matters, the whole reflecting only irregular fragments of Rathenau's many activities. There is nothing on the years 1909, 1910, and 1919. Most useful for this study were Rathenau's detailed notes on his negotiations in London at the end of 1921, but they only emphasize how much is missing.

Rathenau's private papers disappeared during the last war. They may have been shipped to a collection point in eastern Germany which was overrun by Russian troops, according to the archivists in the Deutsches Zentralarchiv. Soviet scholars have published nothing making use of what the Rathenau papers might contain. Most of the important or relevant records in the company Rathenau headed were destroyed when its Berlin main office was annihilated in World War II. There is a collection of material called *Rathenau-Nachlass* (Private Papers) in the Bundes-archiv, but this contains only a few-score letters.

[2] The best biography is still the one by Harry Kessler, *Walther Rathenau: Sein Leben und sein Werk* (1928). A recent edition has as an appendix the reminiscence of Hans Fürstenberg, "Erinnerung an Walther Rathenau" (1963[?]). All references here are to this newer edition. An English translation was published in London in 1929. A wealthy, cultivated diplomat and aesthete, Kessler had been an acquaintance of Rathenau's and his book is sensitive and sympathetically objective in spirit. Kessler could not be entirely objective in effect, since the book was evidently inspired and its research clearly assisted by leaders of the Weimar Republic who were seeking to develop that great rarity, a republican hero. In his *Tagebücher 1918–1937* (1961), Kessler is more critical of Rathenau. In the biography, the section by Fürstenberg, whose family was closely associated with Rathenau's, provides friendly additions and corrections. Etta Federn-Kohlhaas, *Walther Rathenau: Sein Leben und Wirken* (1928), is worshipful, but gives some useful details.

[3] Accounts in Allgemeine Elektricitäts-Gesellschaft, *50 Jahre AEG: Als Manuskript Gedruckt* (1956, 1st ed. 1933[?]), and Artur Fürst, *Emil Rathenau: Der Mann und sein Werk* (1915).

importance, with 61,000 employees and 40 subsidiary firms.[4] Emil Rathenau's wife, Mathilde, was the cultivated daughter of a Frankfurt banker. She was in her own way as forceful as her husband. A bitter, melancholy, and jealous person, she was especially possessive about her elder son. When Walther was an adult he had to arrange secret meetings with his sister, Edith, who was 15 years younger and looked upon him as another parent.[5] Walther tended to take his mother's side in the marital conflicts that frequently erupted, but he knew how to protect himself against maternal excesses, withdrawing behind a wall he lowered for no one more than temporarily. Doing justice to both parents, he became an engineer with an active interest in art and ideas. When he was 25 years old Walther Rathenau listed his strengths in a letter: "My capacity to see through people and deal with them, to talk, to write, and to work up combinations." He was writing to his mother.[6]

Walther Rathenau worked in AEG subsidiaries in various parts of Germany and in other countries, and returned to Berlin in 1899 at the age of 32. He joined the *Vorstand*, the group of five or six officers who ruled the company.[7] Relations between Walther Rathenau and his father were difficult. In 1902 the young man left the AEG[8] and joined a bank, the Berliner Handelsgesellschaft, as an expert in industrial investment. The alienation had its strict limits, since the head of the bank, Carl Fürstenberg, was a close friend of Emil Rathenau's and vice-chairman of the AEG board of directors. A few months later, in January, 1903, Walther Rathenau's younger brother died. Erich Rathenau had been the father's favorite. For a period Emil Rathenau was incapacitated by grief and leaned on Walther for comfort and efficient seconding. Walther spent more and more time with the AEG, leaving the bank in 1907.

[4] *50 Jahre AEG*, p. 184; Fürst, *Emil Rathenau*, p. 36. The AEG was then—and has remained—about two-thirds of the size of Siemens und Halske, Germany's electrical pioneer and developer of the dynamo.

[5] Statement of Edith Rathenau Andreae to Kessler on November 23, 1927, Kessler, *Tagebücher*, pp. 555–58.

[6] Rathenau, *Ein preussischer Europäer: Briefe*, edited by Margarete von Eynern (1955), January 1, 1893, p. 58.

[7] *Vorstand*, for which there is no English equivalent, is the collectivity of leading company officers, i.e., what we might call a board of *officers* as compared with the board of *directors*.

[8] His father failed to support him in a difference with other company officers, according to his vague account in *Kritik der dreifachen Revolution* (first published in 1919), in *Gesammelte Schriften* (hereafter cited as *GS*), vol. 6, *Schriften aus Kriegs- und Nachkriegszeit* (1929), p. 424.

In 1912, when his father fell gravely ill of diabetes, Walther became chairman of the board of directors (*Vorsitzender des Aufsichtsrats*), formally the father's superior, since Emil remained chief executive officer (*Vorsitzender des Vorstands*). Walther Rathenau accepted more responsibility. He was also elected a director of many other companies; the total eventually exceeded one hundred. Emil Rathenau died on June 20, 1915. Felix Deutsch, his closest associate, succeeded him as chief executive officer. Walther Rathenau, continuing as chairman of the board of directors, was then elected *Präsident* (a foreign word in German and generally unknown in the nation's business). The title suggested that his position was analogous to that of a constitutional monarch, with vague powers and important representational duties. One of his most important functions was the negotiation of mergers or trust agreements. He worked amicably with Felix Deutsch.

Rathenau was developing his presence in other worlds. In 1910 he began building a villa in the Grunewald, a prosperous suburb of Berlin, where his neighbors included Gerhart Hauptmann, Fritz Kreisler and the descendants of the composer Felix Mendelssohn, the Fürstenbergs and other members of the banking and industrial community, the Ullstein publishing family and his own publisher, Samuel Fischer, and Maximilian Harden, the editor of the polemical weekly, *Die Zukunft*. A year earlier Rathenau had bought and begun to restore Schloss Freienwalde, which was some 40 miles northeast of Berlin. Chaste but exquisitely royal, it had been the country home of Queen Louise of Prussia (1776–1810). Rathenau was a great admirer of the Prussian classical style; Schloss Freienwalde had been built by Friedrich Gilly, one of its masters, and Rathenau himself tried to design the Grunewald villa in the same style. Severe but undistinguished, the villa was little different from its neighbors, except for a disproportionately narrow entrance. The interior of both residences reminded visitors of museums. When Rathenau entertained he usually had his guests to dinner in the Berlin Automobil-Klub.

Rathenau was making his way in society like the Swann of Proust, but more purposefully. He was one of the first Jews or members of the middle class to become *salonfähig*, socially acceptable, in aristocratic Berlin homes. A bachelor, Rathenau was a valuable extra man. Sensitive to women's sensibilities and a great talker in small groups, he could pour out streams of seductive ideas in his musical baritone. He was a favorite guest of Prince Bernhard von Bülow, Chancellor from 1900 to 1909, and of his Italian-born wife.[9] He also impressed the Kaiser. Wilhelm II had met Rathenau in 1901 and saw him a score of times, drawing on him for his scintillating explications of industry and economics.[10] Rathenau also endured agonizing humiliations.

With affectionate malice Prince von Bülow recalled his first meeting with Rathenau: "A very sympathetic presence. He was flawlessly dressed. He approached with a bow as flawless as his dress—in the manner of a *jeune premier* of the Théâtre Français. ... 'Your Highness,' he said in his pleasant-sounding voice, 'let me, before I am honored by the favor of being received by you, make a statement that is at the same time a confession.' He paused briefly and then, winningly: 'Your Highness, I am a Jew.' "[11] Rathenau was mounting a social triumph on a condition which he experienced as both a social *gaffe* and a sacred illness. He once wrote: "In the youth of every German Jew there is a painful moment which he remembers all of his life: when he becomes aware for the first time that he is a second-class citizen and that all the ability and accomplishment in the world cannot free him from this condition."[12] The hurt was genuine, but Rathenau was dwelling on the minor disadvantages of being a Jew, and also exaggerating them, thus confusing and diluting his tragedy. He was forgetting his fortune, and his directorships and dinner invitations.[13]

Rathenau reacted eccentrically to the problems of being Jewish. While he was in his thirties he met with Martin Buber to discuss the Chassidic movement, which appealed to his taste for mysticism,

[9] Bernhard von Bülow, *Denkwürdigkeiten* (1930), 2: 385.

[10] Rathenau, "Der Kaiser," in *GS*, vol. 6.

[11] *Denkwürdigkeiten* (1931), 3: 40.

[12] In the article, "Staat und Judentum: eine Polemik," originally published in 1911, in *GS*, 1: 188–89.

[13] His sister Edith expressed the sense of their condition better: "What do others know about this loneliness, this magical ring that separates us from the world?" she wrote in her diary. "They admire us, they depend on us, they use us, but they don't love us or understand us. We Rathenaus have always been strangers among them ..." (quoted by her daughter, Ursula [Andreae] von Mangoldt, *Auf der Schwelle zwischen Gestern und Morgen* [1963], p. 24). She was suggesting that the problem of being Jewish was complicated by the difficulties of being a Rathenau.

and he earnestly studied Hebrew.[14] He was drawn by the figure of Christ, however, and talked as if he had accepted the bulk of the Christian teachings. He refused to become a convert. He explained that he preferred to belong to a community of pure belief, an ideal which he thought Judaism approached. In any case, although conversion would have ended any formal career disability, it would have aroused withering attacks by Christians and Jews. Rathenau remained a Jew, but one who was deeply attracted to his enemies. He entertained a remarkably enthusiastic friendship with a racist publisher and even financed the distribution of his books to the troops. He wrote to a lieutenant: "Thank you for your forceful and well-argued letter. . . . I saw you before me, strong, intelligent and solid, and I liked you. . . . You . . . hate—no, disapprove of—us Jews." Rathenau invited the lieutenant to visit him.[15] His biographer remarked on Rathenau's fondness for the young, blond Nordics of the type that would murder him.[16]

In 1897 Rathenau wrote an article on the condition of the Jew in Germany. The article compounded his pain and ambition. From a small town 60 miles in the hinterland, preparing the way for his entry into Berlin, he turned his pain on his fellow Jews. Under the thinly pseudonymous anagram, "W. Hartenau," in *Die Zukunft*, he rapped for attention—"Höre [Listen] Israel!"[17] He told the Jews to stop acting like Jews. "From the first I want to make it known that I am a Jew," he wrote. He showed the Jews how they looked on Tiergartenstrasse or in a theater lobby: "Remarkable sight! In the middle of German life a strange and isolated tribe, glitteringly and ostentatiously decked out, hot-bloodedly mobile of expression. An Asiatic horde on Brandenburg sand . . . not a living part of the nation [*Volk*], but a foreign body in it." Yet how could the Jews continue to exist if they lost all of their distinctiveness? Rathenau proposed that they strive to become "Jews of German character" (*"deutsch geartete Juden"*) and "not imitation Teutons" (*"nicht imitierte Germanen"*). The problem was real; his solution was a verbal trick. The article was characteristic: Rathenau spent the rest of his literary life tactlessly discovering and magically solving real problems.

[14] Kessler, *Rathenau*, pp. 89–90n.
[15] Rathenau, *Briefe: Neue Folge* (1928), October 11, 1919, pp. 201–2.
[16] Kessler, *Rathenau*, p. 72.
[17] Published under his own name in the article collection, *Impressionen* (1902), pp. 3–20.

With his Grunewald neighbor Maximilian Harden as patron and Harden's *Die Zukunft* as platform, Rathenau developed his ideas and his public personality as a literary thinker. He wrote a number of articles for the magazine and then, seeking more solidity for his reputation, published them in two books, *Impressionen* (1902) and *Reflexionen* (1908). Both books were luxury editions, obviously financed by a wealthy amateur, *Reflexionen* in quarto with huge type and chapter headings in red ink. Rathenau expanded widely on these beginnings. The many editions and reprintings, combined with the various collections of his letters and speeches, suggest an even greater bulk to his literary production. In sum, he wrote ten works of greater length than articles, two of them books of more than 300 pages and eight shorter flights of 70 to 140 pages.[18] Many of them sold well and one of them, *Von kommenden Dingen*, became a great best-seller in 1917, going to 100,000 copies. Rathenau wrote or dictated easily, and was said to send off his first drafts without corrections.[19] A busy executive who depended on subordinates to tidy up the details, he expected the same service of his readers. The books were completely lacking in original ideas, self-indulgent, pretentious in style, and disdainful of proof as they proceeded from one arbitrary statement to the next: the sermons of a masterful moralizer who knows better. Each book was a reworking of older materials, so that all of the larger ideas could be contained in one short volume and were indeed covered in the rather long *Von kommenden Dingen*. But the writing served many more purposes than the exposition of ideas.

Rathenau was essentially a moralist, and yet all his ideas came from or through Nietzsche, the enemy of Western morality. Rathenau had begun with a contradiction that could not be resolved. He resolved it with words. His writings were complex sets of logical impossibilities. He attempted to assist the moralism by attaching unassimilable elements from the Hebrew prophets, Jesus Christ, the Romantics, and Karl Marx to the Nietzschean core. Furthermore, while setting intuition above reason, he argued with such

[18] Most of Rathenau's writings were reprinted in his collected works, the *Gesammelte Schriften*, published in Berlin, which appeared in two editions, in 1918 and in 1925–29. The 1918 edition is in five volumes; the later edition reprints those five volumes and adds one more for the writings that came afterward.

[19] According to Fürstenberg's "Erinnerung," Kessler, *Rathenau*, p. 393. Fürstenberg's father, asked about a book of Rathenau's, was reported to have said: "You know, a book like that is easier to write than read" (quoted in Friedrich Rosen, *Aus einem diplomatischen Wanderleben* [1959], 3–4: 315).

intellectual instruments as scholastic or talmudic logic, and analogies drawn from science, pseudoscience, and technology. All this made him vulnerable to annihilating rebuttal. He defended himself artfully. Admitting that he had no talent for "the persuasive art of dialectical proof," he argued: "Every clear idea carries the sign of truth or error on its forehead."[20]

If all of Rathenau's thought derives from Nietzsche, all of its Nietzschean character is reducible to the superman-slave dichotomy. Rathenau went through life drawing up various lists of positive and negative qualities associated with superman or slave. Courage and intuition were characteristics of the superman, according to Nietzsche and Rathenau; fear and calculation were the propensities of the slave. In a series of aphorisms published in 1907 Rathenau attributed to the superman "a sense for the truly important, capacity for pure admiration, trust, good will, imagination, confidence, simplicity, meditativeness, and transcendence." The slave personality was described by "the pleasure in the novel, delight in criticizing, dialectics, skepticism, pleasure in the troubles of others, the drive to outshine others, garrulity, overrefinement, and aestheticism."[21] This was the sum of Rathenau's philosophy.[22]

It was clear that Rathenau used the Nietzschean dichotomy to express his feelings about the Jew—himself. The Jew was the slave.

[20] In dedication (to Gerhart Hauptmann) of *Kritik der Zeit*, in *GS*, vol. 1.

[21] "Blick fürs Wesentliche, Bewunderung, Vertrauen, Wohlwollen, Phantasie, Selbstbewusstsein, Einfachheit, Sinnenfreude, Transzendenz"; and "Freude an der Neuigkeit, Kritiklust, Dialektik, Skeptizismus, Schadenfreude, Sucht zu glänzen, Geschwätzigkeit, Verfeinerung, Asthetizismus" ("Ungeschriebene Schriften," in *GS*, 4: 218–19).

[22] Rathenau tried to build a logical system upon Nietzsche's original dichotomy, producing a curiosity that might interest amateurs of the process of intellection. The system required that his readers accept the claim made in one sweeping sentence about nature and society. In the article, "Von Schwachheit, Furcht und Zweck" ("Weakness, Fear and Purpose"), originally published in 1904 and republished in *GS*, vol. 4, he wrote: "Instinct . . . assures us and reason demands that a regularity, indeed a polarity be discernible" (*GS*, 4: 11). In that one sentence Rathenau made several arbitrary statements about instinct and reason. (He was using reason, incidentally, although he consistently rejected its validity.) Thus he moved without explanation from regularity to polarity, as if the one necessarily followed the other. Obviously Rathenau wanted to arrive at his Nietzschean polarity. He then proceeded to find his polarity in nature in such pairings as granite and clay, and thorns and mimosa. Satisfied with these evidences, he reduced all existence to sets of static polarities or dichotomies. These natural polarities had their social analogues in courage and fear, "the polar protoelements [*sic*] in the temper of human souls" (*GS*, 4: 12). This was the sum of the logic and data serving as a base for all of Rathenau's philosophy.

Beneath all the complexities of his explications lay the simplest form of self-contempt.

Rathenau added one element to his Nietzschean derivatives. Characteristically, it contradicted the sense of Nietzsche. The new element was the soul. Rathenau had ended his first book, the brief *Kritik der Zeit*, with a six-page dithyramb to the soul.[23] He gave it his full attention in his first extended work, *Zur Mechanik des Geistes oder Vom Reich der Seele*, published the next year, in 1913.[24] Nothing that he wrote explained the subject very well. The soul seemed to be a substitute for the emotion Rathenau failed to experience. In the thinking itself the conception of the soul permitted him to avoid the small-minded demands for clarity and data; it was another stroke of verbal magic. The readers were asked to dissolve their thoughts in a contemplation of the ineffable. A mystic might well ask this of his disciples, but it was an extraordinary command from an intellectualizing businessman like Rathenau. Innocently emphasizing the monumental flaws in his views of himself, his work, and his world, Rathenau called the *Mechanik des Geistes* his "major work" ("*Hauptarbeit*") and its ideas the central element of his thought system.[25] It was his emptiest book.

Von kommenden Dingen was Rathenau's major work. It addressed itself to economic and social problems, but retained his moralism. Rathenau built his economics on Marx in approximately the same way he built his moralism on Nietzsche. (He believed that Marxism was out of date and that he had made "the only effective attempt to establish a . . . modern economic system in its place."[26]) He constructed no system. In his usual manner he delivered a series of exhortations: the right of inheritance should be limited, "the equalizing of property and income is a commandment of morality and economics,"[27] the proletariat should be better educated and

[23] *GS*, 1: 242–48.
[24] Comprising all of volume 2 of *GS*. The title might be translated as *The Mechanism of the Spirit or The Realm of the Soul*. *Geist* more frequently means *intelligence*, but it can also mean *spirit*, and Rathenau seems to have used it like a theologian approaching the third personage in the Trinity.
[25] In a letter to Gaston Raphäel, a French scholar who wrote a book on Rathenau's ideas, December 14, 1921, *Briefe* (1926), 2: 339–40.
[26] Letter to a Social Democrat, February 11, 1919, *Briefe*, 2: 121. In the book itself, Rathenau wrote: "This book strikes into the heart of dogmatic socialism" (p. 13).
[27] *GS*, 3: 140.

raised in dignity, and luxury should be sharply restricted. It was revolutionary socialism, but only at first glance. The author's call for sacrifice, furthermore, contrasted oddly with his luxurious way of life. The head of the immensely profitable AEG conceived of an economy organized around nonprofit foundations (*Stiftungen*). He had not credibly explained how they would function without self-interest, leaving them curiously unreal. Also, he defined them as autonomous,[28] although he knew that such powerful economic bodies had to be under some sort of control. The word "autonomous," promising a kind of corporative anarchism, was one more deception. Indeed, in another section of the book, where he discussed the postwar problems to be expected, Rathenau advocated strict regulation of labor and investment.[29] This was the totality of his economics and socialism. He proceeded to more moralizing. Discussing luxury, he drew up a long condemnation of the *Luxusweib*, the female buyer of luxury goods, as if she were a major factor of economic and moral evil.[30] The attack revealed much about Rathenau's relation to women. The book reduced itself to a command to economic man and woman: be good.

Von kommenden Dingen established the author as a figure of some importance in Germany's intellectual life. While the better minds and the cultural establishment smiled over him or ignored him, Rathenau won a wide audience among people who yearned to think and had half the capacity for it. He offered them a Nietzsche and a Marx made harmless. Unfriendly critics might call him the "prophet in a dinner jacket" or "Christ in evening dress."[31] Nevertheless, he gave useful values, if it was often for the worst reasons. His concern for the victims of society had strains of sincerity in it, doubtless deriving from his own conflicts and suffering. His keen executive's intelligence had located many of the problems of the period and applied the ideas of the best thinkers to them.

Besides making his large formulations, Rathenau also suggested specific action on immediate problems in his speeches, articles, letters, memoranda, and salon talk. In later years he claimed to have warned his nation against making her greatest errors. It was true.

[28] *GS*, 3: 153.
[29] *GS*, 3: 295.
[30] *GS*, 3: 198–99.
[31] Quoted in Ernst Gottlieb, *Walther Rathenau—Bibliographie* (1929), pp. 190, 182.

He forgot, however, that he had also urged Germany to make those errors, having managed to be on both sides of almost every question. He had been unhappy about the naval race with England, recognized the dangerous threat in attacking the heart of British security, and pointed out that "little acts of friendliness" were no solution. But then he had his own nonsolution: "With every year that passes the maritime ratio becomes more favorable for us, and this results in a steadying of the balance [of power]."[32] Similarly, while calculating the high costs and doubtful returns of colonies, he argued: "We need land of this earth." He suggested taking over Latin America because "the earth is neither large nor rich enough to permit the luxury of independent demicivilizations at the cost of world productivity."[33] In his depths he was horrified when the war broke out. He cried: "The world has gone mad."[34] But he also enjoyed playing at power, and in a letter of September 7, 1914, to Chancellor Theobald Bethmann-Hollweg, he advocated "the political and economic reduction of France and England" and also "important changes on the map and massive indemnities."[35] Too often, Rathenau permitted himself to be seduced by the warriors. He approved the deportation of Belgian labor to Germany. Freely offering advice to Quartermaster-General Erich von Ludendorff, he supported the establishment, in early 1917, of the semidictatorship of Field Marshall Paul von Hindenburg and Ludendorff. He disagreed with Ludendorff on the issue of unrestricted submarine warfare, however, and broke with him. He then opposed the Ludendorff request for an armistice: the civilian was more warlike than the military man at this moment. The final disagreement inspired a Rathenau article in the *Vossische Zeitung* of October 7, 1918,[36] which called for a new wave of resistance by means of an emergency draft. Rathenau had not been able to defend his sense of proportion against the disproportions of the war.

[32] From a memorandum, "Über Englands gegenwärtige Lage," written in 1908 for Prince Bülow, then Chancellor, in *GS*, 1: 153–69; quotation, p. 169. The memorandum is one of a series of writings in volume 1 under the heading "Mahnung und Warnung"—"Admonition and Warning."

[33] In an article published in 1913, "Deutsche Gefahren und neue Ziele," in *GS*, 1: 267–78; quotation, p. 272.

[34] Letter to a woman friend, end of July, 1914, in *Ein preussischer Europäer*, p. 116.

[35] Rathenau, *Politische Briefe* (1929), p. 9.

[36] "Ein dunkler Tag," reprinted in *GS*, vol. 6.

The thinking, the writing, and the advising were the means to power. "Rathenau's drive was the will to power," the most important woman in his life after his mother said of him. "Everything else about him was just a decorative frame."[37] Rathenau inevitably tended toward politics. His connection with political power began in 1907, and with the help of Prince von Bülow. The Chancellor selected him to accompany Colonial Secretary Bernhard Dernburg on inspection trips in Germany's African colonies in 1907 and 1908. Rathenau published a report of his first trip in *Reflexionen*. Dernburg, who had introduced Rathenau to Bülow as his best friend, was enraged at what he thought was an effort to overshadow him. The report was uncritically and impractically imperialistic, advocating, among other things, a railroad construction program costing 200 million marks in a colony with an annual trade of 24 million marks. Africa was an excursion, professionally as well as theoretically. The war gave Rathenau his first opportunity for important service to the state.

Rathenau's wartime accomplishment was unqualifiedly important, the first in his life that could be so described. He organized the War Materials Administration (*Kriegsrohstoffabteilung*, or *KRA*) of the Prussian War Ministry. Rathenau had gotten the idea from an assistant of his at the AEG, an engineer with an interest in economic administration named Wichard von Moellendorff. In his position Rathenau was able to make an appointment with the War Minister immediately after the war broke out and impress him with the need to act.[38] The purpose of the KRA was to assure the supply of crucial war materials which the army had completely neglected. Creating hundreds of "war companies" to manage all materials necessary to the war, it was an ad hoc administrative stroke of

---

[37] Kessler, *Tagebücher*, interview with Lili Deutsch (*see below*) on November 21, 1927, p. 552. Kessler did not use this comment in his biography.

[38] Innocently imperialistic in his vanity, Rathenau forgot who thought of the idea for the KRA and claimed it for himself. Moellendorff, however, could easily prove his authorship. Furthermore, he could show that Rathenau had denigrated it originally. In a letter of August 8 to Rathenau he sketched the basic conception of a raw materials administration. Rathenau replied the same day. He discounted Moellendorff's idea and instead placed more hope in another idea—namely, mobilization of the resources to be made available in Belgium and France. Two days later Rathenau reported to Moellendorff that he had discussed both ideas with the War Minister and indicated that the Minister had little interest in Moellendorff's. The Minister, however, very quickly saw its importance, and Rathenau was given his assignment to implement it on August 13. Rathenau not only forgot where the idea originated, but resisted Moellendorff's documentary evidence when his former assistant published their letters in 1920. (These and

the first order.[39] The country treated Rathenau shabbily. No longer needed in the KRA after he had established its basic character, he was permitted to resign on April 1, 1915. His abilities and imagination surely promised even greater services to the nation, but the leadership contented itself with assigning a calligrapher to write a letter of thanks. There was no place for a Jewish industrialist on a higher level of responsibility. Rathenau's hopes for power were frustrated.

Rathenau was a distinguished ambiguity at the age of 50, in 1917. Life had been growing more difficult and lonelier despite the accomplishments and social activities. His associates held a birthday party for him, and he talked about himself, showing a certain amount of insight into his problems. Mentioning the conflict between his desire to philosophize and "to act upon the world," he said he suffered "tensions which were very hard to bear for any length of time."[40] A few years earlier the expressionist Edvard Munch had painted a famous portrait of him: dark, cool, masterful, capable of enormities—demoniac in impeccable evening dress. Well over six feet tall, Rathenau liked to put his arm overpoweringly around the shoulders of other—almost always smaller—men. The demoniac aspect had since been softened by the unhappiness in his dark eyes and the white of his goatee. It was this softer Rathenau who was the subject of a literary portrait by the Austrian novelist Robert Musil. In the long, unfinished *Mann ohne Eigenschaften*,[41] Rathenau appears as Paul Arnheim, who pays court to

---

many other letters on the subject are in Moellendorff-Nachlass, BA.) The little controversy had been as unnecessary as it was demeaning. Only Rathenau could have moved the Prussian War Minister so quickly and organized an economic effort of the first magnitude so smoothly. The accomplishment was fine enough.

[39] During the Nazi period an Oberarchivrat of the Reichsarchiv had to give credit to this "member of the Jewish race" for "suggesting extraordinary measures." This was in a long, unpublished study of the KRA (Hermann Cron, "Die Organisation der Kriegswirtschaft im Kriege 1914–1918 und ihre Überleitung in die Friedensverhältnisse sowie Wertung ihrer Akten" [1942], p. 4). The manuscript, which is in the library of the Deutsches Zentralarchiv, Potsdam (hereafter cited as DZA), lists several hundred of the KRA's "war companies," the individual organizations carrying out the detailed work of allocating war materials in the various industries.

[40] "Tischrede zum 50. Geburtstag," in Rathenau, *Gesammelte Reden*, p. 19.

[41] Robert Musil, *Der Mann ohne Eigenschaften* (1952). Musil met Rathenau in January, 1914, writing in his diary: "A wonderful English suit. . . . Somewhat negroid skull. . . . He is accustomed to take over the discussion and swing it to himself immediately. He is a doctrinaire and at the same time the great gentleman" (Frank Trommler, review of the novel, *Frankfurter Allgemeine Zeitung*, December 4, 1965).

a Viennese lady but fails to require more of her than "extreme soul-embraces."[42] Bringing the soul into stock quotations as well as into love, he produces frustrations, but also profits. He incorporates the grandiose impotence of Europe.

Rathenau's sexual character was inevitably as ambiguous as the rest of him. For more than two decades he was almost the official lover of Lili Deutsch, Felix Deutsch's wife, and still she told his biographer in 1927: "To this day I have no idea *what* his love life was like." Kessler noted: "She spoke . . . very frankly about their relationship, which never got to the ultimate . . . although he was very sensual. . . ." Lili Deutsch concluded: "He never had any real feelings. He just had a longing for feelings."[43] Actually, Rathenau responded somewhat more freely to men. An acquaintance of his told me that Rathenau took an active part in a milieu of homosexuals.[44] The theater critic Alfred Kerr, who wrote a book about him, claimed to have seen him make an assignation with a servant girl and theorized that he divided women into two groups, ladies to whom he could talk and lower-class women to whom he could make love.[45] Psychology would not find this irreconcilable with homosexuality. In any case Rathenau's relationships with men were odd. There were, for example, the friendships with the racist publisher, an obscure figure named Wilhelm Schwaner, and with another small editor-publisher, the latter a Jew. Schwaner, attracted by Rathenau's ideas, reacted to his personality in the Nietzschean lingua franca of the period. "I hurl this question down into your soul like a plummet," Schwaner wrote on April 2, 1914, "Are you fond of me? I am fond of you! I am very fond of you!" He wrote in the familiar, and Rathenau replied in the familiar.[46] With the

---

[42] P. 434. Musil's hero finds "Arnheim-Rathenau," as the notes call him in one passage (p. 1619), an unendurable "compound of intelligence, business, luxury, and erudition" (p. 181). The hero adds: "What we all are divided out amongst ourselves—he is that in one person" (p. 195). Musil explained Arnheim-Rathenau's success: "Surrounded by the magic glitter of his wealth and the rumor of his importance, he dealt with men who surpassed him in their fields of expertise but who found him sympathetic as a layman surprisingly knowledgeable in those fields. Then he intimidated them because he embodied the connection of their world to other worlds—worlds about which they knew absolutely nothing" (p. 199).

[43] Kessler, *Tagebücher*, pp. 552–55.

[44] Edwin Redslob, *Kunstwart* (director of ceremonies and art) of the Weimar Republic, interview, November 18, 1966.

[45] Alfred Kerr, *Walther Rathenau* (1935), p. 68.

[46] Correspondence in Rathenau-Nachlass, BA.

Jewish editor, Constantin Brunner, the relationship began with an exchange of letters and works in January, 1919. A month later Rathenau, who had not yet met Brunner, was writing: "How long has it been since I held . . . a letter in my hand and read, and thought, and thought again, and read." He enclosed verses. After a meeting, Rathenau wrote on March 14: "It comforts me to know that you are there. I thought there wasn't anybody any more." On April 8 he wrote: "The house is still full of you."[47] In both cases, however, the relationships very quickly lost their intensity. With Schwaner, Rathenau's letters had become merely polite and kind three or four months after the April beginning. Brunner was commenting on Rathenau's failure to write three months after his first emotional letter. The relationship with Lili Deutsch persevered.

Many of Rathenau's important personal relationships tended to produce explosions of hostility when they were not carefully controlled, and sometimes when they were. Kessler recorded an "undertone of disappointment" in Lili Deutsch's feelings about Rathenau. His erstwhile assistant Moellendorff wrote: "I can well believe that anyone who thought he was Rathenau's friend must have been disappointed to the extent of becoming an enemy."[48] Lili Deutsch's remarks to Kessler showed that she continued to nurture bitterness against Rathenau even after his death. In life she had taken treacherous action against him, showing a letter of his which was critical of Maximilian Harden—the *Zukunft* editor—to Harden himself. Rathenau told Harden this caused him to break off with her for a year,[49] but the friendship of the two men was already deteriorating. The envious, irascible Harden did not need a good reason to get angry with Rathenau. By 1920 Harden had become an active enemy, attacking Rathenau viciously in his correspondence with important people.[50] Other friends, like Gerhart Hauptmann, to whom Rathenau had dedicated his *Kritik der Zeit*, fell away quietly. Still others, recognizing his excellent qualities, learned to tolerate the difficult ones. But Rathenau's talent for arousing resentment was a constant in his life and extended to people who hardly knew him or did not know him at all. This was suggested by

[47] Original letters, Leo Baeck Institute, New York City.
[48] In a handwritten memorandum, entitled "Walther Rathenaus Grösse," dated July, 1922, Moellendorff-Nachlass, BA.
[49] Letter of December 26, 1912, Harden-Nachlass, BA.
[50] E.g., Hugo Stinnes, in Harden-Nachlass, BA.

an episode at an upper-class luncheon during the war, as recalled by Alfred Kerr. Siegfried von Kardorff, a leader of the Prussian Free Conservative Party, suddenly announced the desire to make Rathenau responsible for everything that had gone wrong in Germany, "even for things with which he had nothing to do."[51] The others fell in with it and denounced him in a kind of social lynching. It was not an anti-Semitic exercise, at least, not directly or consciously. Kerr was Jewish and probably there were other Jews at the luncheon.[52] People enjoyed hating Rathenau.

Toward the end of the war Rathenau swung wildly from ambitious hope to depression. "I am like someone in the middle of packing," he wrote to Schwaner on September 24, 1918. "My father and brother are waiting for me in that neutral country to which no railroad leads. They cannot understand why I am delaying."[53] He was, however, writing more and more books and articles. *Von kommenden Dingen* appeared early in 1917 and *Die neue Wirtschaft*, a revision of some of its ideas to fit the immediate situation, at the end of the year. In 1918 he tried to capture the attention of Germany's youth by directing a brief book[54] at it, while Samuel Fischer, his neighbor and publisher, brought out his five-volume collected works. In 1919 Rathenau produced two other derivations of *Von kommenden Dingen*, the short books *Der neue Staat* and *Die neue Gesellschaft*, thus encompassing state and society in the new Germany. This was all literary action, and Rathenau tried to move beyond it. In November, 1918, he founded his own party, the Democratic People's League, but it perished within the month.[55] He sought membership in the (First) Socialization Commission; the Independent Social Democrats blackballed him because of the *Vossische Zeitung* letter calling for an emergency draft.[56] He joined the Democrats; the provincial electoral district to

[51] Kerr, *Rathenau*, p. 185.

[52] Kerr considered Kardorff a decent fellow—hence his puzzlement over the episode. Hans Fürstenberg, in his postscript in Kessler, *Rathenau*, pp. 409–10, remembered that Kardorff was a good friend of Max Liebermann, a second cousin of Rathenau's and the leading Prussian painter of the period, and that Kardorff had the courage and decency to go to Liebermann's funeral during the Nazi period, in 1935.

[53] Rathenau-Nachlass, BA.

[54] *An Deutschlands Jugend*, in *GS*, vol. 6.

[55] Letter of Rathenau, November 27, *Ein preussischer Europäer*, pp. 288–90.

[56] In a letter to Friedrich Ebert on December 16, 1918, he reacted like a hysterical woman scorned: "I beg you not to nominate me on second thought" (*Ein preussischer Europäer*, p. 293).

which he was assigned put him so low on the party listing that he had no chance of being elected to the National Assembly.[57] On February 7, 1919, at the second meeting of the National Assembly, a telegram nominating him for the nation's presidency was read; the delegates reacted with startled laughter. Later in February Kessler visited Rathenau and found him diminished from the figure of a few years ago and profoundly out of joint with the times: "The man of false notes and circumstances gone awry—the Communist in a damask chair, the patriot out of condescension, the avant-garde musicmaker on an old harp." Kessler reflected: "And yet a virtuoso."[58]

Kessler's second thought had recognized that Rathenau's possibilities were not extinguished. A few months later Rathenau said: "When the Revolution came they were all agreed to get me out of the picture."[59] Kessler had been closer to the truth: "they" had not given Rathenau a thought. Having never participated in politics he was not seriously considered as a political figure. Rathenau was also continuing to give reason for mistrust. The left-wing groups thought of his warlike letter and the conservatives disliked his socialistic ideas. Nevertheless, he began to take on political dimension precisely in early 1919. It began with an attack. On March 8 the Economics Minister, the labor leader Rudolf Wissell, gratuitously criticized Rathenau in the National Assembly.[60] Wissell was seeking to cover the pillage and inversion of Rathenau's ideas. Wichard von Moellendorff had become Wissell's assistant and achieved intellectual domination over his mediocre chief. He had persuaded the Minister to sponsor a plan for what they called a social economy (*Gemeinwirtschaft*), a conception deriving from *Von kommenden Dingen*. Rigid and dogmatic, Moellendorff transformed the loose inconsistencies of his former chief into a monolithic system. Although the idiom was socialist, the essence was corporative, quite in the manner of Mussolini's fascist state.[61] Wissell had tried to defend himself against the charge of authoritarianism by accusing Rathenau of it; Rathenau turned the charge back

[57] Kessler was told by Rathenau's secretary that anti-Semitic arguments had been used (Kessler, *Rathenau*, p. 272).

[58] *Tagebücher*, p. 131.

[59] Letter to a well-wisher, November 11, 1919, *Politische Briefe*, p. 267.

[60] Kessler, *Rathenau*, pp. 274–75.

[61] Copy in Wissell-Nachlass, BA. Many details of the issue are in this and in the Moellendorff-Nachlass in the BA; also in the larger Wissell-Nachlass in the Historische Kommission zu Berlin.

upon its author and argued that conditions in any case were too chaotic for a revolutionary reorganization of society. His own sense of reality, a characteristic which persons he influenced often did not share, prevented him from being led too far astray by his own ideas at this moment. The Social Democrats agreed with the practical Rathenau and voted down the plan at their party conference in June. Wissell and Moellendorff resigned the next month, having rendered Rathenau's ambitions important service.

Rathenau was being associated with socialism, his ideas having captured wide attention through the debates in the National Assembly. Those ideas, moreover, had found the great opening between doctrinaire socialism and irresponsible capitalism. Many felt that he was correct in general, whatever error in the details. He was continuing to give public advice, now and then using the *Vossische Zeitung*. In a lead article on January 11, 1920, for example, he attacked the government for failing to solve problems beyond its control; he could be as unfair as his own critics. The outcome of the Kapp Putsch gave him his opportunity.

The militarist-authoritarian conspiracy, operating with a Free Corps unit, put the government to flight and held Berlin for four days, from March 13 to 17, 1920. It failed after the bureaucracy refused to function and the capital's workers went on general strike. In April, 1920, the (Second) Socialization Commission was organized to reward the workers. It was only reasonable that Rathenau, the socialistically minded industrialist, should become a member. He was also named to the (Temporary) National Economic Council, which was meant to be a kind of economic parliament. He had to wait to fill a vacancy, but it came quickly enough for him to attend the council's third meeting on July 22. Both positions attested to Rathenau's new political or semipolitical character, but the strength of rival business leaders like Stinnes in the National Economic Council prevented him from being effective there.[62] The Socialization Commission, on the other hand, was the ideal platform. It provided precisely that combination of the hopeful, the technical, the trivial, and the unreal, of which Rathenau was the master.

Many persons felt that the government was morally obliged to

62 Germany, *Stenographische Berichte über die Verhandlungen des vorläufigen Reichswirtschaftsrats* (1920–23).

introduce socialism or, at least, more socialism. The commission represented a renewal of the socialization efforts initiated with the revolution. By December, 1918, the Workers' and Soldiers' Councils, modeled on the Russian soviets, had failed to take command of the country and lead it into socialism. In January, 1919, government troops and Free Corps formations killed hundreds of radicals in Berlin and crushed the socialist ambitions associated with Rosa Luxemburg and Karl Liebknecht. In April, 1919, the (First) Socialization Commission resigned after failing to get anything done. Then came the Wissell-Moellendorff failure. In 1920, with the second commission, the prognosis was hardly more favorable. Two months after the commission began life, on June 6, new elections were held and the result was a victory for the middle-class parties. The elections brought the Centrist Konstantin Fehrenbach into office and a new coalition with him. The Social Democrats dropped out of the government on the Left, and the People's Party joined it on the Right. Fehrenbach's government had no mandate for a socialization program. That made little difference, as it turned out.

The new Socialization Commission, meeting for the first time on April 17 and thus before the conservative electoral expression, had set the modest objectives of socializing the coal industry and drawing upon a program for the municipal ownership of utilities. These objectives were so limited that they were not affected by the election results, and the commission went on sincerely talking, the businessmen in it as sincerely as the Social Democrats and the socializing bureaucrats. At the first meeting Rathenau made sensible proposals for the coal organization and also intervened tactfully to keep the other commission members from bringing up too many irrelevant subjects.[63] On April 28 he was elected a member of the most important of the four committees, the Coal-Potash-Iron Committee. A week later, at the meeting of May 5, he had already produced a complete coal scheme, which was henceforth known as the Rathenau Proposal. The Rathenau Proposal became the subject of the commission's most important debates. Rathenau had established his leadership in one governmental area.

Rathenau's plan provided for a mixed public and private corpo-

[63] Sozialisierungskommission (minutes), DZA, item no. 94.

ration. It had to compete with the plan of a doctrinaire socialist expert, who wanted to expropriate the coal mines without compensation to the owners. On May 10 Rathenau argued: "I am far from being an enemy of complete socialization—absolutely not—but it would be impractical and unfeasible under the present circumstances. . . . Coal production would collapse if you eliminated the mine owners suddenly." With his generalist's sense of the wider issues Rathenau took the occasion to mention another problem: "The reparation question is becoming more and more urgent. . . ."[64] Over the next months he fought the expropriation plan with the help of Rudolf Wissell, who was a labor representative on the commission. The former Economics Minister, no longer under Moellendorff's influence, was happy to accept Rathenau's compromise with capitalism. Rathenau achieved the victory of his proposal before the summer adjournment.[65]

The Rathenau Proposal went to the government and the victory vanished. Under the leadership of Hugo Stinnes the mine owners bypassed the Socialization Commission and introduced a coal plan of their own in the National Economic Council. They wanted a coal cartel under governmental aegis—capitalism with all the advantages of socialism. In the Economic Council the Stinnes Proposal easily overcame Rathenau's plan, the latter receiving less than a third of the votes. At a meeting of the Socialization Commission on November 20 Rathenau admitted defeat.[66] Once more a socialization effort had failed, but Rathenau has made the acquaintance of Joseph Wirth.

Rathenau impressed Wirth immensely. "The cabinet ministers did a lot of babbling without getting through to any real understanding of the problems," Wirth told Kessler in 1928. "So [Kessler's note continued] he got into the habit of calling Rathenau and discussing questions of finances and reparations. . . ." The leverage point was reparations.

"There soon," Kessler went on, "developed a half-political, half-intellectual friendship between them."[67] It was a special friendship, surely political, but more personal than Wirth was willing to admit,

[64] *Ibid.*, no. 104. The expert was Professor Emil Lederer of the University of Heidelberg.
[65] July 31, 1920, *ibid.*, no. 127.
[66] *Ibid.*, no. 146.
[67] *Tagebücher*, interview, February 27, 1928, p. 559.

and hardly intellectual. Politically, Rathenau could be very useful to Wirth, as shown by his reparation plan at the time of the London Conference. The plan had been impossible, but its egregious impossibility was an important part of its value. It had an aura of moralizing that was the best defense against the moralizing destructiveness of Allied reparation policy. Rathenau promised to be an Ariel to Wirth's Caliban. Wirth, who was barely forty and also a bachelor, had proved his capability in dealing with the more conventional problems of domestic politics. After teaching mathematics in a secondary school, he entered politics in Baden and became a dedicated professional politician. A Reichstag member by 1914, he got through the war as a medical orderly and became Baden's Finance Minister following the 1918 revolution. Establishing himself on the left-wing of the Center, he became a favorite speaker of the Catholic workers. Confident of his own talents, which were entirely different, Wirth could enjoy being dazzled by Rathenau without suffering from his condescension. Rathenau, for his part, could act somewhat like an older brother, since he was a dozen years Wirth's senior, and somewhat like a son, since he was the political subordinate. Rathenau's relationship with his own brother had been excellent, while he had worked well with his father after Erich had died. Here, the specific character of the Rathenau family relationships were helpful. Personally as well as politically the Rathenau-Wirth association went deep.

The connection between the two men was strong enough by July, 1920, for Wirth to insist on adding Rathenau to the delegation to the Spa Conference. Wirth had to overcome the "rabid" resistance of the Foreign Ministry, he told Kessler in 1928.[68] It was at the Spa Conference that Rathenau first dealt actively with reparations.

Wirth constructed a legend about Rathenau at Spa. Referring to a speech of Rathenau's, he told Kessler: "At that moment the fulfillment policy was born."[69] Neither the records nor Rathenau quite make that claim.

The Spa Conference was another stage in the slow and tentative development of the fulfillment policy. Kessler, taking his facts from Wirth, would have the policy given its complete form during a confrontation between Rathenau and Hugo Stinnes. There had in-

[68] *Ibid.*, p. 559.
[69] Kessler, *Rathenau*, p. 297.

deed been a debate between the two men at a meeting of the German delegation on July 14.[70] The Wirth-Kessler account of it establishes a hero-villain pattern in perfect balance: the conciliatory, democratic internationalist Rathenau and the recalcitrant, nationalistic, and domineering Stinnes. Yet, as Kessler admitted, Stinnes was a convinced republican, enjoyed excellent relations with labor because of his genuinely enlightened policies, and was no more nationalistic than Rathenau. It was true that Stinnes and Rathenau took the opposite views on whether or not Germany should accept the Allied ultimatum, which demanded the delivery of two million tons of coal a month. It was also true that Stinnes had fired a provocative speech at the heads of the Allies four days earlier in which he told them they were making ridiculous demands.[71] Kessler did not mention the fact that Rathenau was only an expert adviser to the actual negotiators and that two other experts had preceded him in debating with Stinnes. With uncharacteristic modesty Rathenau himself said he had a small position at Spa, adding inaccurately that he had "no influence on the decisions."[72] According to the minutes of the meeting, Rathenau's former friend Bernhard Dernburg as well as Chancellor Fehrenbach's consultant on reparations, Professor M. J. Bonn, had also urged yielding to the ultimatum. Rathenau, in fact, had insisted on making a condition about Upper Silesia which the Allies would have found unacceptable. Bonn gave his version of the debate in his book and said he himself had been the first to contradict Stinnes.[73] All this does not deny that Rathenau's opinion was a significant factor, as Kessler would have it, in convincing the German delegation, including General von Seeckt, of the need to make an effort toward fulfillment. Nevertheless Germany had to undergo many experiences before she formulated a true fulfillment policy. Rathenau was not being inconsistent—not betraying his position at Spa—when he opposed the policy almost a year later, in May, 1921, during those days when Wirth was trying to form his government of fulfillment. Furthermore, while Rathenau always qualified his definition of fulfillment, Stinnes, for his part, represented a policy that was much more constructive than

[70] Minutes, Reichskanzlei: Spa, Allgemeines, BA, R43I/403.
[71] Copy of speech, Büro des Reichsministers: Spa, Deutsche Sitzungsprotokolle, Politisches Archiv, Auswärtiges Amt, Bonn (hereafter cited as PA, AA).
[72] Letter to Schwaner, July 19, 1920, Briefe, 2: 246.
[73] M. J. Bonn, So Macht Man Geschichte (1953), p. 247.

mere recalcitrance. Stinnes was so important that Alexandre Millerand had a secret meeting with him in Brussels before the Spa Conference began, treating him as if he were a foreign power.[74] The
French Premier, who was concerned about the coal requirements
of the steel plants in Lorraine, respected his command over coal
resources and was not unwilling to consider Stinnes a good European. At the Spa Conference itself the Allies reacted to Stinnes's
speech with a show of indignation, but the industrialist, supported
by the union leader Otto Hue, was important in winning their respect and in forcing them to lend Germany the $90 million to im-
port food for the miners. Two days after the Stinnes uproar Viscount Edgar d'Abernon, the British Ambassador to Germany,
recorded in his diary: "A turning point in European history was
reached this afternoon, when M. Millerand described Germany as
a 'necessary and useful member of the European community.' "[75]
He would hardly have done so, had he taken Stinnes's remarks so
tragically. At a German cabinet meeting on July 19, Foreign Minister Simons "paid warm tribute to the positive effect of the intervention of Stinnes and Hue."[76] Men like Stinnes were as necessary
as the Rathenaus in dealing with the Allies, a fact which Rathenau
always recognized. Rathenau spent the last night of his life arguing with Stinnes over fulfillment policy. They were differing, but
only to a precisely limited extent; they were partners in the German
concern. To the end Rathenau, like Stinnes, believed the fulfillment
policy to be tentative.

The ambiguities of Spa were in accord with Rathenau's style.
The conference meant an important advance in his career. His giving of advice, so central an element in his functioning, began to
extend beyond Wirth to the government itself. A Rathenau proposal had naturally been part of the Spa delegation's armament. It
was eloquent and impractical.[77] After the summer of 1920 Rathenau continued to be active in the Socialization Commission, but he
was addressing himself more and more to greater questions. The

[74] Handwritten letter by Stinnes to Foreign Minister Simons, July 4, 1920, in
Büro des Reichsministers: Spa, Kohlenfrage, PA, AA.

[75] Viscount Edgar Vincent d'Abernon, *The Diary of an Ambassador: Versailles
to Rapallo 1920–1922* (1929), p. 69.

[76] Diary entry of Interior Minister Erich Koch-Weser, Koch-Weser-Nachlass,
BA.

[77] Copy in Büro des Reichsministers: Spa, Allgemeines, PA, AA.

London Conference showed how far he had progressed by March of 1921. It had been extraordinary for Chancellor and cabinet to tell the Foreign Minister to break up his own negotiating pattern in favor of a proposal drafted by a private person. At that moment Simons had been able to ignore the advice from Berlin. A moment later he was out of the government and Rathenau was making policy.

Wirth's ability to identify himself with an approach to a fulfillment policy had made him a logical candidate for the chancellorship. Owing this largely to Rathenau, Wirth wanted him for the reconstruction post very badly. Rathenau's own reluctance prevented Wirth from making the nomination immediately. The political situation required the creation of a new government as soon as possible, and Wirth, who was charged with the chancellorship at noon on May 10, presented his cabinet to the Reichstag by eleven that evening. At the time he carefully avoided mentioning the Reconstruction Ministry, although it was one of the most important posts because of the fulfillment crisis that had put him in power. It was clearly on his mind. The day after he formed his government Wirth took the time to lunch with Rathenau. He offered Rathenau the Reconstruction Ministry. Rathenau refused. His vanity and his tendency to errors of instinct misled him. He wanted the Foreign Ministry.[78] It was utterly impossible at that point in German history. Aside from the fact that Rathenau was a Jew and a Jew with numerous enemies, he was a man of no political experience and undefined political character. His qualifications for Reconstruction Minister, on the other hand, were splendid. One could forget his opposition to the London Ultimatum, or rather, such was the pathology of domestic politics and international relations that one could use the opposition to advantage. To the German nation one could argue that it had proved his patriotism; to the Allies his change of mind could demonstrate his deeper wisdom and sense of responsibility. Now, all the factors that had previously handicapped Rathenau's political career came to his aid. The industrialist clearly had the technical competence to deal with reconstruction and reparations generally; the economic and social philosopher

---

[78] A mutual acquaintance, a Geheimrat Kreuter, was with them and reported on the luncheon to Ernst Laubach, author of *Die Politik der Kabinette Wirth 1921–1922*, Historische Studien (1968), 402: 36n.

could claim a broader sweep to his competence; the idealist could represent a trustworthy, democratic, and peaceful Germany to the world, and a Jew could minimize Germany's German character. On May 11, 1921, however, Wirth had to accept Rathenau's refusal. Wirth then discussed the reconstruction post with the director of a large manufacturing company who had won a doubtful and, in any case, irrelevant reputation as an expert in reconstruction, and a Social Democratic member of the Reichstag who was a leader of the Construction Workers Union and thus had a similarly unnecessary relation to a Reconstruction Ministry that would reconstruct nothing.[79] Wirth also spoke vaguely with Otto Wiedfeldt, a Krupp director with an interest in government, about the Reconstruction Ministry, but he mentioned the Finance and Foreign Ministries to him as well.[80] Everything indicates that Wirth did not really want any one of these three for the Reconstruction Ministry. Meanwhile, on May 23, after a number of candidates had refused or shown themselves to be unacceptable, the Chancellor named Friedrich Rosen, the 66-year-old Minister to the Netherlands, to the Foreign Ministry. Rosen was a professional diplomat and a scholar of Persian literature, but he had neither imagination nor a real understanding of foreign relations. He promised to be harmless, and Wirth, who had set the main direction in foreign policy by accepting the principle of fulfillment, expected to continue making the major decisions. If someone else were also to become important in that area it would not be Rosen, but Rathenau as Reconstruction Minister. Now with a Foreign Minister snapped into position, Wirth devoted his best energy to capturing him. He used Rosen himself in the wooing. When Rosen told Wirth that Rathenau was "not to be taken seriously," Wirth tried to get him to withdraw the remark by asking if he would say it to Rathenau's face. Rosen said he would, and he did. Wirth then got President Ebert to talk to Rosen. Ebert asked Rosen to give up his objections and to try himself to persuade Rathenau to take the position. Rosen thereupon lunched with Rathenau, who "gave no evidence of ill-feeling against me." Rosen's reminiscences continue: "[He] brought up an

---

[79] Laubach, *Die Politik der Kabinette Wirth*, pp. 36–37. One rumor, however, had been sufficiently forceful to persuade *Le Temps* of May 12 to list the Social Democrat, Hermann Silberschmidt, as Wirth's Reconstruction Minister.

[80] Lothar Albertin, "Die Verantwortung der liberalen Parteien für das Scheitern der grossen Koalition im Herbst 1921," *Historische Zeitschrift* 205 (1967): 571.

overwhelming mass of arguments against joining the cabinet—in the midst of which there was clearly evident his desire nevertheless to get into the cabinet, if at all possible."[81] Rathenau also asked the opinion of his fellow Democrat Eugen Schiffer, who had joined the cabinet as Minister of Justice. Schiffer, who was not enthusiastic, suggested that Rathenau ask another opinion, and Rathenau talked to Defense Minister Gessler in Schiffer's presence. Gessler was negative. Rathenau responded: "Now that I have learned your reasons, my dear Minister Gessler, my self-respect obliges me despite my own misgivings to accept the post in order to prove those reasons wrong."[82] Schiffer felt certain that Rathenau was going to accept and that he only wanted encouragement. On May 29, a Sunday, Wirth nominated Rathenau. It was two days after Rathenau had written to his mother that he was going to refuse.[83] On June 1 he wrote her again: "The decision was really very, very difficult."[84] Viscount d'Abernon, who saw Wirth after Rathenau had finally accepted, noted the Chancellor's words: "Do not let us discuss current affairs today. There is a great, most important event: Rathenau has joined the Ministry."[85]

[81] Rosen, *Aus einem diplomatischen Wanderleben*, 3–4: 319; Rosen's account of Rathenau's nomination may be found on pp. 314–19.

[82] Schiffer-Nachlass, memoirs in manuscript, p. 23, Hauptarchiv (Berlin-Dahlem).

[83] Rathenau, *Ein preussischer Europäer*, p. 391.

[84] *Ibid.*, p. 392.

[85] Versailles to Rapallo, p. 42.

CHAPTER IV

Reparations:
Germany and France

The first necessity of the new government was to convince the Allies that it was serious about fulfillment. Wirth and Rathenau, each in his own way, did so as eloquently as possible in their Reichstag speeches of June 1 and June 2.[1] Leaving most of the specifics of reparations to Rathenau, Wirth spoke about fulfillment in general. He promised to surrender the stocks of weapons left over from the war and to dissolve some of the irregular military units, although he was carefully vague about implementation.[2] At the same time, attempting to comfort the electorate, he felt obliged to hope pathetically for a favorable decision on Upper Silesia;[3] the Allies would understand the domestic pressures and refuse to take that brief part of the speech too seriously. Wirth went on to say that he would lead Germany in a spirit of international cooperation. The next day Rathenau elaborated on the theme of international cooperation through reparations. "We must find ways of coming together with the other nations," he said.[4] He emphasized that reparations meant not only financial payments, but also reconstruction

---

[1] In Wirth, *Reden während der Kanzlerschaft* (1925), pp. 41–65; and Rathenau, *Gesammelte Reden*, pp. 199–204. Also: Germany, *Reichstag: Stenographische Berichte* (hereafter cited as *Stenographische Berichte*), 349: 3709–17, 3742–45.
[2] *Reden während der Kanzlerschaft*, pp. 42–45.
[3] *Ibid.*, pp. 53–58.
[4] *Gesammelte Reden*, p. 200.

work in France. "Another factor that persuaded me [to join the government] was the conviction that France really wants reconstruction," Rathenau said. "I have convinced myself that reconstruction is a reality."[5] The belief, he virtually admitted, owed more to his own will than any real evidence of what France wanted. Nevertheless, the speech enunciated a policy that could let Germany develop the image of international virtue.

Behind Rathenau's speech was a great deal of his most expansive and ambitious postwar thinking. He had propounded his ideas on reconstruction almost two years earlier to Matthias Erzberger, then Finance Minister and the dominant figure in the cabinet. Their talk took place on July 6, 1919, and Rathenau followed it with a letter: "I mentioned these factors:—In our desperate situation we must find the leverage point which will permit us to roll up the whole flank. This point is located in Belgium and northern France, and in the context of the problem of reconstruction. It will permit us to (1) get our relationship with France straightened out, (2) correct the Peace Treaty, (3) transform and reduce the kind of payments demanded, (4) indirectly influence the domestic situation in a salutary way, (5) win back Germany's moral position." Speculating on sending as many as a half-million German workers to France, possibly by means of a draft, Rathenau said he hoped to use the reconstruction effort in a way that would make it overshadow the war in world public opinion. "When people set it over against the war," he said, "it will take on the character—even after centuries—of Germany's greatest accomplishment."[6]

The Wirth-Rathenau government, meanwhile, was collecting and paying the billion marks as evidence of its good will. Of course the action weakened the currency and the economy. It brought Wirth and Rathenau closer to the real objective of their fulfillment policy —getting reparations reduced—but it also encouraged extremism.

Other contradictions appeared in the relations with the two major Allied powers. Some persons debated the comparative merits of pro-British or pro-French policies. Foreign Minister Rosen, a straightforward person, favored the British because they were more sympathetic than the French.[7] Georg Bernhard, editor of the *Vossi-*

[5] *Ibid.*, pp. 200–201.
[6] Letter of July 16, 1919, Rathenau, *Briefe*, 2: 167–71.
[7] The account of his stewardship in Rosen, *Aus einem diplomatischen Wanderleben* (1959), 3–4: 349–89.

sche Zeitung, urged a pro-French policy on the ground that France was less perfidious than Great Britain and could be persuaded to recognize the common interests of continental powers.[8] Neither so simple nor so subtle, the best policy had nothing to do with such constructions as sympathy or perfidy among nations. The British were moving steadily toward a better understanding of the German economic situation, as German exports, under the pressure of reparations, undersold British goods. At the moment there was little that had to be done or could be done about Great Britain. The opposite was true of France and her representatives. "The French deputy . . . continued . . . to cherish the passions and the financial hopes which in 1919 his British counterpart had shared," a student of British-French-German relations has written.[9] Germany had to do something about the French situation immediately, if she could hope to save herself before reparation payments caused a final collapse of the currency. While Rosen made unavailing gestures toward Britain, Rathenau addressed himself to France.

The real determinant of French policy was the need for security and solvency. The problem of security for France could be put simply. Even with Germany's losses, her population was 50 percent greater than that of France. This was the proportion against which Clemenceau had fought so fiercely at the Paris Peace Conference. Another consideration was the fact that German industry had survived the war essentially intact and all the more efficient. The problem of solvency has been discussed in Chapter II. French finances, weakened by the war, were under the pressing threat of American (and British) demands for war-debt payment. The truths in the French situation were distorted in expressions of policy by an entirely human mixture of nationalistic resentment, fear, ambition, ignorance, and skilled rationalization. If fear about security was only reasonable, France reacted by overcompensating. She was trying to dominate the continent—not an immoral ambition surely, but an impossible one. In any case France refused to admit that there could be other security threats besides Germany. Concerning the financial problems, the French economist Alfred Sauvy has made several references to his countrymen's "predominantly legal

---

[8] In lead articles on January 21 and 30, and September 4, 1921, supported by continuing references in the news columns.

[9] W. M. Jordan, *Great Britain, France, and the German Problem 1918–1939* (1943), p. 113.

and literary education . . . and very slight knowledge of economics" in his *Histoire économique de la France entre les deux guerres*.[10] Without the corrective of competence in economics, all the French weaknesses led to huge errors, and Louis Loucheur, after making the usual reparation demands in the Chamber of Deputies in 1919, remarked: "I couldn't tell the truth—they would have killed me."[11]

The *Bloc national*, a grouping of the more conservative parties, had won the election of November, 1919, and tried to hold the government in a firm posture vis-à-vis Germany. Its large majority, however, was unstable, the Bloc having gathered in many conflicting interests. Its more reasonable members also knew that Great Britain disagreed about the degree of sacrifice to be expected of Germany. France might have to choose between German cash, assuming she could get her hands on it, and the association with Britain. In view of this it was not surprising that Aristide Briand, the great conciliator, should come to power at the beginning of 1921. One deputy, a man of principle, disconsolately said to Briand: "You are carrying out left-wing policy with a right-wing majority."[12]

Raymond Poincaré was developing a responsible alternative to Briand's policy. He argued that France must maintain herself against the threat of American war-debt demands. He pointed out that Great Britain refused to commit herself to a firm guarantee of French security. France, he said, could afford neither to be gentle with Germany nor cooperative with her old ally. Poincaré would not admit the extent of the dangers of isolation, but then Briand was less than frank about the disadvantages of his management of foreign affairs.

A nationalistic Lorrainer, Poincaré represented a guarantee that French interests would be assured against German cheating. He stood comfortably close to most of the important French prejudices. He was conservative about money and taxes, and yet his anticlerical past made him sympathetic to many French on the Left, particularly since they, too, were conservative about money and taxes. Retired in February, 1920, after seven years as President of France,

---

[10] Alfred Sauvy, *Histoire économique de la France entre les deux guerres*, 2 vols. (1965–67); this reference in 1: 7; others, also in 1: 129, 167, and 430.
[11] Quoted in Sauvy, *Histoire économique*, 1: 148.
[12] Quoted in Suarez, *Briand*, 5: 218.

he had permitted himself to be named president of the Reparation Commission. He knew how important reparations were. He remained with the commission three months, just long enough to acquaint himself with the issue and not so long as to suffer loss of stature. As a senator and chairman of the Senate's Foreign Affairs Committee, he was in an immensely favorable position, with great standing and no responsibility. Briand could do nothing without first asking what Poincaré would say or do.

Poincaré knew precisely what to say in his frequent expressions of opinion. He mentioned his fundamental arguments only perfunctorily. The effects upon France of British and especially American policy could not arouse his readers. Instead, he dwelt on the obvious German evils and French sufferings, mixing hardy commonplaces with conventional hyperboles. He was writing weekly articles for *Le Matin*, the conservative newspaper, and a regular feature, the "Fortnightly Chronicle," in the *Revue des deux mondes*, the important periodical. His first statement in the *Revue*, on March 15, 1920, was a model of everything to come: "When Germany signed the Versailles Treaty, she recognized in writing, on the honor of her plenipotentiaries, that she was guilty of having unleashed the war, and that, out of respect for justice, she had to make reparation for the evil of which she was the author. But the ink was hardly dry . . . when she began . . . a campaign, with the fine art of mendacity, to liberate herself from her obligations. She had insidiously broadcast the idea in all countries that she and her allies could not be solely responsible for the war . . . ," while her government "tried to paint her economic situation in the blackest colors."[13] Poincaré continued each fortnight: "real disarmament, reparations truly equal to the damages" (May 1, 1920, p. 240), "the gaping roofs, the crumbled walls of the war-devastated regions" (May 15, p. 469), and "behind her camouflage of misery, Germany is busily occupied in reestablishing herself" (July 15, p. 447). On February 1, 1921, commenting on Briand's accession to office, Poincaré praised Briand for promising to be firm.[14]

Poincaré had exaggerated, but not too much for France. It was possible to go too far. The speech of an obscure deputy in the Chamber lent itself to satirical reportage in *Le Temps* of May 21,

13 Pp. 472–73.
14 Pp. 661–62.

1921. Discussing reparations, the deputy had "brought those . . . billions to life . . . with the help of his prodigious magician's wand . . . those billions owed to our tragically disabled veterans, to our widows, to our orphans, those billions still in suspense. . . . The breathless audience saw them come, go, be born, live, die, tremble, shake, demand their rights, bewail their wretchedness and betrayal, huddle—maimed themselves, insecure, and as if ashamed of themselves—in the hollows of devastated valleys, in the shade of melancholy ruins, and rise up again, incensed to see themselves required to justify themselves, quibbled at, haggled over by a conniving Germany, or—crueler agony—by allies become—already!—indifferent." *Le Temps* was taking advantage of an extreme statement to defend the government. The point was to set up a contrast between the manifestly magical claims of the deputy and those of the government's policy. The reader might be persuaded that the somewhat smaller official demands were reasonable, even if these also assumed the impossible.

Beyond Poincaré on one side and Briand on the other there were voices indignantly demanding even more firmness or timorously suggesting a little more understanding of German problems. Those who tended toward a milder policy had to be cautious. The Socialists were trying to return to their internationalism after having emphasized their patriotic Jacobin sources. They had called for the usual high reparations at the time of the Peace Conference, repeating their demand in a resolution of October, 1919.[15] By 1921 they were trying to make things easier for their fellow Socialists in Germany, but they could not let France be second to the other Allies in exploiting reparations. Commenting on the London Conference, *Le Populaire*, the Socialist Party organ, avoided the real problem by falsely accusing Foreign Minister Simons of being a spokesman for German industry.[16] Even the most conciliatory among the French required much more of Germany than she could give. Two forceful groups were counterweights to the inhibited advocates of mildness. Clemenceau's former lieutenants, a half-dozen able men, never forgot that Briand had frustrated the war leader's presidential candidacy. Their principal figure was the formidable André Tardieu, who had drafted the Versailles Treaty for France and was

[15] Weill-Raynal, *Les réparations allemandes*, 2: 581.
[16] March 3, 1921.

committed to defending its integrity. On the far Right the *Action française,* the royalist-nationalist league, regretted and anticipated a separatist Rhineland under French tutelage while demanding the maximum in reparations. If these groups were only on the fringes of power, they still had the effect of weakening Briand and strengthening Poincaré. The natural eloquence of French politics favored Poincaré, but, for the moment, the nation's natural prudence prevailed.

Briand had won a series of successes, beginning with the Paris Conference in January and culminating with the acceptance of the London Ultimatum by a new German government. Their content, however, was largely gesture and promise, and he would need more substance. The situation was all the more difficult because France would get nothing from the first billion marks remitted by Germany: the inter-Allied balance of credits and obligations would force France to let Britain and Belgium divide the billion between themselves. This was to compensate those powers for French possession of the Saar and its mines. The Saar, however, had been used up as a political satisfaction, and to fend off his enemies Briand had to show that France was getting something more—and this before the next important installments under the London Payments Plan would be paid. These were not due until January and February, 1922; Briand had advisers clear-sighted enough to doubt that Germany could or would pay the 1922 installments. In the spring of 1921 the French government found one palpable advantage in the logic of reparations and international economics. Germany was delivering to France a few items, chiefly coal, timber, and dyes, that were as good as money. Transfer was no problem: Germany had these products and France needed them. A year earlier Millerand had taken political advantage of this to win a temporary easing of pressures through the coal provisions of the Spa Agreement. The coal had temporarily satisfied public opinion. Even before Wirth's government of fulfillment had taken office, Briand's people had worked out a new plan promising the advantage that Briand needed politically.

Rathenau's Reichstag speech of June 2 and, long before that, his talk with Erzberger, had conceived of something sublimely different from the French plan. It was typical of Rathenau, however, that he could keep two contradictory ideas vigorously alive in his mind at the same time. Less than three months before making his speech he had expressed a much more realistic view of the French attitude. He had been a member of a group of businessmen who met with officials of the Reconstruction Ministry on March 19. French reconstruction was mentioned. "The romantic prospect of rebuilding all of northern France . . . cannot be carried out," Rathenau coolly said. "The French don't want it."[17] Such opposed views would have paralyzed the effectiveness of most men. Rathenau functioned differently. His imaginative side made the most of the public relations value of the dream of reconstruction. The practical Rathenau seized upon the operational details of the French plan.

The files of the Reconstruction Ministry contained more opinions and much evidence supporting the practical approach. On May 28, 1921, anticipating a new Reconstruction Minister, State Secretary Gustav Müller prepared a report on the reparation situation. Müller told of the Ministry's inability to get France to take anything besides coal, timber, and dyes. There was the matter of the 60,000 wooden sheds which the Allies had solemnly demanded shortly after the peace. In October, 1919, Louis Loucheur, then Clemenceau's under secretary of state responsible for reparations and reconstruction, refused to accept delivery of the sheds. Subsequently, Loucheur simply failed to reply to German questions about construction material. In the spring of 1920 the Reparation Commission handed to Germany unexamined lists of articles requested by war-damaged French factories. To give one example of what had been requested, "there were enough driving belts to go around the equator." As Müller summed it up, all the evidence so far had shown that neither the Reparation Commission nor the French were serious about taking materials. The needs of those who had suffered from the war had little influence on decisions.[18] Carl Bergmann, reporting from Paris as a member of the War Payments Office, dismissed the idea of reconstruction. In a memorandum on April 4, 1920, he said it was "simply impossible."[19] Loucheur himself would revise the French position, but only after a year.

A new series of negotiations began shortly before the Fehrenbach government fell. On April 23, 1921, the Chancellor formally

[17] Reichskanzlei: Wiederaufbau der Feindgebiete, BA, R43I/342.
[18] Ausführung, BA, R43I/20.
[19] *Ibid.*, R43I/14.

renewed Germany's offer to provide equipment and workers for French reconstruction. On May 12, Loucheur, now Briand's Minister of the Liberated Regions, took up the idea. He told Dr. Wolf of the War Payments Office that France would be prepared to accept 25,000 wooden sheds in 1921. On May 31, in another talk with Wolf after Rathenau was named to the Reconstruction Ministry, he said that France was willing to consider taking goods in general. On June 3, in a third interview, Loucheur expressed a keen interest in Rathenau's views.[20] Obviously anxious to proceed, Loucheur went on to make an important point. He reminded Wolf that France, according to the agreement made among the Allies at the Spa Conference, was to receive 52 percent of German reparation payments. If she made a special arrangement with Germany, France would have to compensate the other members of the Entente to the extent that it gave her more than 52 percent of reparations in any given year. Loucheur wanted to keep France from losing to her friends what she would get from her old enemy. He suggested that France and Germany work out a formula that would spread the reparation credit to Germany over future years. He was conceiving of a situation in which Germany might, for example, give France coal and other products worth a billion marks in 1921. During the year, however, Germany would get credit for perhaps 350 million gold marks or, in any case, a figure that would just fail to put France's total reparation receipts over 52 percent. This was the reasoning behind the Wiesbaden Agreement, the negotiation of which represented Rathenau's first important act in office. Rathenau was heavily praised and blamed for Wiesbaden. The idea was purely French.

Less than two weeks after taking office, on June 12–13, Rathenau met with Loucheur in Wiesbaden, talked with him for a total of eight or nine hours, and accepted the principle of the Wiesbaden Agreement.[21]

---

[20] Reports by Dr. Wolf, *ibid.*, R43I/20.

[21] Detailed accounts by Rathenau in *Tagebuch*, pp. 171–87, and his report to cabinet on June 14, in Kabinettsprotokolle, BA, R43I/1368. Further details of this and other meetings, copies of Wiesbaden Agreement, supplementary agreements, and other relevant material are in Ausführung, BA, R43I/20 and 21; and Wiederaufbauministerium: Reparationsverhandlungen mit Frankreich, BA, R38/169. Also, Büro des Reichspräsidenten: Politische Abteilung, Ausführung des Friedensvertrags, DZA, vols. 673 and 674.

Loucheur was as well prepared as Rathenau to deal with the shifting realities and fantasies of reparations. Briand's biographer remarked that Briand appreciated Loucheur's "skill . . . in pirouetting away from the denials of the evidence . . ." as he "manipulated his figures like dice—with intuition, speed, and optimism."[22] Loucheur had the optimism of the self-made man who could become the owner of the chateau of Louveciennes, Madame du Barry's country residence. Outstandingly different from Rathenau in style, tall but massive, furiously energetic, he had a number of similar qualities and had been engaged in some parallel functions. He was five years younger than Rathenau. A railway engineer and later co-owner of an engineering construction firm, Loucheur had entered the government during the war as an expert in military production. He became an important member of Clemenceau's group of assistants, with special responsibility for reparations during the peace talks. He gave frequent evidence of the talents Briand's biographer mentioned. On September 11, 1919, he told the Chamber of Deputies that Germany could not pay the 800 billion gold marks he himself had earlier claimed, and that a more reasonable figure would be 300 billion gold marks, to be paid at a rate of 18 billion gold marks annually. He blamed France's allies for having forced her to make the old demand. As for paying the 18 billion gold marks, Germany would have to expand her sales to the Americas. With all its excesses, the speech was an attempt to move France toward a more sensible position on reparations. At the time, it also took courage to say, as Loucheur did, that "there is a limit to [Germany's] capacity to pay."[23] Unlike Tardieu, he was not so rigid in principle nor so closely identified with the Versailles Treaty as to remain tied to the aged and politically moribund Clemenceau. He was happy to join Briand when Briand returned to office, and both men contributed another decade of valuable service to their country. Loucheur was further recommended for his present position by his continuing association with the construction industry in northern France. French businessmen could be confident that he would not permit reparation deliveries to deprive them of customers.

[22] Suarez, *Briand*, 5: 105 and 104.
[23] France, *Annales: Chambre des députés*, 108: 3rd sect., 3849; the speech, pp. 3849–57.

The negotiations for the Wiesbaden Agreement took another four months. Rathenau and Loucheur met again on August 25–26, when they initialed a draft treaty, and on October 6–7, when they signed the agreement and four supplementary agreements. Rathenau had won a few small concessions by hard negotiating, but Loucheur got the essence of what he had originally demanded. Nothing was left of Rathenau's schemes, the reconstruction work in France, the demonstration of German good will in an international labor of brotherhood—nothing but the aura. In the workings of international politics the aura was very useful.

The Wiesbaden Agreement was the perfection of harmlessness. Its general provisions vaporized the specific and concrete terms. According to the latter, France and Germany would create complex administrations managing the transfer of great lists of products, a total of 7 billion gold marks in four and one-half years, from October 1, 1921, to May 1, 1926. Germany would get reparation credit up to 35 percent during any one year, but in no case so much that France would have to admit receiving more than her 52-percent share. This provision, however, created a problem which was never solved. If France was receiving the full 52 percent from other reparation payments—and there was no reason to suppose she would not—then Germany would get no credit for deliveries under the Wiesbaden Agreement—at least, not until after the agreement had expired in 1926. The German economy could hardly wait that long for relief. The provision was so clever and protected France so completely that it destroyed the agreement's announced sense. The agreement was not meant to provide for the delivery of 7 billion gold marks of German goods to France in four and one-half years, giving France valuable products on the one hand, and permitting Germany to substitute goods for desperately needed gold or foreign currency. This was what the public was told. French business and labor, however, refused to permit the import of anything except coal, timber, and dyes, which were in short supply in France. Since these were being shipped anyway—as provided in the Versailles Treaty—the Wiesbaden Agreement introduced no change whatsoever. The agreement was meant to confuse the French electorate and give the French and German governments a little more time to maneuver among the impossibilities. In one of his last statements, on June 9, 1922, Rathenau said: "Up to now [the agreement] has had no effect on economic reality, but a most valuable effect [on] economic insight."[24]

The question of Upper Silesia illustrated the limited value of any arrangement with France. While Rathenau had been negotiating the Wiesbaden Agreement, France had been aggressively supporting the Polish interest in that province. Rathenau had taken the occasion to suggest to Loucheur that a kinder French attitude would improve the chances for German reparations, but the argument had no effect.[25] In October, less than a week after Rathenau and Loucheur signed the agreement, the decision on Upper Silesia became known. It made Germany exceedingly unhappy with France, but then France had her reasons for being unhappy with Germany. The unhappiness was due to the same reciprocal reason, excessive weakness in dealing with the other. By October it had become clear to the French that Wiesbaden would give them no real advantage. They were getting no cash from Germany and could see only doubtful prospects of it. They reacted bitterly.

A great debate began in the Chamber of Deputies on October 18. Briand, defending himself against the accusation that he was practicing a *"politique d'abandons,"* had to fight for his government's life. Furthermore he was preparing to leave for the Washington Naval Conference before the end of the month, and the conference promised nothing good. Briand did not trust his full weight upon the Wiesbaden Agreement. In a long speech on October 21 he mentioned it briefly as helping to produce a "favorable atmosphere."[26] But that was all. There was little else he could say about it. After getting nothing from the first reparation payment, France was now watching the mark decline more and more, a process that took dismal effect on its own economy. Guided by orthodox economic thinking, the nation found it easy to blame Germany for the German inflation. "Germany is undergoing planned bankruptcy in order to evade her contractual obligations. . . . *La faillite équivaudra*

[24] Rathenau, *Gesammelte Reden*, p. 405, in a speech (pp. 404–18) in Stuttgart before a group invited from "all the parties." The Reparation Commission did not approve the agreement until March 31, 1922. The Chamber of Deputies ratified it only on July 6, 1922, and the four supplementary agreements on December 20, 1922—after Rathenau was dead. Nothing was ever delivered under it.

[25] Ernst Laubach, "Die Politik der Kabinette Wirth 1921–1922" (dissertation, 1966), p. 78. The published version, previously mentioned, does not carry this passage.

[26] Suarez, *Briand*, 5: 222; the full text of the speech, pp. 209–30.

à une victoire." This was how the German Ambassador had summarized French press opinion in a report on September 20. "The
German government is responsible for the inflation because it
constantly prints up new paper money while refusing to get its
hands on the nation's real wealth," the Ambassador continued.
"The hateful judgments predominate by far."[27] In the *Revue des
deux mondes* Poincaré was tirelessly demanding that Germany slow
down its currency printing press and balance its budget. The Ambassador found a few mild exceptions; the radical *Ère nouvelle*,
for example, pointed out that a German bankruptcy might be painful to the Germans as well as to the French. He did not report that
Le Figaro was hinting at the value of peaceful coexistence. In the
spring of 1921 it had begun to carry a number of articles on German subjects and personalities, friendly reviews of Rathenau's ideas,
interviews with Erzberger and Stresemann, and, during September,
a series called, "A Survey of Germany," which included an interview with Rathenau. This effort to understand Germany was ex-
ceptional. Few persons dared say anything objective about her. In
the debate in the Chamber, Léon Daudet called Briand weak on
Upper Silesia, while Maurice Barrès urged a more energetic encouragement to separatism in the occupied Rhineland. Tardieu
concentrated his contempt in a killing phrase; the government, he
said, was as decisive as "a dead dog floating downstream."[28]
Briand had to use all his skill to placate Chamber and nation. His
objective, he said, was "to disengage from the corpus of Germany
a Germany with whom we can live."[29] For the moment the majority
of the Chamber agreed with Briand, who went to Washington with
its formal support. But the limits were set.

For Germany, and in a way that was more essential, the limits
had also been set. French policy, if it did not change for the better,
meant German bankruptcy. The only reasonable expectation was
that it would change for the worse. The Wirth-Rathenau government had to maintain itself against the dangerous effects of French
demands upon domestic politics and engage the understanding of
the other major Allied power.

[27] Wilhelm Mayer, in a telegram to the Foreign Ministry, Wiederaufbauministerium: Londoner Ultimatum vom Mai 1921, BA, R38/118.
[28] Suarez, *Briand*, 5: 217, 218, and 232.
[29] *Ibid.*, 5: 222.

CHAPTER V

Germany:
The Politics of Reparations

In their programmatic speeches of June, Wirth and Rathenau had tried to reassure the country that fulfillment would destroy neither its security nor its finances. They were saying that their fulfillment policy did not constitute fulfillment. Wirth's promises about military compliance were imprecise enough to suggest that he would practice as much evasion as possible. About reparations Wirth said: "We must try through deeds and good will to show just how great our productive ability is." He meant this as a limiting statement. By extending herself to the utmost, Germany would show the limits of her productive ability, thus proving she could not pay what the Allies were demanding. Wirth was asking the Germans to contribute the "deeds and good will" that would earn eventual Allied understanding. With those materials he could hardly be inspiring.

Rathenau, trying to get beyond the harsh sense of it, developed a mystique of fulfillment. He called fulfillment "an autonomous, self-assigned task" that would serve the cause of international peace. Into this general fulfillment mystique he tried to infuse a business mystique: "When a document has my signature on it . . . then I look upon that signature as [a pledge of] my honor and the honor of my people." Germany, however, had been thrashed into assigning herself a task she believed to be impossible, and the London

Payments Plan surely had no claim upon honor, as in the case of a contract freely entered upon. Rathenau was asking the nation to follow him in suspending disbelief. He supplemented his arguments with music. He mentioned the last movement of Beethoven's last string quartet: "It begins slowly, 'Must it be?' and ends with a decisive and powerful 'It must be!' "[1] The Reichstag applauded appreciatively.

The Wirth-Rathenau formula and the Allied tractations had their effect. Most Germans who would stop to think about the ungrateful problem of fulfillment accepted the government's program. Coherent opposition did not exist in mid-1921, and indeed never would develop completely. The Nationalists and other rightists were helpless before the blind necessity. They could only fall back upon the strategy they used in confronting all the unpleasantness of existence in a republic: they tacitly admitted the basic wisdom of the policy but tried to cover that by quarreling over the details. Thus a Nationalist spokesman told the Reichstag that Wirth should have obtained concessions from the Allies.[2] A less responsible rightist reaction was expressed on June 2 by the *Deutsche Zeitung*, a racist newspaper close to the Pan-German League. The *Deutsche Zeitung* actually started similarly with the implicit admission that there was no alternative to fulfillment. It then stopped reasoning and fell into mindless emotion: "But we turn red with shame at the sight of a chancellor . . . boasting to the world how obediently he has done everything, how punctually he is paying the billion marks . . . how conscientiously he is turning us into slaves. . . ." The newspaper was condemning Wirth not for doing what he was doing, but for presumably enjoying it. Actually the Social Democrats had been no less patriotic, if more humane, in their rhetorical flourishes. Their spokesman in the Reichstag excoriated the Allied leaders for forcing German democracy into a posture of "complete submission"; he added that his party's support of the government had been the result of "a difficult decision."[3] *Germania*, the organ of Wirth's Center Party, commented with resignation on June 3:

---

[1] Wirth, *Reden während der Kanzlerschaft*, p. 45, and *Stenographische Berichte*, 349: 3711. Rathenau, *Gesammelte Reden*, p. 203, and *Stenographische Berichte*, 349: 3744.

[2] Friedrich Edler von Braun, in *Stenographische Berichte*, 349: 3733–42.

[3] Otto Wels, in *Stenographische Berichte*, 349: 3722.

"A Wirth government could never become popular as long as it does what has to be done at this time."

The government proceeded to carry out its unpopular and difficult tasks. The Justice Ministry, functioning with real motivation for the first time, began the war crimes trials before the end of May. The restriction of the Reichswehr to 100,000 men had already been specified in legislation passed on two occasions, August 8, 1920, and, during the last days of the Fehrenbach government, on March 23, 1921. Wirth put through a definitive law on June 18 as a further proof of German good will and pacific intentions. Before then, beginning on his first full day in office, he carried out another reassuring demonstration in the military area. On May 11 be began negotiations with the government of Bavaria about the irregulars being sheltered there. They were important to his own government in many ways, at this moment especially in Upper Silesia, and he had no desire to eliminate or cripple them. Nevertheless he had to produce an acceptable fiction of compliance. Wirth had Bavaria order the disarmament of the Civil Guards on June 4 and their dissolution on June 28.[4] The action did not apply to the Free Corps, and the Civil Guards went on existing illegally anyway. Some weapons were given up, while others—perhaps 50 percent—were kept, according to a recent study.[5] The Allies, respecting Germany's need for a minimum of force, declared themselves officially satisfied. Through the Military Control Commission they would continue to press the Germans to avoid obvious violations, but, as the author of the study has remarked, the military aspects of fulfillment henceforth almost disappeared under the shadow of reparations.[6]

[4] Laubach, *Die Politik der Kabinette Wirth*, 402: 33. Laubach's book, to which I have already referred, deserves notice at this point when I treat German domestic politics under the Wirth government. A detailed study of precisely this subject, the book is based on wide research in the government archives and is most helpful to any student of the Weimar Republic of this period. Laubach also reviewed the press, and his original dissertation, which was available to me, carried an annex with many long quotations on the major issues from a wide range of newspaper and periodical opinion. There was little direct analysis of the economic and financial problems, which were treated as they were verbalized by opinion in the twenties. On the politics the author was reluctant to make any extended judgments or develop broader meanings in the context of German history.

[5] Salewski, *Entwaffnung und Militärkontrolle*, p. 176. This was the opinion of the Weimar government's representative in Bavaria.

[6] Salewski, *Entwaffnung und Militärkontrolle*, p. 172. This is confirmed by implication, when not explicitly, in the highly uninformative memoirs of Otto

It was an important accomplishment of the Wirth-Rathenau government, although Germans and Allies united in refusing to admit its significance. There would be many other problems for Wirth and Rathenau, but their predominant concern would remain reparations.

While Rathenau was negotiating the Wiesbaden Agreement, the government was dealing with the various other details of its reparation program. The first was the payment of the promised billion marks. A nation of Germany's size, whatever her financial difficulties, could always collect a certain amount of cash. Actually, Germany had gold reserves worth almost exactly the sum demanded, but they were her last defense against the annihilation of the mark. The Reparation Commission showed more understanding of that point than it would express publicly. On the deadline date of May 31 the commission got only 150 million gold marks in cash, which the Reichsbank transferred from its receipts of foreign currency. For the remainder, the commission accepted three-month notes endorsed by the four leading private banks of Germany. This had allowed Wirth, in his speech of June 1, to tell the Reichstag that the billion had been paid.[7] The Reichsbank then commenced selling great amounts of paper marks, collecting a total of 439 million gold marks in foreign currencies. The bank had to supplement this by using 68 million gold marks of its gold and 58 million gold marks of its silver reserves. The silver, when melted down, required ninety railroad cars for land transport. At the point of transfer, one shipment was held up when a barge was delayed by low water, causing some anxiety that the payment would fail to arrive on time. These sums were still not enough. With German export revenues as security, the Reichsbank borrowed 270 million

---

Gessler, the Democratic Defense Minister from 1920 to 1928, *Reichswehrpolitik in der Weimarer Zeit.* Gessler made no effort to deny that he was doing his best to evade the Versailles Treaty, although he was defensive about some details of his administration. He regarded himself as an exponent of the fulfillment policy: "Before history I freely admit my part in it" (p. 182). He had, in fact, been the first Reconstruction Minister, thus Rathenau's predecessor. Writing in the 1950's, this survivor of so much history still believed in the wisdom of Wirth's fulfillment policy and justified it with the same reasoning Wirth and Rathenau had used. Gessler saw no inconsistency in supporting Seeckt and the generals in building up arms, on the one hand, and Wirth and Rathenau in paying reparations, on the other.

[7] *Reden während der Kanzlerschaft,* p. 42; *Stenographische Berichte,* 349: 3710.

gold marks from Mendelssohn & Co., an Amsterdam bank. Mendelssohn & Co. shared the loan with other banks in The Netherlands, Switzerland, Great Britain, and France. Thus Germany's two great reparation creditors, Great Britain and France, lent her money to pay reparations, Lazard Frères having gotten permission from the French government to cover 50 million gold marks. It was good business, since the loan combined a high interest rate with reassuring security. The loan was repaid as Germany received her payments from exports in the next few months. Transferring the billion gold marks had been a delicate and complex operation; the Reichsbank used all its skill to reduce the damage to the economy as much as possible.[8] The bank's money traders could do little; in fiscal 1921–22 the German economy was losing almost 3 billion gold marks through other uncovered expenses. The mark went from 58.3 to the dollar on May 13, to an average of 70 in June, to 81 on August 1, to 86 on August 15, 91 on September 5, and 100 by September 10. With the Upper Silesian situation adding its unsettling effect, the rate was 310 by November.

The Wiesbaden Agreement, like the cash payment, was purchasing French forbearance at the cost of German distress. Rathenau defended the agreement at home with the same tact he had used in negotiating it abroad.

The disabused realism which had guided Rathenau in accepting the French demands made his domestic assignment all the more difficult. He had conceded very much, at least in words. Thus he agreed to count the free deliveries of coal and other products as part of Germany's export total. As a result, according to the export index clause of the London Payments Plan, Germany would be obligated to pay 26 percent of the value of these deliveries as additional cash reparations. On the face of it this was double indemnity. Similarly, he was willing to calculate the credit Germany would receive for the coal deliveries on the basis of the domestic German price, although subsidies kept it to about half of the international price. It was also true that the only products France would take would be those easily salable for cash on the world markets. None of these details mattered, since they could not be carried out. Rathenau, however, could not quite say so. He had to mix a measure of illusion into his explanations.

[8] Described in a Reichsbank report, dated October 5, 1921, prepared for Wirth, in Ausführung, BA, R43I/21.

Rathenau applied his persuasions upon the cabinet, the business community, the press, and the nation at large. He interpreted the agreement selectively. He got the cabinet's support on the day he returned from his first meeting in Wiesbaden. Almost two months later he overwhelmed his ministerial colleagues with a brilliant performance, lecturing on such details as the 26 percent index, coupons, prices, duties, and the selection of goods. He described the service organizations which were to collect orders and make deliveries under the agreement, and then discussed such broader themes as the immediate reactions in the economy, industrial demand in France and Germany, and economic and political developments to 1935. On October 3 he defended the agreement against an unexpected proposal by Foreign Minister Rosen, who wanted to make Germany's signature conditional on the cancellation of the military sanctions (the occupation of Düsseldorf, Duisburg, and Ruhrort) imposed in March.[9] Rathenau easily prevailed upon the cabinet to reject that futile effort at blackmail. Going beyond the cabinet to the business community, Rathenau spoke three times—on June 16, July 27, and November 9—to the Reparation Committee of the National Economic Council.[10] To his audience of businessmen he had to admit that the French would resist importing German goods, but he reminded them that cash reparations were weakening the mark. The implication was false—that Wiesbaden promised relief by transforming future payments from cash to goods. But then the person objecting to Rathenau's reasoning would be forced to suggest an alternative, and no one could think of any. The point was that the business community, as represented in the National Economic Council, had to live with Rathenau's arguments, even if it did not believe them. Rathenau would continue to spin out fantasies because of the agreement's nature as well as his own inclinations, but he could also talk hard sense. The latter was evident in two talks in early July, one to a business group and the other to the Congress of the German Press, in which he emphasized the importance of the United States. He told the businessmen: "European conditions cannot be cured as long as an economic complex of the magnitude of the United States keeps its

---

[9] Kabinettsprotokolle, BA, R43I/1368 (June 14), 1370 (August 3), and 1371 (October 3).

[10] Reichswirtschaftsrat II: Reparationsausschuss (Minutes), DZA, vols. 611–13. The July talk is also in his *Gesammelte Reden*, pp. 225–40. Rathenau was no longer in office in November, but he was still important in the government.

hands off."[11] For the press he drew a precise diagram of the world's
finances: All nations were tied to each other by the international
debts—whether war debts or reparations—the United States as the
great creditor, Germany as the great debtor, and the other nations
fixed at various points between the two.[12] Of all persons responsible
for policy no one understood or expressed the true proportions
better than Rathenau. Continuing the family argument among industrialists he replied firmly to a letter from Hugo Stinnes: "Your
objections are wrong and . . . irrelevant."[13] Rathenau also went
to Munich to speak at a meeting of the National Industrial Association on September 28. Georg Bernhard, who was a member of
the National Economic Council and deeply interested in economic
questions, reported on the speech himself for the *Vossische Zeitung*,
of which he was editor. Bernhard noted that the industrialists had
been hostile to Wirth and Rathenau, although primarily because
of Wirth's somewhat demagogic past. By now, he said, the hostility
had declined as a result of the Wirth-Rathenau statesmanship, while
Rathenau's speech helped reduce it much further. The record of
the speech noted many "Bravos" and "stormy, lengthy applause"
at the end. The association's chairman, Kurt Sorge, had introduced
Rathenau cautiously. When the speech ended he spoke more warmly
and assured the members that Rathenau had gotten the prior approval of the organization's leadership for every important provision of the agreement.[14] A speech taking issue with Rathenau was
ironical proof of his effectiveness. It was given by Jakob Reichert,
a Nationalist Reichstag member, an important association leader,
and president of the Union of German Iron and Steel Industrialists.
A few months later Reichert published a book attacking Rathenau's
reparation policy.[15] At the meeting he had to admit that he approved the principle of the agreement before he went on to make
the obvious objections. The members were so nearly perfect in
their ambivalence that they responded to Reichert with the same

[11] *Hamburger Ausschuss für den Friedenswirtschaft*, on July 7, *Gesammelte
Reden*, p. 214.
[12] On July 4, report in *Le Figaro*, July 6.
[13] *Ein preussischer Europäer*, November 24, p. 405.
[14] Minutes of the two-day meeting (September 28 and 29), *Sondersammlung
zur industriellen Verbandsgeschichte*, Deutsches Industrie-Institut, Frankfurt,
Veröffentlichungen des Reichsverbands der deutschen Industrie, vol. 17 (1921).
Rathenau's speech also in *Gesammelte Reden*, pp. 243–64. *Vossische Zeitung* report, September 29 (A.M.).
[15] Jakob Reichert, *Rathenaus Reparationspolitik* (1922).

"stürmischer, langanhaltender Beifall" they had granted Rathenau. The meeting then passed a resolution supporting the Wiesbaden conception of deliveries in kind. To have got that much from the industrialists was a great accomplishment. Rathenau's use of the Wiesbaden Agreement had been a masterpiece of the politics of reparations.

Rathenau's skillful manipulation of the agreement was also evident in his dealings with Great Britain. The provision for delayed credit meant that Germany was helping France cheat her allies, and the British might well have objected. Rathenau kept them informed at every step.[16] On September 23, after talking with Lord d'Abernon, Rathenau sent him a copy of the agreement and used the covering letter to argue that reparations were driving Germany to compete all the more keenly with Great Britain.[17] Rathenau could not rest with the reasonable, and in his talk with the Ambassador he suggested that Britain take goods from Germany and pass them on to Russia, who would then pay England.[18] He did not explain where Russia would get the money. It was not necessary for D'Abernon to enter into these thought processes to get the point, and he noted: "The Wiesbaden Agreement . . . may be fairly characterized as a swindle based on a fallacy. . . . But even so, it may pacify Europe, and we had better use our blind eye."[19]

In July Lord d'Abernon had recorded: "Rathenau appears to have gained great influence in the cabinet lately and to have become something like Vice-Chancellor with special responsibility for the reparation question, and to some extent for foreign affairs."[20] All the circumstances assisted this development—Rathenau's personal relationship with Wirth, the centrality of reparations in government policy (Rathenau to young Democrats: "The greatest part of our future [foreign] policy will have to be reparation policy."),[21] the close marriage of his peculiar excellences and the specifics of the situation, and Rosen's incompetence as Foreign Minister. It was true, as noted by his fellow Democrat, Justice

---

[16] Letter to Alfred Kerr, in *Ein preussischer Europäer*, November 19, p. 405.
[17] Letter to D'Abernon, September 23, 1921, in *ibid.*, p. 402.
[18] D'Abernon, *Versailles to Rapallo*, entry, September 23, p. 217. Rathenau's letter did not mention that point.
[19] *Ibid.*, entry, October 7, pp. 223–24.
[20] *Ibid.*, entry, July 20, p. 204.
[21] In Mannheim, October 27, in *Gesammelte Reden*, p. 278.

Minister Eugen Schiffer, that "in the cabinet meetings he takes the floor on most questions, argues about this or that trivial point after a forceful, profound-seeming introduction, and as a result makes his colleagues impatient. Rosen in particular suffers. . . ." Schiffer also remarked: "Quite often you can see that there is nothing behind all those glittering and glistening phrases but a very ordinary detail."[22] It was true enough. Yet Schiffer's judgment of Rathenau's contribution to the government, as reflected in his memoirs, was strongly favorable. Most members of the cabinet showed by their actions that they agreed with Schiffer. They listened to Rathenau with respect and supported him whenever he made a stand, thus on the Rosen intervention. Even Rosen, with all his remembered distress, made a generous assessment of Rathenau in his own memoirs.

There had been an initial uncertainty in 1921 as the Germans tried to understand what the Allies wanted of them. Then the billion-mark payment and the negotiation of the Wiesbaden Agreement began to have their effects on public opinion. The enemies of fulfillment became more active. In general the enemies of fulfillment were the enemies of the Weimar Republic. There were pervasive ambiguities in either position as well as in the relation of the one to the other.

The Weimar Republic had not been an accident of history. It was the most reasonable response to the realities of the situation and the demands of the overwhelming majority of Germans, no matter what they thought they wanted.

The first elections, held two months after the revolution, were misleading indications of what the Germans wanted. In January, 1919, the coalition of parties supporting the republic, the Weimar Coalition of Social Democrats, Democrats, and the Catholic Center, got more than 75 percent of the vote. In the next election, on June 6, 1920, the Weimar Coalition parties got less than half of the vote. This did not mean that the Germans had first accepted the republic and then rejected it a year and a half later. In 1919 they were voting for the best alternative to the failure represented by the imperial regime and the chaos promised by the radicals. This meant a republic. In 1920, with conditions somewhat more normal, most Germans were making specific demands in defense of their inter-

22 Schiffer-Nachlass, p. 24, Hauptarchiv Berlin-Dahlem.

ests, but without direct reference to the question of the republic's continued existence. Government policy changed little after the second election. Despite the party slogans most Germans assumed that the republic would continue to exist. Some of them despised it, many of them disliked it, but few conceived of anything to replace it.

The actions of the parties maintained the republic better than their beliefs or public statements. Among all the parties, only the Democrats—a party of professors, editors, and enlightened businessmen like Rathenau—completely accepted the republic on principle, and their career was discouraging. Representing no definable special interest, they went from 5.6 million votes and 75 seats in 1919 to 2.3 million votes and 45 seats in 1920. The Center, also losing votes in 1920 but still a substantial party, brought together Catholic workers, employers, and peasants in a confessional party. If religion distorted its representation of secular interests, it also gave the Center a helpful bias in the circumstances. The position of the Catholics as a minority made the party sympathetic to the republic, particularly with its unhappy memories of a Protestant monarchy and Bismarck's *Kulturkampf*. The Catholic situation was more important than Catholic tradition in encouraging its republicanism, but the republicanism was assisted by selected parts of a newer tradition, the social welfare policies deriving from Pope Leo XIII's encyclicals of the 1890's. Wirth was a sincere representative of this combination of Catholic interests and ideals. The Social Democrats, still the largest party, had to violate Marxist principle to become good republicans. They found it not at all difficult, although it made them vulnerable to attacks from the further Left. Most of the working class gave no evidence that it wanted socialism, and the Social Democratic leadership was content to support a middle-class republic with social welfare easements. The contradictions on the Right were a mirror image of those among the parties of the Weimar Coalition. The Nationalists, who got 2.2 million votes in 1919 and a million more in 1920, lamented the monarchy passionately, but not even in 1920 did their program call unequivocally for its return.[23] They had a range of interests which the republic served and which a concentration on the

[23] Party statement of December 27, 1918, in Wilhelm Mommsen and Günther Franz, *Die deutschen Parteiprogramme 1918–1930* (1931), pp. 9–10; party statement of principles in 1920, *ibid.*, pp. 82–91.

monarchy's return could neglect. In moments of crisis they would compromise their principles ungraciously but helpfully. In June, 1919, when the nation balked against the humiliations of the Versailles Treaty, the Nationalists agreed to a formula permitting its acceptance by the National Assembly. They also promised not to attack the patriotism of the assembly members who took the responsibility for voting affirmatively upon themselves.[24] Of course the Nationalists failed to keep their promise, but it inhibited their verbal excesses. The role of the German People's Party was another illustration of the seductive powers of the republic. Gustav Stresemann, rejected by the Democrats as an expansionistic imperialist, organized the party among right-wing National Liberals representing monarchical attachments and conservative business. Stresemann remained a sentimental monarchist but he began moving toward a position of support for the republic, dragging a half-reluctant party with him. He would become its ablest statesman and the most successful exponent of fulfillment. Until the holocaust, the republic grew stronger upon the ambiguities of its situation.

Underlying all the ambiguities was a reality that favored the republic. Germany had outgrown its feudal and military aristocracy. A parliamentary government worked best under the present circumstances. Both the middle class, which replaced the aristocracy in the powerful positions in society, and the working class, guided by leaders inevitably borne upward into the middle class, functioned naturally in a republic. Until the holocaust. But that is another matter, which can be better studied after we have seen the effects of reparations and the other Versailles Treaty provisions, and those of the Great Depression, on the weaknesses in German society. Until the Depression the question of governmental form—a republic or not—was not quite a true question.

Another doubtful question, and one interwoven with the problems of fulfillment, was that of the class war and economic conflict generally. There was not one important confrontation between capital and labor throughout the whole period of the Weimar Republic. Labor never used the general strike for either economic gain or political power. Capital, for its part, made no effort to cancel out any important labor gain and permitted the further development of social welfare services. On November 15, 1918,

[24] Eyck, *A History of the Weimar Republic*, 1: 105.

the important labor leaders and industrialists, Hugo Stinnes and Walther Rathenau among them, signed an agreement which established the Industrial Community (*Arbeitsgemeinschaft*) as a body for capital-labor cooperation. The agreement stipulated capital's acceptance of the principle of collective bargaining and of the eight-hour day, and its promise to desist from organizing company unions. The Industrial Community was neither a guarantee of industrial peace, nor important, but its existence showed a real desire for social peace. Strikes were comparatively rare. The greatest industrial strikes occurred in the latter part of the twenties, the republic's most prosperous time. These conflicts emphasized the overriding force of the general agreement, with the combatants carefully avoiding extreme positions. With all the hardship directly and indirectly caused by reparations, strikes never once gave Wirth real concern during his chancellorship. He did have to give his attention to one strike—in February, 1922. The working class had nothing to do with it, the strikers being clerical and supervisory employees of the railroads whose incomes had been cruelly reduced by inflation. Blustering and compromising, Wirth got them back to work after a week. Fulfillment and reparations had meant a new overlay of contradictions upon the basic contradictions of the Weimar Republic. Reparations meant more sacrifices which each group tried to pass on to the other groups. But then all of them, flung together by foreign harshness, frequently halted their struggles to cooperate against the Allies. These contradictions were acted out intensely during the months after Wirth accepted the London Ultimatum.

The two theoretical sources for paying reparations were either current revenues or the national wealth. The German economy was in deficit, however, and the Allies did not propose to let it develop favorable trade balances with them: there were simply no current revenues and no prospects of any. This left the German national wealth, which could be attacked either by special levies or by more taxes.

One idea which had many attractions was to confiscate part of the value of property. Socialist views affected almost everyone, and many people on the Left thought that the Weimar Republic had failed the egalitarian promises of the revolution of 1918. Even more people felt that businessmen had profited from the war and war sufferings. If anybody had the money, it was the rich. Why noι make them pay reparations? Wirth, who represented the Catholic workers in the Center, wanted to impose the greater sacrifice on property. The Socialist Economics Minister, Robert Schmidt, was enthusiastic about it.

Immediately after accepting the chancellorship, Wirth attempted to move the government in a left-wing direction. He discussed property confiscation at the cabinet meeting of May 30, when he introduced Rathenau to the other members.[25] In his Reichstag speech of June 1 he had also vaguely mentioned the idea.[26] Earlier, at the cabinet meeting of May 17, Robert Schmidt suggested a 5-percent share of property and another special levy on profits.[27] That was only an unformed idea, but on May 19 he submitted a detailed plan. Schmidt now called for a compulsory mortgage on 20 percent of the value of German property, the mortgage notes to be sold in foreign markets and the cash returns to flow into a reparation fund.[28] Keeping the 20-percent principle, he submitted a more elaborate draft to Wirth on June 27.[29] This latter was known as the Schmidt Plan. Wirth, however, had already begun to have doubts, which he mentioned to the cabinet on June 24.[30] He said that it might be easier to extend the National Emergency Contribution (Reichsnotstandsopfer), a wartime tax measure that had produced substantial revenues. Rathenau had strong ideas about the Schmidt Plan himself. Seeing many dangers in it, he took the leadership in opposing Schmidt at an extended cabinet discussion on June 29.[31] The Economics Minister's plan meant "socialization [but] the present economic situation does not permit experiments," Rathenau said. Besides, he added, the Allies might simply seize the money without crediting Germany. By now Wirth was firmly opposed to property confiscation. With Rathenau's help, he maneuvered to destroy the Schmidt Plan. At that meeting on June 29 Rathenau had suggested another way of getting money, namely by a tax on capital increment. In point of fact, the existing

[25] Kabinettsprotokolle, BA, R43I/1367.
[26] Reden während der Kanzlerschaft, pp. 47–50; Stenographische Berichte, 349: 3711–16.
[27] Kabinettsprotokolle, BA, R43I/1367.
[28] Copy in Ausführung, BA, R43I/20.
[29] Copy in ibid., R43I/20.
[30] Kabinettsprotokolle, BA, R43I/1368.
[31] Ibid., R43I/1368.

taxes, including the Emergency Contribution, exploited that general area, but the idea gave Wirth his opportunity. He found difficulties in Rathenau's conception, and permitted it to disappear in the next two or three weeks, but he found even more difficulties in Schmidt's idea. He got the cabinet to make a Solomonic decision: the cabinet assigned a subcommittee headed by Rathenau to examine the Schmidt Plan further. In effect, Rathenau was charged with destroying it. Supported by Rathenau's subsequent recommendations, Wirth finally made his decision at a cabinet meeting on July 30. The Schmidt Plan had to be dropped because it was too complicated and certain to cause destructive class conflict.[32] The Economics Minister had resisted vigorously. He had tried to outflank Rathenau's study subcommittee by sending still another version of his original plan directly to Wirth on July 28.[33] At the cabinet meeting on July 29 he offered an alternative idea, the capitalization of taxes for 40 years. Wirth, however, remained negative at the cabinet meetings on July 29 and 30. He had tested the possibilities of the left-wing approach to collecting reparations and found only discouragement.

Nowhere did firm support for property confiscation appear. The Social Democrats, Robert Schmidt's own party, refused to commit themselves to it. They did not need Rathenau to tell them of the political and administrative problems, and they had too many other concerns requiring their attention and energy. Julius Hirsch, Schmidt's chief assistant as State Secretary in the Economics Ministry, later admitted the Ministry's doubts about its own project. In a lecture series he gave in 1924 he mentioned the plan briefly and with obvious embarrassment, neither defending nor mourning it.[34] If support was equivocal at best, resistance was hard and clear. A typical expression came in a letter addressed to the new Reconstruction Minister on June 20 by the National Committee of German Agriculture, representing twelve important agricultural organizations.[35] The Committee assured Rathenau that it was

[32] *Ibid.*, R43I/1369.

[33] Appended to minutes of July 29, Kabinettsprotokolle, BA, R43I/1369.

[34] "Kiel Lectures," published as a book, *Die deutsche Währungsfrage*; discussion of project, pp. 13–14.

[35] Copy in Wiederaufbauministerium: Londoner Ultimatum vom Mai 1921, BA, R38/118. The committee—the *Reichsausschuss der deutschen Landwirtschaft* —represented these groups: *Deutscher Landwirtschaftsrat, Bezugsvereinigung der deutschen Landwirte, Bund der Landwirte, Deutsche Landwirtschaftsgesellschaft,*

prepared to help the government meet its obligations under the London Payments Plan, but it argued that a mortgage on farm property would destroy the economic base of German agriculture. Accordingly, it "was summoning all agricultural groups to join in a battle union against the government's ruinous plans." After the acceptance of the principle of fulfillment came the rejection of the detail of implementation. The sacrifice would be borne by others. Urban property owners were threatening similar action on the basis of similar arguments. Wirth could only change direction.

The Chancellor moved along two lines. One was familiar. On July 6 he went before the Reichstag and reminded the members as gently as possible that the government was running enormous deficits and that it might reasonably increase taxes.[36] An expert in the politics of taxation, he found it natural enough to return to the tax measures he had drafted. The Reichstag speech was anticlimactic and disappointing; many persons had been hoping for a miracle. A month later, just before the government and the nation went on vacation, Wirth announced a supplementary tax program requiring fifteen new drafts of the major tax laws. He had simply increased the old taxes as much as he thought the economy could bear. This revision held until October, when the government submitted a new series of tax drafts which required more negotiations. From October until January Reichstag tax committees bargained over the allocation of the burdens. Middle-class members had reduced the taxes to such an extent that Wirth had to go to the committee meetings in mid-January and beg for reconsideration. He won a new compromise which held until March, 1922.[37] Through it all the deficits mounted.

Wirth, meanwhile, had been pursuing a somewhat more attractive objective. The effort to use compulsion upon the sources of wealth had failed. Perhaps a voluntary action might succeed, particularly since it did not mean the threat of socialization. On

---

Deutscher Landbund, Deutsche milchwirtschaftlicher Reichsverband, Generalverband der deutschen Raiffeisengenossenschaften, Kartoffelbaugesellschaft, Reichsverband der deutschen land- und forstwirtschaftlichen Arbeitgebervereinigungen, Reichsverband der deutschen landwirtschaftlichen Genossenschaften, Verband deutscher Gartenbaubetriebe, and the *Vereinigung der deutschen Bauernvereine.*

[36] *Reden während der Kanzlerschaft,* pp. 111–30; *Stenographische Berichte,* 351: 4467–73.

[37] Discussed by Georg Bernhard in *Vossische Zeitung,* January 26, 1922 (A.M.).

July 30 Wirth told the cabinet that he would approach industry directly for a loan from its reserves.[38] The most prosperous part of the economy might be persuaded to show its patriotism by bearing a greater part of the burden. In the normal order of things, specifically through export, industry managed to obtain foreign currency. Could it not lend some of that money to the government? Beginning in July, Wirth and Rathenau negotiated with the leaders of the National Industrial Association. On July 17 Wirth asked several industrial leaders to discuss the "transfer of certain sums of foreign currency to the Reich." The leaders included Hugo Stinnes, the Krupp director Otto Wiedfeldt whom Wirth had considered for a ministerial post and who would later become Ambassador to the United States, and Wilhelm Cuno, the managing director of the Hamburg-America Line and Wirth's successor as Chancellor.[39] There was a great deal of understanding for the government's position among the association's leaders in the fall of 1921, according to a recent student of German politics.[40] At a meeting of the executive committee on June 14, Wiedfeldt supported the industry loan with great enthusiasm.[41] Even Alfred Hugenberg, the Nationalist newspaper magnate and future Vice-Chancellor to Hitler, was initially sympathetic to the idea, although he soon changed his mind.[42] The subject came to public discussion at the Munich conference of the association in September, the same conference at which Rathenau had explained the Wiesbaden Agreement. Chairman Sorge used a frank argument: Germany still had to purchase Allied understanding, and the government, if it could not get the money through a loan, might follow the advice of people like Economics Minister Schmidt and confiscate private property outright.[43] Speaking for the association's cautious leadership, however, Sorge made a condition that virtually annihilated any real chance of an industry loan. The government must make a credible effort to balance its budget. Most particularly, it should

---

[38] Kabinettsprotokolle, BA, R43I/1369.
[39] Telegram with list of addressees, Wiederaufbauministerium: Londoner Ultimatum vom Mai 1921, BA, R38/118.
[40] Albertin, "Die Verantwortung der liberalen Parteien," p. 580.
[41] Ibid., pp. 578–79.
[42] According to Karl Helfferich, Die Politik der Erfüllung (1922), p. 64.
[43] Deutsches Industrie-Institut, Frankfurt, Sondersammlung zur industriellen Verbandsgeschichte, pp. 3–7.

prove its sense of financial responsibility by eliminating the enormous deficit in the federal railroad system. This prepared the way for the ultimate rejection of the loan, but meanwhile the association members passed a resolution supporting the loan in principle. By the time of the September meeting, furthermore, the conception had changed from an outright transfer of business funds to a guarantee by business of a loan the government itself would contract abroad. This was given form in the next weeks in the National Economic Council.[44] Max Hachenburg, a council member and leading provincial lawyer, was asked to draft legislation providing for a credit union of property owners in business, industry, agriculture, and real estate. This organization would guarantee a loan of 2 billion gold marks, the loan to be raised on the foreign money markets. Hachenburg, who told the story of the plan in his autobiography, approached the idea like a legal draftsman, with no understanding of its economic aspect.[45] The Hachenburg Plan was redundantly defective. It was voluntary, and no rational property owner would risk his property to support a government that might go bankrupt. Then there was the problem of gaining entry to the foreign money markets and attracting foreign credit. Stinnes put this kindly to Hachenburg: "You won't get a foreign loan—not even with your guarantee," he told Hachenburg—"and smiled in his friendly, quiet way."[46] A debate in the National Economic Council on November 4 showed that the representatives of industry were negative.[47] At a Berlin meeting on the next day the National Industrial Association rejected the Hachenburg Plan under the influence of Stinnes and Alfred Hugenberg. Otto Wiedfeldt thought this was a betrayal of the Munich resolution and part of a Nationalist intrigue to take over the association,[48] but Stinnes was a People's Party member, and Wiedfeldt never gave evidence of having studied the economics of a loan. The future Ambassador

---

[44] *Stenographische Berichte . . . Reichswirtschaftsrats*, meetings no. 27 (November 3, 1921), no. 28 (November 4), no. 32 (December 10), and no. 33 (December 13).

[45] Max Hachenburg, *Lebenserinnerungen eines Rechtsanwalts* (1929), pp. 311–409. The plan is in Ausführung, BA, R43I/26. Hachenburg discussed the plan in detail at meetings of the National Economic Council on November 3 and 4, *Stenographische Berichte . . . Reichswirtschaftsrats*, meetings no. 27 and 28.

[46] Hachenburg, *Lebenserinnerungen*, p. 335.

[47] *Stenographische Berichte . . . Reichswirtschaftsrats*, meeting no. 28.

[48] According to a letter in the Krupp archive, quoted in Albertin, "Die Verantwortung der liberalen Parteien," p. 609.

was thinking more like a political man than a business representative. The association's rejection called up a sharp reaction, the government and left-wing newspapers carrying indignant comments. *Vorwärts* on November 12 threatened socialization and Georg Bernhard in the *Vossische Zeitung* of November 13 demanded a return to the idea of property confiscation as the Schmidt Plan had provided. Bernhard's response was slow and his indignation forced; he had attended the National Economic Council meeting of November 4 and he knew the attitude of industry. In the debate he had been unable to produce any valid arguments. The real proportions of the issue were evident at a cabinet meeting on November 14.[49] By then Germany was facing a new urgency. The Reparation Commission had come to Berlin and was demanding assurances that Germany would not default on the next reparation payment. In view of that, the government's hopes had swung away from the Hachenburg Plan and the inevitable delays it promised, and back to the idea of a simple loan. Wirth had been thinking of getting 500 million gold marks for the next major payment out of industry's foreign currency reserves. He began the November 14 cabinet meeting by saying that he had tried and failed to get the 500 million. Furthermore he was neither surprised nor angry. He said he doubted that private interests had the money anyway. Indeed, he had already attempted an alternative, and that, too, had failed. The idea had been for industry itself to borrow the money abroad on its own account and hand it over to the government. He had shown a letter making that request to Hermann Bücher, the executive secretary of the National Industrial Association, and had gotten his response. Industry refused, saying that it could not risk using up its last foreign credit. Gustav Bauer, Wirth's Vice-Chancellor and a Socialist, reacted with indignation and called the association's attitude a mockery of the government. He then paused, his thought processes showing themselves clearly. He wondered if the Reich should have the money in its possession in view of the risk of losing it to the Allies for no good reason. Economics Minister Schmidt cast off the whole doctrinaire weight of his earlier attitude and agreed with Bauer. Clearly, he had never really believed in his own scheme for property confiscation. Wirth remarked

---

[49] Kabinettsprotokolle, BA, R43I/1371.

that he saw no mockery in the association's attitude. Germany, he said, would have gained very little if she were in a similar position when she had to make the next reparation payment. The cabinet discussion marked the suspension of the struggle between Left and Right. Both united against the Allies, planning to show the Reparation Commission that the nation had tried everything to get the money. The letter to the association and its refusal were to be part of the documentation. In December, a month later, the documentation was further strengthened when all parties and interest groups united to revive a version of the Hachenburg Plan which was even weaker than the original. There was no chance that it would produce any revenue. Hachenburg remembered that Wirth called it "a harp on which he could play."[50] According to the official minutes, Wirth pointed out to the council that Rathenau was in London at that moment engaged in important negotiations. The Hachenburg Plan would furnish him with one more proof of Germany's good will. The National Economic Council passed the Hachenburg Plan unanimously on December 13,[51] and the idea of an industry loan vanished as a real possibility.

The loan idea was revived once again, but in even less credible form. Wirth developed it partially to appease the Social Democrats for his concessions to the middle-class parties in the tax compromise of January, 1922.[52] Another purpose was to use it as a counter in Germany's negotiations with the Reparation Commission, one more hollow proof of her good will. The compulsory feature was restored, while the sum was set at 1 billion gold marks. As the discussions extended through February and March the loan became less and less substantial. Conservatives had won the agreement that the original figure in paper marks—70 billion—was to be inviolable, even if the mark rate declined. Of course the rate declined. In the end the government collected the equivalent of 50 million gold marks, a twentieth of the announced value.[53]

The conservatives took the offensive for free-enterprise principle

[50] Hachenburg, *Lebenserinnerungen*, p. 336.
[51] *Stenographische Berichte . . . Reichswirtschaftsrats*, meeting no. 33.
[52] Laubach, *Die Politik der Kabinette Wirth*, pp. 147–48, 157–59. On June 14, 1922, Georg Bernhard reported on its slow progress at a meeting of the National Economic Council, *Stenographische Berichte . . . Reichswirtschaftsrats*, meeting no. 40.
[53] According to Hirsch, *Die deutsche Währungsfrage*, p. 14.

and fell into hypocrisy corresponding to that of the Left. At its Berlin meeting in November, the National Industrial Association had demanded that the railroads be returned to private business. When it developed its idea, however, it produced an admission of failure. Its plan, which foresaw an autonomous stock company, gave the control to representatives of a range of organizations, including professional groups and even unions. It had produced just another socialistic form,[54] although the slogans had originally called for the "privatization" (*Privatisierung*) of the railroads. A kind of reversal of the Schmidt Plan, it also perished quietly.

Like the question of a governmental form, the question of sacrifice had proved to be not quite a true question. Men of politics or pure theory might formulate it for their own purposes: who should make the greater sacrifices, capital or labor, business or agriculture, city or country, producer or consumer? Merely to express it that way exposed the defects in the proposition, since no German citizen had a singular and perfect identity. He was a consumer— and a working man, clerk, peasant, or anyone else; he was a farm laborer, combining the interests of agriculture and labor; he was a small-town resident, impossible to classify firmly as urban or rural. The experience of the Wirth government illuminated all the defects of theory. Any interest group was best served by shifting alliances among the other groups, depending on the issue. Business and labor had opposed each other on socialization and "privatization" —and not with entire sincerity. At the same time they were cooperating against agriculture and consumers by easily agreeing on wage increases that were transformed into price increases. Business and agriculture, combining politically in conservative parties, supported each other in opposing property confiscation and increased property taxes. No party or person had the right to be sure that a given policy advanced his interest.

Other factors confused the situation all the more. The failure to resolve the international transfer problem increased the element of the irrational in the economies of Germany and the world. Germany had paid the billion marks not out of its own resources, but by getting foreigners to speculate in paper marks. Within the coun-

---

[54] Dated March 31, 1922, and signed by the leaders of the association, in the brochure, *Die deutsche Eisenbahnfrage* (Berlin, 1922), in archive of Deutsches Industrie-Institut.

try the result was more inflation, and inflation multiplied the distortions. The mark's loss of a large part of its value on a single day would wipe out the usefulness of a tax schedule which had taken months of hard negotiations. The Berlin correspondent of *The Times* reported on November 7, 1921: "The low value of the mark is . . . rendering the work of the taxation committees almost ludicrous." The correspondent had been careful to make a qualification. He had properly done so.

An arbitrary act of the Allies, made without reference to German needs, could affect conditions more profoundly than anything done by a responsible domestic leadership. Nevertheless, the little that Wirth and his colleagues could do meant a great deal. It might mean a few ounces more or less of meat in a working-class household, or a small wholesaler's rescue from business failure. The struggles among the interest groups were no less bitter or necessary for all the unpredictable results.

Another effect of these uncertainties was the premium on demagoguery. The political parties could survive only by outbidding each other with promises and protestations that they could not believe themselves. Wirth and Rathenau had made claims which nothing justified. On the Left the Independent Social Democrats continually emitted Marxist criticism. A typical statement was made by Rudolf Breitscheid, one of their orators, in the Reichstag debate following a speech of Rathenau's on March 29, 1922. He argued: "Fulfillment is carried out at the cost of labor income and to the advantage of property interests." He was really trying to defend his party against the charge that it was failing to defend the working class. He had begun by saying: "We call the principle of fulfillment a good principle—" He had finished his sentence weakly: "but we cannot approve of the way it is being implemented."[55] In fact the Independents had been supporting fulfillment almost enthusiastically and to the detriment of the party's concern for labor's interests. Revolutionaries of the immediate postwar period, the Independents made no attempt to lead the workers in forceful action on a reparation issue. On the Right the Nationalists and their confederates were accusing the government of selling out to the Entente. This dishonest disillusionment caused great

[55] *Stenographische Berichte,* 354: 6660.

damage to the republic. At the same time, however, the Nationalists were tending toward responsibility. Almost half of their Reichstag deputies would vote for an important bill in 1924 permitting a renewed fulfillment policy, and the party would enter the government in 1925. There were restrictions, equivocal though they might be, upon the destructive tendencies of all the major economic and political groupings.

Unfortunately, other sources of danger existed beyond the limits respected by the organized and generally responsible enemies of fulfillment. These were apathy and a rejection of all order, rancors turned in upon themselves. The Free Corps, developing a culture of unending war, sought excuses for nihilistic violence. Other paramilitary organizations, Hitler's Brown Shirts among them, were expanding. To them fulfillment was another betrayal by a degenerate republic. The irresponsibles could draw upon Germany's military and authoritarian bias and the deep resources of 19th-century racism and anti-Semitism as well as all the backwash of war suffering.

Fulfillment also required that Germany accept the judgment of the Allies on Upper Silesia, as Wirth and Rathenau were acutely reminded in October, 1921. Here was another matter that brought them under vicious domestic attack. Wirth was doing his best to frustrate the Allies. "As if we were only fulfillment people!" he exclaimed in a Reichstag speech at the end of 1926. "The government . . . kept its mouth shut, but it acted patriotically. We organized the defense [of Upper Silesia]."[56] He said that all the major parties cooperated, from the Social Democrats to the Nationalists. President Ebert knew about the government's secret operations and unannounced objectives. Rathenau also knew: "Patriotism glowed in the heart of this Jew."[57] The defense, besides local units, had included the Free Corps formations from Bavaria which Wirth had managed not to disband. In his speech Wirth mysteriously mentioned the *Organisation Consul*, a mysterious military office functioning as a kind of general staff for all the Free Corps. It was headed by Captain Hermann Ehrhardt, a former naval officer, who had led his own Free Corps, the Ehrhardt Brigade, in support of

[56] December 16, *Stenographische Berichte*, 391: 8589, 8590; the speech, pp. 8588–93.
[57] *Ibid.*, p. 8591.

the Kapp Putsch in 1920. In 1921 Ehrhardt was an outlaw carefully overlooked by the Bavarian and Reich governments. Wirth and his government directed the military action in Upper Silesia through Defense Minister Gessler and General von Seeckt of the Reichswehr. On May 18 Wirth assigned Karl Hoefer, a retired general, as chief of operations in the area.[58] On May 23 German units captured strategic Annaberg, and Hoefer, while holding back the Poles, also resisted the efforts of his conventionally superpatriotic officers to continue their drive into Polish territory. With the line stabilized, some of the formations were officially dissolved to quiet French protests. The struggle continued on the diplomatic level, as Wirth and Rathenau dealt with their other problems. The Poles and the French would have agreed that the German government had acted patriotically.

The negotiations concerning Upper Silesia moved toward their petty denouement. The Annaberg victory had simply kept Germany from losing more territory in Upper Silesia than had been indicated in the Versailles Treaty. Wirth had to do something, if only to convince the Germans that he was not failing the fatherland. In an interview with the New York *World* on July 31 he said that he would resign in case of an unfavorable decision. Meanwhile, he was making loud, loose speeches. In Bremen on August 1 he tactlessly warned the Allies against turning Upper Silesia into another *casus belli* like Alsace-Lorraine.[59] No one could say to what extent the German reaction was real and to what extent it was forced. The government was encouraging the Upper Silesians to demonstrate, and Foreign Minister Rosen had been astonished to find two officials in his own ministry coordinating the protest actions under Wirth's direct orders.[60] Earlier, the government had helped transport former residents back to the province for the plebiscite, but Wirth was building upon authentic feeling within Upper Silesia and Germany at large. The nation itself, with all its other economic problems, was threatened with the loss of a valuable industrial region. The Germans of the border region, frankly racist, looked with horror at the prospect of living in a Polish state. The nation sympathized crudely. Within Germany, agreement was

[58] See Hoefer's *Oberschlesien in der Aufstandszeit* (1938).
[59] *Reden während der Kanzlerschaft*, p. 148.
[60] *Aus einem diplomatischen Wanderleben*, 3–4: 323–24.

so complete that the Germans, who could see what was happening, refused to believe what they saw. They were putting too much faith in Great Britain. It was true that the British wanted to restrain French power expansion on the continent, but they had no effective means of influencing the decision on Upper Silesia. Lloyd George went to Paris to confer with Briand, failed to move him, and departed angrily on August 12. His Foreign Minister, Lord Curzon, had to make the official farewells and accept diplomatic defeat the next day. The Allied decision was a transparently masked French victory. The division of Upper Silesia would be carried out not by the Allied leaders, who could not agree, but by the League of Nations. Since France dominated the league, she could get what she—and Poland—wanted.

On October 10 Foreign Minister Rosen told the cabinet to expect the loss of much of Upper Silesia. Rathenau wanted the government to resign immediately, but Ebert and Wirth preferred to await the league statement.[61] Two days later, Ebert, trying to avoid the wearying business of building a new cabinet, argued that the government should not resign, but simply threaten to do so. Rathenau, usually cautious about opposing superior authority, came out directly and forcefully against Ebert. He argued that the government would lose "moral credit" if it stopped short of resigning.[62] Wirth did nothing. Although the league decision was actually known by October 12, the government remained cramped in a waiting position, its leaders repeating a series of futile arguments among themselves.

On October 20, finally, the league officially announced that there would be a partition. The details were favorable to Poland. The new frontier line was drawn in a way that gave her most of the Upper Silesian industrial area, including the important towns of Katowice (Kattowitz) and Chorzow (Königshütte). Germany lost 18 percent of her coal reserves, 28 percent of her iron ore, and 70 percent of her zinc. Inevitably, many Germans and Poles found themselves on the hostile side of the frontier, Poland receiving 220,000 Germans and 280,000 Poles, while 131,000 Germans and 109,000 Poles went to Germany. The Germans insisted upon being shocked. The cabinet debates now appeared meaningless, and

[61] Kabinettsprotokolle, BA, R43I/1371.
[62] *Ibid.*, R43I/1371.

to maintain his connection with a patriotically frantic nation Wirth resigned on October 22. Four days later he reconstituted the government.

The death and revival of the Wirth government permitted a saving catharsis in the German electorate. After the first violence of feeling had exhausted itself, it was generally recognized that no other government combination would work. No one, surely not the leaders of the right-wing parties, could show how Germany could resist. Despairingly, the Germans had to recognize fulfillment as their only possible policy, however much they hated it.

The best hope of the Wirth government lay in forgetting Upper Silesia and achieving a reduction of reparations. Much of this hope was associated with the figure of Rathenau, but he was not in the new government. The Democrats had dissociated themselves from the responsibility, ordering Rathenau and Justice Minister Schiffer to resign. They had left Otto Gessler as Defense Minister, but only as an expert and without commitment of the party to Wirth's policy. The action was dictated by the Democrats' weak position and the nation's exacerbated patriotism. Particularly sensitive because they lacked the support of any interest groups, the Democrats thought they would flee yet another humiliation. The exception made for Gessler could be given a patriotic gloss, since he was the civilian cover for the military's violations of the Versailles Treaty. There was no such justification for keeping Rathenau.

Rathenau was nevertheless indispensable. On October 27 Briand told the Senate: "I saw with disquiet that Rathenau has not been brought in."[63] The government of fulfillment could not do without the man who personified fulfillment. Rathenau would continue to carry out important functions in the character of an expert adviser. His most urgent assignment would be to negotiate with the English for relief. Rosen had been dropped from the Foreign Ministry because of his incompetence and uncomprehending resistance to Wirth's policy, but he had not been replaced. The vacant post suggested Rathenau's future dignity. More than ever before, the most important concern of the government was foreign policy and fulfillment: reparations.

[63] *Le Figaro*, October 28, 1921.

CHAPTER VI

Reparations:
Germany and Great Britain

Wirth and Rathenau had been right in expecting events to bring Great Britain nearer. While trying to accommodate France, they could see the British finding their own reasons to appreciate the German situation. At the same time an increasing distance developed between Great Britain and France.

A dialogue between *The Times* and *Le Temps* courteously marked off the distance less than a month after the London Ultimatum had purchased unity for their two countries. On June 3, 1921, an editorial in *The Times* expressed no sympathy at all for France's reparation demands and only sympathy for her security requirements. About the latter, it promised that Britain would "again . . . hurry to the help of France if . . . Germany were again to make a wanton attack upon her." The assurance was worthless, as *The Times* very well knew, since there were many threats to French security besides the extreme case of an overt attack. In any event, *Le Temps,* replying two days later, said that Britain was demanding too high a price for her aid. The British newspaper had admitted that a treaty of mutual assistance was out of the question, and the French organ, for its part, acknowledged differences which were impossible to resolve. Security had clearly become ambiguous.

The Times thereupon addressed itself to reparations. The occasion was provided by a speech of Reginald McKenna, a former Chancellor of the Exchequer and now chairman of the London Joint City and Midland Bank. As *The Times* reported in detail on June 16, McKenna told an accountant's association that exports were Germany's only real source of income, while her "highly developed manufacturing and commercial power brings her in direct competition with us, more than any other nation in the world." He argued: "It is our trade that will mainly be affected." McKenna's only solution was to restrict German reparations to raw materials needed by the Allies; he mentioned coal, timber, potash, and sugar. The attempt to be concrete simply emphasized the nonsense in the reparation situation: the only item of financial importance was coal, which England did not want (coals to Newcastle!). All these items together, including coal, would have produced a risible figure anyway, something like 500 million gold marks annually. Furthermore, Germany was presently shipping as much reparation coal as she could dig and the Allies, mainly France, were willing to receive.[1] Absurdities aside, McKenna was telling Great Britain she could expect nothing positive and a great deal that was negative from reparation payments. *The Times* associated itself with his ideas in a long editorial. Unable to admit the full rigor of his arguments, however, it sought another solution to the problem of permissible reparations. The editorial produced the verbal formula "complementary and not competitive" for reparation items, but failed to specify which items were indeed complementary to the British economy without being competitive to its producers. There were none such. For the next few months, however, *The Times* would make do with the formula, as the British public was being exposed to more reason on reparations.

The thinking of the British government, faithfully reflected by *The Times*, was undergoing a series of dull shocks. "It is useless to disguise the fact that profound unrest and bitter feelings are grow-

---

[1] The deliveries were ordered under the provisions of the Versailles Treaty originally, and then under the Spa Agreement of July, 1920. Although the latter expired after six months, Germany continued to deliver coal. The annual figures for the early years were: 1919, 2.4 million (long) tons; 1920, 15.15 million tons; 1921, 17.82 million tons; and 1922, 17.91 million tons (according to Baptist Gradl, *Die Reparations-Sachleistungen von Versailles bis zur Bank internationaler Zahlungen* [1933], p. 106). In 1921 the 17.82 million tons were worth about $170 million or 680 million gold marks at the international price, but Germany was given reparation credit according to the domestic price within the country, which was about half of the international price.

ing among the unemployed," a cabinet committee on unemployment reported to the cabinet on October 6.[2] Winston Churchill, the Colonial Secretary, could have provided supporting facts out of his own experience. Mounted police had to disperse a group of unemployed bearing red flags when, on September 24, he gave an important speech in Dundee.[3] The cabinet discussion on unemployment continued earlier talks on the subject going back to February 11 and May 26. Those discussions had resulted in the formation of the cabinet's Unemployment Committee, as well as a Treasury Committee on the same subject which also gave the cabinet a discouraging report. Britain was becoming aware of the connection between unemployment and poor trade on the one hand, and reparations on the other. British businessmen were impressing it further upon the government,[4] their arguments supported by their bookkeeping, and the government would be forced to act to save some of them from bankruptcy. At a cabinet meeting on June 13, 1922, Stanley Baldwin, President of the Board of Trade, "urged that the fabric glove industry . . . was now threatened with extinction, largely owing to the advantage which German manufacturers derived from the collapsed German exchange."[5] At that late date he obtained a cabinet order to protect the industry. Meanwhile, the fall of the mark, accelerated by the expected partition of Upper Silesia, intensified British concern. *The Times* remarked on its "very unsettling effect upon other exchanges." On November 8 the title of an editorial admitted a cause-and-effect relationship which *The Times* had hitherto denied, "Reparations and the Mark." The editorial tried once more to discover acceptable reparation imports, mentioning "iron ore, certain chemicals we do not manufacture [and] some supplementary 'capital' goods." It communicated little conviction. *The Times* was really suggesting that there would have to be a change in reparations.

The experts were beginning to change their minds—and to admit it. Lord d'Abernon, while condemning Germany's financial practices, was advocating a temporary surcease in the pressure to

[2] Cabinet Conclusions, PRO, CAB 23/24.
[3] *The Times*, September 26.
[4] E.g., letter of December 28, 1921, to Lloyd George from P. W. Robson, manufacturer, who carefully elucidated the relation of German exports and the transfer problem, and urged a "sensible" reparation policy, in Private Papers of David Lloyd George, Beaverbrook Library, London, F/25/2/56.
[5] Cabinet Conclusions, PRO, CAB 23/30.

pay. The Committee of Guarantees, a subcommittee of the Reparation Commission charged with assuring German honesty on reparation payments, spent several weeks in Berlin beginning in September. James A. Logan, a committee member as well as deputy representative of the United States on the commission, wrote an annex to the committee's report, and the Foreign Office received a copy and applied some thought to it. Logan's annex said that "there is some considerable foundation [for the] opinion . . . that Germany is being required to make payments beyond capacity. . . ." He warned: "The maintenance of vast charges . . . can only end in prejudicing the possibility of substantial payments. . . ."[6] The Reparation Commission itself came to Berlin on November 9 and remained for nearly two weeks. The visit had many results, and one of them was reported to the cabinet's Finance Committee by Robert Horne, Chancellor of the Exchequer: "Sir John Bradbury has formed a definite view that Germany would be unable to meet the coming obligations and it was clear that if Germany was to default the effect on the whole of Europe would be a disaster of the most appalling character, the consequences of which no man could estimate."[7] It was an important moment in the economic education of John Bradbury and of his country.

Bradbury was a good indicator of British thinking, as well as an important personage in reparation policy. Almost 50 and educated at Oxford, he had been a government official all his adult life. He was an insurance commissioner and a member of the National Health Insurance Joint Committee from 1911 to 1913, Joint Permanent Secretary to the Treasury from 1913 to 1919, and now, and until 1925, principal British representative on the Reparation Commission. His communications show that he understood the technical operations of finance well enough, but applied a few well-worn dogmas to general economic questions. His opinion on reparations in late 1921 was at the midpoint in its long trajectory. At the London Conference, on April 30, he had told Lloyd George that the reparation sum of 132 billion gold marks "was not an excessive one, and was similar in character to that which would

---

[6] Foreign Office [Documents] 371 (hereafter cited as Foreign Office 371), PRO, item 6038C21868. The report by the Committee of Guarantees, dated October 29, was the usual denunciation of German dishonesty and financial irresponsibility, reflecting the opinions of the French and Belgian members.

[7] Cabinet: War Cabinet, Finance Committee, Minutes, PRO, CAB 27/71.

have been fixed by an impartial jury in a claim against a railroad company."[8] In a letter to Bonar Law, who was succeeding Lloyd George, Bradbury wrote on October 23, 1922: "The present total of 132 [billion] . . . has the advantage of being ridiculous as well as absurd. . . ." He pressed his point further: "But if the Allies set themselves to collect 40 [billion] we should be passing from pure to applied lunacy."[9] It had taken a great deal of history to move Bradbury's thinking so far.

Lloyd George, who was making the decisions on the advice of experts like Bradbury, was later frank and even apologetic about the errors, although he blamed the experts. In his *Truth about Reparations and War Debts*, published in 1932, he recalled the great expectations of people like Lord Cunliffe and Louis Loucheur.[10] He did not mention Bradbury or John Maynard Keynes. Yet the insights of 1932, or even 1922, were politically useless in 1921.

Bradbury's economic reasoning had been properly subordinate to the politics of reparations. This was particularly evident in his memorandum of November 7, 1921,[11] which was a reply to a question by the Chancellor of the Exchequer about Germany's capacity to pay during the next few years. Bradbury made heavy use of two-part statements that enabled him to take back with the left hand what the right hand had just given. At one point he said that Germany could pay 2 billion gold marks annually, but then he admitted that his estimates were based on an annual productivity which had not yet been reached. Similarly, he made reparation payments conditional upon "financial and industrial order in Germany," as if reparations were not helping to destroy that financial and industrial order. Sharing many of the errors of public opinion and unadjusted economic thinking, Bradbury could exercise his moderating influence on the more extreme misconceptions. His opinion was now helping to prepare a change in British policy.

By mid-November the British government had decided to grant Germany relief on her reparation payments. It also decided to call an international economic conference.

[8] *Documents on BFP*, 1st ser., 15: 494.
[9] Copy of letter, Foreign Office 371, PRO, 7486C14819.
[10] David Lloyd George, *The Truth about Reparations and War Debts* (1932), pp. 11–14.
[11] Cabinet: War Cabinet, Finance Committee, Memoranda, PRO, CAB 23/72.

The British position on reparations was worked out in a series of papers. A Treasury memorandum, dated November 16, got to the point: "Germany threatens to collapse financially, socially, and politically. . . . In her frantic efforts to produce and sell exportable goods Germany may destroy the export trade of her neighbors, and in particular that of the United Kingdom."[12] A covering letter written by Basil Blackett, the Treasury's chief reparations expert, said: "The British aim must be to give Germany a considerable breathing space—say two years at least without payments other than deliveries in kind—as soon as possible. . . ."[13] In point of fact, the British government was not willing to dispense entirely with German cash payments, but it had accepted the idea that Germany needed substantial relief. Under the force of this conviction Britain set about arranging the necessary international agreement.

The idea of an international conference was inseparable from that of relief for Germany. Only such a conference would permit the necessary broad discussions and the complex trading of favors and threats. The British government could never agree to relenting on the reparations (and war debts) owed Great Britain without securing a comparable reduction of the war debt the country owed the United States. Somehow this might come about through the international mechanism and the genius of Lloyd George. There had been many international conferences since the war, and Lord Curzon, the Foreign Secretary, recalled them in a penciled remark on the Blackett letter: "I note with horror that we are to have it all over again, London Lympne Brussels Belgium Spa Paris—a dreadful cycle."[14]

Churchill had suggested the idea in his Dundee speech of September 24. Soberly reasoned and meant to be important, the speech put reparations in the context of the world's political economy: "What a curious spectacle! . . . The great . . . nations in the civilized world . . . all hoping to get enormous sums out of each other

---

[12] Cabinet: Cabinet Papers, PRO, vol. 36, no. 3556. The memorandum also included a comment of the kind that would have driven the Germans frantic: it said they had "rather foolishly offered" the billion-mark payment.

[13] War Cabinet, Finance Committee, Memoranda, PRO, CAB 23/72.

[14] Lympne, near Dover, was the location of the country residence of Sir Philip Sassoon, which Lloyd George used for his meetings with Briand on April 23–24, 1921.

or out of Germany. In fact you may say that debt collecting has become a principal industry. . . ." It was not a sudden insight. Churchill had been objecting to reparations while Lloyd George was preparing the London Ultimatum in April.[15] In Dundee he referred to the Washington Naval Conference: "A conference on the establishment of normal exchanges would be found valuable, and is even more urgent."

This was the situation when the German government drew up its request for relief. As imagined by the British, however, the details of relief could be as dangerous to Germany as the principle was beneficial. Basil Blackett was recommending that Germany first pay the January and February installments, 500 and 260 million gold marks. The January payment alone would have taken all the proceeds from the moribund industry loan. Furthermore, Germany owed still more money under other provisions of the London Payments Plan. She would let the dates of December 1 and December 15 go by without paying 85 million gold marks due each time on the export percentage, besides also falling behind on payments under the Clearing Operation.[16] The Allied leadership, however, preferred not to notice, since these small complications only made the more important problems more difficult. To thrash Germany for a few million marks would have satirized the whole reparation process. The British did not really want the January and February installments either, but felt they had to keep the French content. Another payment or two would be an eloquent expression of German good will. The German government, adding up its resources, was sure that the price of this expression would be bankruptcy.

During the next weeks the negotiators were using the word "moratorium," although the British really meant a temporary re-

[15] Cabinet Conclusions, PRO, CAB 23/25. At the cabinet meeting of April 27: "The Secretary of State for Colonies asked that his view be recorded that in these new suggestions [2 billion gold marks plus the export percentage] the British government were still trying to extract from Germany in the way of reparations more than it was possible to obtain."

[16] Undated memorandum by State Secretary Ernst von Simson of the Foreign Ministry to Wirth, in Ausführung, BA, R43I/22; also minutes of cabinet meeting of November 24 and memorandum of Finance Minister for cabinet, December 12, in Kabinettsprotokolle, BA, R43I/1371 and 1373. The cabinet debated using foreign exchange reserved for the bread-grain subsidy, but Wirth refused to take the money. This would have meant an increase in the bread price, a real hardship for poorer people and a political inconvenience for the government.

duction and not a complete postponement for a given period. A reduction, if it were substantial, would enormously improve Germany's international credit. The negotiators were really working toward an arrangement that compounded a partial moratorium with a reduction. In any case, and with little damage to the sense, the promised reduction would be unanimously called a moratorium.

The word "moratorium" was still unmentionable. The French were not ready to hear of a postponement or even a reduction of reparation payments. With Poincaré's tireless comments as reminders, they were insisting on the inviolability of the Versailles Treaty and the London Payments Plan. The talents of Walther Rathenau were exquisitely appropriate to the requirements of the situation. Personally invited by the British government,[17] he arrived in London on November 28 as the chief German actor in the scenario of the unmentionable moratorium. The next day he met with Sir Robert Horne, Basil Blackett, Stanley Baldwin, and Robert Kindersley, the latter a director of the Bank of England who had been brought into the reparation problem.[18] On November 30 *The Times*, cooperating in the deceptions of diplomacy, was careful to report that it was only a loan that Rathenau was pursuing in England.

The loan conception was a useful element in Rathenau's efforts. No sane creditor could be expected to lend Germany money as long as large sums poured out in the form of reparations. The inevitable refusal would be a powerful argument for the moratorium.

Rathenau discussed a loan with the usual sources. On December 1 he noted: "City negative. Everything else to follow from that."[19] On December 2 he got the final refusal from Montague Norman, governor of the Bank of England.[20] Actually, his talk with Norman had itself paralleled a quieter action of the Reichsbank. Sir Robert Kindersley had accompanied Bradbury when the Reparation Commission made its November visit to Berlin, and while there had suggested that the bank make a formal loan request of the Bank of England. On November 25 Rudolf Havenstein, its president, had accordingly done so. Havenstein proposed a loan of the equivalent

---

[17] According to his comment at a cabinet committee meeting, December 12, Ausführung, BA, R431/23.

[18] Much of this account is drawn from Rathenau's *Tagebuch*, which has a series of notes on the London negotiations, pp. 263–75.

[19] *Ibid.*, p. 264: "City ablehnend. Davon abhängig alles weitere."

[20] *Ibid.*, p. 267.

of 550 million gold marks, the money to be secured by Germany's customs receipts or its reserves of foreign currency. Montague Norman made his official reply the day after he had informally refused Rathenau. On December 3 he wrote Havenstein that the priority of reparation claims eliminated any chance of granting either a short-term or long-term credit.[21] This made the logic of the loan request perfect and officially impeccable. The negotiators were now able to deal more straightforwardly with the real objective, the moratorium.

Rathenau still had to use his best persuasions against the demand for 500 or 760 million gold marks, the final good will payment as envisaged by the British. At a meeting of the British cabinet's Finance Committee on December 1, Horne reported that he "had had several interviews with Herr Rathenau and had been very favorably impressed with his strength of character [and] ability. . . ." It was indicative of his importance as an embodiment of German good will that the Chancellor of the Exchequer also told his colleagues: "Herr Rathenau would only be prepared to resume office in the German government if he could see some sign of hope. . . ."[22] Rathenau himself had recorded the interchange: "Horne's wish that I should reenter the government. My doubt that England interested in democratic government. Assurance, yes."[23] Thus Rathenau's willingness to participate in the German government was a factor in Britain's willingness to make concessions to the Germans. He understood this well and used it to get the maximum advantage for his country. Lloyd George was also impressed. He had Rathenau to dinner in the Park Lane town residence of Philip Sassoon on December 2, and he recalled later: "I was of the opinion he had made out his case. . . ."[24] In his best popularizing style Rathenau had explained the pathological character of Germany's high employment.[25] But the sympathy of the British leaders did not settle Germany's problem. The Finance Committee meeting of December 1 had been called to discuss a paper of Horne's which recommended a moratorium, but only "subject to the payment by the German government . . . of the two installments

[21] Copy of Norman's letter, Ausführung, BA, R43I/23.
[22] War Cabinet, Finance Committee, Minutes, PRO, CAB 27/71.
[23] *Tagebuch*, p. 265.
[24] *The Truth about Reparations*, p. 405.
[25] Rathenau's notes on the dinner, at which Sassoon was not present, *Tagebuch*, pp. 266–70. He reminded Lloyd George that "Germany had saved the world

due on the 15th of January and the 15th of February next." On December 6 a telegram from Rathenau to Wirth marked "secret" and "personal" indicated that the question was not resolved: "Everything else depends on talks between the Allies."[26]

France was angry and suspicious. The idea of a moratorium had appeared publicly at last in the headline of a *Times* article on December 1: "A Reparation Holiday." It was a clear admission that France's ally was plotting with Germany behind its back. On December 1 the French Ambassador had an interview with Lord Curzon and asked pointedly about the Rathenau visit. Curzon blandly told him he knew nothing about any proposals Rathenau might be making. Referring to the Wiesbaden Agreement, he said: "I imagine they would be closely analogous to the discussions which had taken place between that gentleman and Loucheur." That was how Curzon reported it in a letter to Lord Hardinge, the British Ambassador in Paris.[27] Briand, returning from the Washington Naval Conference, was still on the high seas. He debarked at Le Havre on December 2. He was in his office in the Quai d'Orsay that afternoon and received Hardinge the next day. Hardinge, accepting the guidance implicit in Curzon's letter, repeated the Wiesbaden story to Briand when the Premier demanded explanations.[28] The Wiesbaden Agreement represented an original deceit between partners, and a diplomatic mendacity constructed out of it had its instructive point. Briand got the point. He could not gainsay the British initiative without causing a break with Britain. His leadership had functioned on the premise that the British association, however uncomfortable, was an absolute necessity. He had to accede to an invitation, sent on December 5, calling Loucheur to London.[29]

---

from Bolshevism," a comment that won his host's "complete agreement." Lloyd George declared himself "deeply ashamed" about Upper Silesia and expressed his desire to see a "strong, healthy, blooming Germany." Rathenau noted that Lloyd George was not always to be believed. He recorded the Lloyd George statements in English.

[26] Ausführung, BA, R43I/23.

[27] December 1, Foreign Office 371, PRO, 5979C22662.

[28] Telegram, Hardinge to Curzon, December 3, Foreign Office 371, PRO, 6039C23049.

[29] Foreign Office telegram to Hardinge: "Prime Minister and Chancellor of the Exchequer think that solution of reparation question would be facilitated if they could have a preliminary personal and informal discussion with M. Loucheur . . ." (Foreign Office 371, PRO, 6039C22953).

On December 5 Great Britain intensified the pressure on her ally. That day Robert Horne put the weight of the government behind the moratorium in a long speech in Manchester. He mentioned his talks with "Dr. Rathenau, a distinguished citizen of Germany," and incidentally discussed reparations in such a way as to bring the British a few steps closer to recognizing the fact that they would never see reparation cash. The force of his argument lay in his reading of the present economic danger: "The collapse of Germany, if that were unfortunately caused by any action on the part of the Allies, would be a misfortune, not only for Germany, but also for Europe and for the world."[30] A long article in *Le Temps* of December 7 reflected France's weakness in the face of British realism and decisiveness. The newspaper could only comfort its readers by telling them that no decision on reparations would be taken without "prior consultation" between the Allies. France was so unnerved that *Le Temps* was constrained to go back and justify Wiesbaden: "*En somme* France was making a sacrifice so that Germany could pay her debts more easily." And so, on December 8, Loucheur came to London.

Loucheur's visit served one purpose. Through him Lloyd George invited Briand to Britain "to discuss the economic situation of the world."[31]

The extent of the Lloyd George–Briand talks, held at 10 Downing Street from December 19 to 22,[32] gave the French submission the appearance of dignity and even of generosity. On the first day of the conference Lloyd George advanced upon Briand with overwhelming optimism: "If German trade could be reestablished [with Russia] and one-half to two-thirds of the proceeds definitely allocated to reparations, the problem of reparations would be very considerably advanced."[33] That would be arranged at an international economic conference. Briand could not help being sympathetic to the idea. He, too, thought in pacific and global images that promised something for everybody. Rathenau himself served the two Allied leaders as an idea man, although Briand, aware of his nation's suspicions, avoided any meeting with the German. At-

[30] *The Times*, December 6.
[31] *The Times*, December 10.
[32] Official British notes in *Documents on BFP*, 15: 760–805.
[33] *Ibid.*, 15: 765.

tribution of the conference idea itself would be impossible to make. It had been such an obvious possibility that Churchill can claim no particular credit for having mentioned it in Dundee almost three months earlier. Rathenau had been thinking along these lines even before the end of the war. More specifically, his views on Russia, which he had discussed at length at the Park Lane dinner, appear to have influenced the Prime Minister.[34] They had talked about aiding Russia as part of international economic cooperation. With Russia they had brought in the last major component of the world's economy. Rathenau's secretary, who accompanied him to London, claimed that the thought of reconstructing Russia with Western capital and German expertise was Rathenau's.[35] Lloyd George, seeking support from the Prime Ministers of the dominions, drew them a picture in a telegram on December 21. Remarking that "advantage has been taken of Rathenau's visits to learn something of German point of view," Lloyd George said: "The reparation question can no longer be satisfactorily dealt with apart from the general economic position of the world including possible international action for the reconstruction in central Europe and Russia. . . ." He went on: "We are determined to take the lead in bringing together the nations for the purpose of general cooperation in rebuilding the shattered economic system of Europe, as we are very strongly of opinion that time has passed for a policy of threats and exactions leading to European crises every few months."[36] Briand's biographer communicates his subject's embarrassment by emphasizing other matters in his account of the talks, thus Briand's attempt to revive the Anglo-French mutual defense treaty.[37] Lloyd George's telegram ignores the treaty and continues its thought about the international economic situation: "It is now possible hopefully to count on France's participation and ready concurrence in this policy. Ends."

And so Lloyd George and Briand worked out an agreement on the moratorium. It would be a reduction, of course, and not, strictly speaking, a moratorium, but the relief for Germany would be great.

---

[34] Rathenau's notes in *Tagebuch*, pp. 269–70. Lloyd George referred to Rathenau when he discussed the Russian scheme in detail with Briand on December 20 (*Documents on BFP*, 15: 768–74).

[35] Hugo F. Simon, in his book, *Reparation und Wiederaufbau* (1925), p. 120.

[36] Foreign Office 371, PRO, 6040C23069.

[37] Suarez, *Briand*, 5: 349–51.

In 1922 reparations were to be reduced to 720 million gold marks in cash and not more than 1.25 billion gold marks of deliveries in kind.[38] The London Payments Plan had vanished. Germany's cash payments had shrunk to less than a quarter of the more than 3 billion gold marks originally demanded. The new provision about deliveries in kind, moreover, was not to be believed, since the Allies did not propose to import so many competitive products. Lloyd George and Briand had also resolved in Germany's favor the question of the installments due in January and February, Rathenau's arguments having at last taken effect. At the cabinet meeting on December 16, two days before Briand arrived in London, Horne brought them up as if he were just beginning to believe them.[39] The Germans, however, had to wait until the last moment to be told that they would be saved in fact as well as in principle, that the conditions of the moratorium would not destroy its effect.

The Lloyd George–Briand London agreement also provided for an approximate schedule of international action. It would be necessary to have a preparatory conference and only then proceed to the conference proper. The preparatory conference would meet very soon in Cannes, where it would do what had to be done quickly. This conference would be officially defined as a meeting of the Supreme Allied Council, now an incompetent anachronism that was still trying to manage the postwar world. Afterward, the world's leaders, less confined by the past, could confront the new problems.

The most urgent matter awaiting the preparatory conference at Cannes was a review of the Lloyd George–Briand agreement on reparations. Briand's assent did not mean his nation's, and Cannes would have to provide the public ratification. A glance at the political scene in Paris would, however, show how tenuous the agreement was.

Briand's biographer wrote: "At the end of the year 1921 all the fuses were lit to blow up the Briand ministry."[40] He saw the situation as an intrigue, but it was an entirely public plot. A substantial

---

[38] Lloyd George, in a memorandum dated December 22, 1921, and entitled "German Reparations"; copy in *Documents on BFP*, 15: 800–803. Actually the 720 million gold marks was divided between 500 million, defined as reparations, and 220 million, defined as occupation costs. This might have misled the Germans into thinking that they would have to pay only the 500 million, an assumption made by Bergmann and Kessler in their books.

[39] Cabinet Conclusions, PRO, CAB 23/27.

[40] Suarez, *Briand*, 5: 318.

body of public opinion, increasingly distressed about security and reparations, was turning away from Briand and looking toward Poincaré. The Washington conference, still continuing, was producing the appearance of an Anglo-American arrangement at the cost of France. Briand's London excursion, coming after his hasty return from Washington, meant more uncompensated concessions. A *Times* article on December 5 mentioned Poincaré as the logical successor to Briand and tried to make the best of it. The same day *Le Matin* published an article of Poincaré's expressing courteous regard for the British point of view, but insisting rigidly on guarantees that would have meant an Allied financial dictatorship of Germany, something completely unacceptable to Britain. Poincaré, however, was being patient. Briand, returning from London, easily withstood a flurry of objections in the Chamber from December 24 to 27. The French government and the London agreement survived into the new year.

The distinguished private citizen Rathenau was being extraordinarily active in the international councils of government. He was in London from November 28 to December 10, when he negotiated for reparation relief;[41] back in Berlin to discuss the relief request with Wirth and the other government leaders; again in London from December 18 to 23, when he tried to influence the Lloyd George–Briand talks and spoke to Loucheur; in Berlin then to brief the government on the London agreement; in Paris from December 29 to January 6, where he spoke with members of the Reparation Commission, and, irrelevantly, with André Gide;[42] back once again to Berlin to attend a cabinet meeting on January 8, when he was made leader of the German delegation to the Cannes Conference; and in Cannes on January 11. The activity had been effective. Rathenau's tact and persuasiveness had not only succeeded in eliminating the January and February payments, but also made harmless a number of other ideas dangerous to Germany. These were deflationary measures which Horne and Bradbury wanted

[41] He also spoke with Winston Churchill on December 3, according to *Tagebuch*, p. 270. Churchill, cordial and an enemy of reparations, told him: "You cannot frame an indictment against a nation." Rathenau did not, however, understand the key word in the comforting statement: *"Debet? oder Schuld? Klang wie Dike."*

[42] He saw Gide on January 2, according to *Tagebuch*, p. 276. Gide, who had met Rathenau earlier, was critical, mentioning *"manières trop cordiales."* He noted: "The refrain was 'All Europe is plunging into the abyss' " (*Journal 1889–1939* [Paris, 1948], p. 713).

Germany to carry out: balance the budget, make the Reichsbank independent (thus permitting its management to refuse to discount government bills), and stop all subsidies. Any one of these classical measures would have caused the immediate collapse of the economy. Without giving offense to the well-wishing but doctrinaire British, Rathenau managed to entangle their advice in an endless series of promises and excuses. Whatever they may have thought about Rathenau's evasions, the British experts were aware of the practical value of the Lloyd George–Briand agreement, and for the moment they did not insist. With the promise of aid, the mark began to improve radically from its Upper Silesian nadir. From 310 to the dollar on November 8, it rose to 190 by December 1, and it would hover around the 200 level into March. The world financial community—unsentimental, unpatriotic, sophisticated, but not always correct—had a cautious belief, or willingness to suspend disbelief, in German solvency. Yet anyone could see that Germany was still in the process of going bankrupt, as shown by the increases in the general operating deficit. In the fiscal year April 1, 1921, to March 31, 1922, the deficit expanded by 3.7 billion gold marks, a tenth of national income. Germany needed more than a reduction in reparation payments; she needed financial aid. No one, except Keynes and a few dreamers, could imagine anything so radical. Rathenau could only continue to do his best.

The Anglo-French agreement subsumed other difficulties. Lloyd George, who had the will of a leader, often bent men and circumstances to his desires, but he was setting his will against that of the United States. Horne had told the cabinet on December 16, just before Briand came to London: "It had been contemplated as possible that the representatives of the United States, France, and Great Britain, would have entered upon a general discussion of the various outstanding economic questions, including the question of inter-Allied debts." The result would have been: "Great Britain in the event of the U.S. of America agreeing to a cancellation of her European indebtedness to have simultaneously cancelled the debts owed to her by the Allies. . . ." Any junior diplomatic officer could have told Lloyd George that, as Horne now reported, the United States would have given a "very hostile reception to the idea."[43] The Prime Minister met the same resistance from Soviet Russia. The

Russians were being asked to the international conference and promised help, but the invitation was associated with a demand that was absolutely unacceptable, that they recognize the tsarist government's debts. The United States, the only nation with excess funds, would not provide the money, and the Russians would refuse to be the subject of aid under such conditions.

A *Times* editorial on the last day of 1921 remarked that "the auguries for Cannes are not wholly promising." Referring to Lloyd George's idea of economic reconstruction and cooperation, it said frankly: "The plan wears even a timorous and hesitating air." On January 5 the headline over an article by the newspaper's special correspondent read: "Pessimism at Cannes." The correspondent complained that the conference was taking "an unconscionable time in being born" and speculated on a possible breakup. Lloyd George had arrived in Cannes early, on December 26. He was spending the next days playing golf, going on picnics, and exploring the countryside.[44] He was still playing with the idea of an Anglo-French mutual assistance treaty, having discussed it in Paris with Briand on his way to Cannes.[45] He was playing. Briand, arriving in Cannes on January 4, was under tremendous pressure. Millerand, who had been a conciliatory Premier at Spa a year and a half before, was now the President, and difficult. From Paris he was telegraphing daily admonitions to Briand about the danger of betraying French interests.[46] This is where the Briand biographer found many details to support his thesis of a conspiracy, but at one point, in addition to Millerand's machinations, he saw one other obstacle to Briand's success: "the character of [public] opinion."[47]

On January 6, in a bow-windowed room with a magnificent Mediterranean view, Lloyd George began expansively: "I am proposing that there should be a conference summoned of all the powers of Europe to consider the reconstruction of Europe, East and West. . . . I consider this conference as, perhaps, the most important held since the Armistice. . . ." He had to defend his mildness toward Germany: "When Great Britain . . . has put in a plea for

[44] *The Times*, January 2.
[45] Suarez, *Briand*, 5: 352.
[46] Many useful details on the next days to Briand's resignation are in Suarez, *Briand*, 5: 353–430. Suarez is not entirely trustworthy, but he reproduces many messages, memoranda, and the like.
[47] *Ibid.*, 5: 376.

not rushing Germany into anarchy and bankruptcy, we are not doing it in the interest of Germany. . . ." He avoided direct comments on the discouragements of American policy, while holding Russia to capitalistic integrity: "We can only trade with her if she recognizes the honorable obligations of every civilized country."[48] This was a particular concession to France because of her numerous holders of Russian bonds, but France was demanding much more from Britain, Germany, and the world. Lloyd George articulated the difficulties of the objective situation as much as his own optimism.

On Sunday, January 8, Lloyd George introduced Briand to golf, and photographs of the French leader taking instruction from the Prime Minister were a few more pebbles in the hands of his enemies in Paris. On January 9, defending himself, Briand wired Millerand about the problem of getting more money out of Germany: "We have run into an absolute impossibility." He was irritated enough to remind Millerand about Spa.[49] At a cabinet council meeting on January 10 Millerand strengthened the opposition within the government to Briand's policy, the majority objecting to any moratorium and complaining of insufficient guarantees for future payments.[50] A telegram from Millerand on January 11 was forceful enough to bring Briand to Paris on the night train.[51] On the morning of January 12 Briand had an agitated interview with the President and got through an indecisive cabinet council meeting. In the afternoon he defended his actions before the Chamber of Deputies, enduring several interruptions. "He waited, however, until the Chamber had heard what he wanted to say," the *Times* Paris correspondent reported. "And then, he suddenly stopped, threw his resignation in the face of the House, and walked out, without even asking for a vote." Three days later Poincaré formed his government.

The news from Paris reached Cannes as Rathenau was making a speech that took advantage of Germany's great opportunity, as her journalists were saying, to put her case before the world. The *Times* correspondent reported, however: "With M. Briand in Paris, and

[48] *The Times*, January 7, 1922.
[49] Suarez, *Briand*, 5: 382, 383.
[50] *Ibid.*, 5: 388.
[51] *Ibid.*, 5: 396–97.

with everyone in Cannes hanging on . . . to the end of a telephone line with the capital, the proceedings . . . were manifestly lacking in reality." Except for Lloyd George, who had opened the meeting as chairman, Rathenau had been the sole speaker, and his technical virtuosity helped him dominate the long, unreal day. When his interpreter began to have difficulties, Rathenau relieved him and proceeded to deliver the speech in French and English as well. The speech did have direct reference to reality, but the conference was too distracted to notice. Rathenau gave a straightforward lecture on the German economy and supported his arguments with statistics on trade, deficits, and the rest. He said that the Lloyd George–Briand agreement, with all its concessions to Germany, would nevertheless require enough reparations to mean doubling or tripling taxes in 1922. The implication was that the Allies would have to go further to relieve Germany. He had been explicit the day before at a meeting of the Reparation Commission, which had come to Cannes. In that more restricted group, advancing beyond the London Agreement, he had said: "Leave Germany at peace for the whole year." All of this was sensible and substantial enough. Rathenau then indulged himself. He followed Lloyd George in imagining Germany as a sorcerer's apprentice in restoring Russia to health and free enterprise. With polylingual repetitions the fantasies became an interminable fugue.

Briand's fall changed the situation sharply. Loucheur came into the room with a telegram about 5 P.M. and whispered to Lloyd George, who thereupon suspended the session for a half-hour. The Prime Minister then asked Rathenau to finish, and when Rathenau had at last finished, at 6 P.M., he adjourned the conference sine die. France had no government at the moment, and everything seemed to hang in midair: the Cannes Conference itself, the agreement on reparations it had to ratify, the decision about the future economic conference this conference was meant to prepare—some of the most important decisions for Germany, Europe, and the world.[52]

The negotiators were nevertheless able to create a working sub-

---

[52] Rathenau's speech in his *Gesammelte Reden*, pp. 361–74. Reports on the conference in Ausführung, BA, R43I/24 (including telegrams of Rathenau to Wirth, and unsigned minutes of all important meetings), and in Büro des Reichsministers: Cannes, PA, AA. Accounts also in Weill-Raynal, *Les réparations allemandes*, 2: 115–50, and Bergmann, *Der Weg der Reparationen*, pp. 145–53.

stitute for the decision-making. One must assume that the French delegates discovered what Poincaré wanted. Poincaré was opposed to the spirit of the Lloyd George–Briand agreement, Cannes itself, and the projected international conference, but he wanted time.

The London Payments Plan was in force and the Germans were still obliged to pay the installment of 500 million gold marks on January 15. On the evening of January 12, however, the English were confident enough about Poincaré's cooperation to tell them not to worry about it. On January 13 the Reparation Commission held its second formal meeting in Cannes. As the agency responsible for reparations it would announce as its own any determination made by the Allied leadership. Despite all the uncertainties in Paris the commission had a clear decision to announce. Germany was to pay 31 million gold marks every ten days, beginning on January 18. This arrangement of January 13 was only temporary, but it eliminated the last threat that Germany would be required to pay the 500 million-gold marks installment. The next installment, the 260 million due February 15, also disappeared, as did the more imaginary sum of another 500 million fixed for April 15 and the variable sums calculated on exports. The relief had been discounted since the previous November, when the mark began to rise. It was still important. A refusal to grant it at this moment would have struck the German economy with incalculable force. The arrangement of January 13 would hold the Germans in suspense until March 21, when the Reparation Commission granted them what was called the provisional moratorium. This was provisional until May 31, when the commission would confirm or withdraw it, depending upon compliance with certain conditions. The provisional moratorium ordered them to pay approximately the sum Lloyd George and Briand had agreed upon in December. The figures were 720 million gold marks in cash, exactly the cash terms of London, and 1,450 million gold marks in deliveries in kind, thus a little more than the original total of 1.25 billion gold marks. By the time the commission made this decision in March, these sums had developed many new meanings, but the Cannes arrangement of January saved Germany.

Rathenau had reached a position of power in Germany and Europe. In Berlin, the cabinet postponed all major decisions until he could return. On January 14 a cabinet committee meeting refused to reply to the Reparation Commission, which had put an urgent question to the German government.[53] The answer would await Rathenau's opinion. At the Reichstag session of January 26 Wirth began a long speech on reparations: "Dr. Rathenau devoted himself—in the most valuable way imaginable and by contributing all of his knowledge and talents—to helping the German government . . . come into closer contact with its former enemies,—helping it remove the many misunderstandings about our situation."[54] It was an extraordinary statement about a private citizen.

The Nationalists, now assured that the nation would not collapse, felt confident enough to accuse Wirth and Rathenau of granting too much to the Allies. One of their first attacks appeared in an article by Karl Helfferich in the *Deutsche Tageszeitung* of January 14. Helfferich demanded an end to the "back-room politics of Wirth and Rathenau." Still unable to suggest an alternative policy, he got his best arguments from Rathenau, quoting Rathenau's old words on the London Ultimatum: "Germany should whine and beg, apologize and promise every year. . . ." In the Reichstag another Nationalist leader, Cuno von Westarp, demanded a " '*Nein*' . . . not only spoken out but transformed into truth and deed."[55] Like Helfferich, Westarp was closer to Rathenau than he would have liked to admit. He could only conclude by saying what Rathenau himself was saying—that the new conditions announced at Cannes were also unfulfillable. Helfferich and Westarp had carefully failed to put any real strength into their attacks. Wirth and Rathenau still held the initiative.

With the economy surviving and the mark improved, it was only reasonable that Rathenau should have the official responsibility of carrying out the reparation policy. On January 28 the *Frankfurter Zeitung* flatly predicted his nomination to the Foreign Ministry. On January 30 the *Kölnische Zeitung* took it for granted and went on to support it. He was named the next day, and on February 1 the Pan-German *Tägliche Rundschau* commented without bitterness: "In view of the way things were, the nomination of Rathenau as Foreign Minister was an absolute inevitability."

[53] Kabinettsprotokolle, BA, R43I/1374.
[54] *Reden während der Kanzlerschaft*, p. 251; *Stenographische Berichte*, 352: 5558.
[55] January 26, *Stenographische Berichte*, 352: 5565.

Rathenau had written to Lili Deutsch: "My heart is heavy and I think of you in this night hour. You have heard . . . what decision I had to make this evening. I look ahead to the task with deep and grave doubt. A man alone—knowing his limits and weaknesses— what can a man like that do in this paralyzed world, with enemies all around?"[56] It was an accurate reading of his situation. Now that he had indeed been named, the Germans could swing over to an indulgence of their resentments and misgivings. The *Kölnische Zeitung*, which was close to Stresemann's People's Party, had to defend the nomination against the objections of party members. It felt obliged to chide them for "prejudices" that would deprive their nation of a valuable leader. An organ of the industry of the Rhine, it reflected the mixture of appreciation, respect, resentment, dislike, and real bafflement that Rathenau inspired in industrial circles and in the German bourgeoisie generally. The rightist press was bringing a vague enmity to expression, but the Right was still unsure of itself and crippled by an irreducible regard for him. More and more the Germans were coming to see him as an active symbol of sacrifice—necessary or useless, but ineluctably sacrifice, something helpless and deeply wretched—and the nation continued to live in an atmosphere of violence remaining from the war, the revolution, and the various uprisings of Left and Right, an atmosphere that had just been renewed by the military action in Upper Silesia. A number of political leaders had been killed. On the night of January 15–16, 1919, after the failure of the left-wing rebellion they had led, Karl Liebknecht and Rosa Luxemburg had died violently at the hands of government troops. On February 21, 1919, Kurt Eisner, the Independent Social Democrat who headed the Bavarian government, was murdered by a young student. Also in Munich Karl Gareis, a deputy in the Bavarian legislature and also an Independent, was assassinated on June 9, 1921, during the first days of the Wirth government. Gareis had made a speech in the Landtag attacking the irregular Civil Guards. On August 26, 1921, as Rathenau was concluding his second series of negotiations with Loucheur, Matthias Erzberger was murdered in a Black Forest resort town. Erzberger, signer of the Armistice and a Finance Minister who had levied high taxes on business, had been an object

---

[56] Quoted in Kessler, *Rathenau*, p. 323.

of monumental and vicious rightist hatred. His killers, two young men who escaped to Hungary, were known to belong to Organisation Consul, the Bavaria-based secret military office which had been useful to Wirth in the defense of Upper Silesia. Erzberger had personified an earlier sacrifice. His enemies could enjoy hating Rathenau.

In the past months Rathenau had been experiencing the narrowing of the area in which German foreign policy could operate. He himself had used up its best opportunities. An article in *Le Figaro* on February 2 showed how far the French had withdrawn from the spirit of Wiesbaden. The newspaper now took its guidance from Poincaré. Its summer friendliness was gone and, with it, the articles suggesting the values of peaceful coexistence with Germany. It commented: "The nomination of M. Rathenau . . . could argue for a certain good will on the part of the German government, and the newspapers of the Right have not failed to attack the new minister vigorously." But it objected: "In fact Dr. Wirth is perfecting a system which has permitted him to keep the confidence of the Allies at little cost." *Le Figaro* attached its disappointment to the new minister: "M. Rathenau has the reputation of being a man with whom one can talk. *En effet.* The dialogues with him will be interminable. . . ." Reflectively it concluded: "He will . . . take precautions that the Pan-Germans do not execute him like Erzberger." The British were friendlier in their reactions. They had wanted to see Rathenau in the government, but Rathenau knew how little they could help him.

CHAPTER VII

The Anti-Conference

The Genoa Conference had been meant, as Lloyd George told the House of Commons, to reconstruct "economic Europe devastated and broken into fragments by the desolating agency of war."[1] Genoa utterly lacked the means to carry out its plan. It was dominated by irrelevant and doctrinaire economic ideas. Even if the conference had been wiser, it still faced the problem of trying to do a job without money. Only the United States had the money and the United States was not participating. The thirty-four participating powers had only debts to shunt about among themselves.

American politics, reacting to an autonomous domestic logic, was arriving at a definition of war debt policy. On January 31, 1922, the Senate passed a bill creating the World War Foreign Debt Commission. The purpose of the commission, which was to be formed from members of the House, the Senate, and the executive branch, was to prevent the executive from being too mild on the debt question. Controlled by the legislative branch and more sensitive to public opinion, the commission would make sure it got its money. The bill became law as the Debt Funding Act on February 9.[2] Charles Evans Hughes, the American Secretary of State, dis-

[1] April 3, quoted in John Saxon Mills, *The Genoa Conference* (1922), p. 10.
[2] See discussion in Harold G. Moulton and Leo Pasvolsky, *War Debts and World Prosperity* (1932), pp. 71–82.

cussed the sense of it a few days later with an American journalist. The result was a long article that appeared in a number of newspapers, including the London *Times* of March 2. Hughes made it clear that the United States would not attend and, furthermore, disliked the idea of the Genoa Conference itself. "Sooner or later an international conference must deal with the whole subject of international indebtedness, which includes German reparations and Allied debts to the United States," the article said. Hughes was making an extraordinary admission for the American government—that the Europeans were right about the need for an economic conference and about the connection between reparations and war debts. "But—" the article went on—"at the moment neither the people of the United States nor France are adequately educated to the facts of the situation. Until this education is achieved little real good can flow from the Conference." *The Times* gave additional emphasis to the thought in an accompanying editorial: "Europe is invisible from the Mississippi Valley." The American farmer could not be expected to understand a "Europe, whose discontents and wranglings [he] knows only as the strange murmurings of a far-off world. . . ."

It was not surprising, in view of this, that the leading powers of the Genoa Conference should unite to eliminate any residual life-giving elements. One might argue that the negativism of the United States need not completely overwhelm the conference. If Genoa had only debts to adjust, intelligent debt management, arranged in a spirit of European solidarity, could make things better instead of worse. Here, however, doctrinaire economics and anxiety-ridden nationalism came into play. A few years ago a European historian commented: "The only positive solution would have been by means of a constructive European policy, but Great Britain, France, and Germany were still a long way from anything of the sort."[3] Europe found it easier to cooperate in destructive policy.

The preliminaries clearly showed the direction the conference would take. Poincaré was functioning as an instrument of French public opinion, confirmed in its stubbornness by American policy. He saw no advantage for France in participating. Unable, however, to disengage France totally and abruptly, he set out to make the

[3] Rudolf von Albertini, professor of modern history at the University of Heidelberg and a native of Zurich, in a lecture to the Antiquarische Gesellschaft of Zurich, reported in *Neue Zürcher Zeitung*, November 30, 1955.

conference harmless. Lloyd George, because of the urgencies, had wanted to begin in February or March. On February 9 Poincaré sent a resistant note to the British government. Pointing out the many problems—to which he was actively contributing—the note asked for a postponement of three months "at least" and threatened that France would otherwise not attend. Poincaré was arguing the principle of the sanctity of contracts with "pitiless logic," compared with Lloyd George's "brilliant improvisations," in the judgment of the *Times* correspondent.[4] Conventional economic belief, looking upon the Versailles Treaty and the tsarist debts as solemn contracts, had to agree with Poincaré. This meant that German reparations, as a *chose jugée*, should not even be discussed, and the Soviet government would, for its part, have to accept responsibility for the old Russian debts. Lloyd George, who reflected the opinion of the British financial community, took the same position as Poincaré on claims against Russia. At a cabinet meeting on March 28 he meticulously impaled himself upon the Soviet dilemma. He began by remarking on the importance of Russian trade to Britain, but then he said: "Payment of debt . . . was at the root of civilized government."[5] German reparations were another matter. After all, they were an important part of the conference's *raison d'être*. Poincaré, however, had been no less firm about them. He forced Lloyd George to arrange a meeting at Boulogne on February 25. The leaders debated for four hours, causing Poincaré to miss his train—and Lloyd George capitulated. A *Times* correspondent might report that both men emerged "vividly content," but the Premier won his point. Reparations would not be on the agenda at Genoa.[6] And so the sense of Genoa was destroyed.

All of these failures had their effect on British politics. Returning from Boulogne, Lloyd George had to act forcefully to reduce a near revolt among his supporters. Some of the young Conservatives were opposing his policies. He threatened to resign, and Austen Chamberlain and Sir Laming Worthington-Evans both made speeches on March 3 pointing out that there was no one to take his place. The reasoning was effective, if uninspiring. The House of Commons resolution of April 3, which empowered the government to act in Genoa, suspiciously fixed precise limits on what it could do

---

[4] *The Times*, February 10.
[5] Cabinet Conclusions, PRO, CAB 23/29.
[6] February 26.

there. Lloyd George had never been treated this way before, but he was losing his confidence. He "warned the country that it was a mistake to believe that if the Conference did not achieve anything . . . it was a failure."[7] He needed a great success to maintain his position, and he could see little reason to expect one.

A few days earlier, on March 29, *The Times* had said: "The European governments are now going to the Conference unprepared, disunited, with unconcealed rivalries and unsolved conflicts, with specious schemes and formulas in which not one of them at heart believes. . . ." All the messages about Genoa that reached Germany were unhappy. On February 25 the Hamburg banker Carl Melchior reported to Rathenau on what Sir Robert Horne had privately told him. The Chancellor of the Exchequer said that Genoa "will produce no positive results for Germany." Horne doubted that there was any chance for relief in 1922: "Germany must try to keep her head above water during this time."[8] How?

Rathenau alternated between faint optimism and hopelessness. On March 7 he tried to comfort the Reichstag Committee of Committees (*Hauptausschuss*). The prospects were certainly not promising, he said, but other conferences would succeed Genoa and could eventually bring relief.[9] He pursued this possibility in a letter to Lloyd George on April 2. Rathenau begged the Prime Minister to discuss reparations privately with him in Genoa and went on to suggest a small conference afterward. He warned of economic disaster: "We are rapidly approaching Austrian conditions"—and of political disaster: "The general discontent with existing conditions is assuming more and more menacing forms. . . ."[10] He was seeing less and less reason for expecting anything good. Three days after writing Lloyd George and less than a week before the conference opened, Rathenau told a cabinet council: "Genoa is . . . a conference from which the chief creditor of the world stays away, at which the reparation question cannot be dealt with . . . at which the Russian situation will get much more attention than that of

[7] *The Times*, April 4.

[8] Letter in Büro des Reichsministers: Collection entitled "Genua," microfilmed records of Auswärtiges Amt, National Archives, Washington (hereafter cited as NA), container 1734, serial 3398, frame 738120.

[9] *Vossische Zeitung*, March 7 (P.M.).

[10] Foreign Office 371, PRO, item 7473C1338. The letter is in Rathenau's almost faultless English.

Germany." He concluded: "It therefore does not hold much hope for us."[11]

The Wirth-Rathenau government, meanwhile, was being whipsawed by the Reparation Commission and the economic problems of fulfillment. When the commission had granted the temporary reparation relief in Cannes on January 13, it demanded that Germany carry through a series of classic deflationary measures. Wirth and Rathenau had to give the commission some kind of satisfaction, and Wirth delegated the domestic details to Andreas Hermes, Acting Finance Minister in the reconstituted cabinet. This meant new legislation to modify the tax program Wirth had completed only in October, when his first cabinet had fallen on the Upper Silesian issue. Now, more taxes were required to reduce the deficits, and Hermes labored to persuade the political parties to allocate new sacrifices among the interest groups they represented. Wirth had been led originally to giving the finance responsibility to Hermes because Hermes had the confidence of important business groups and the German People's Party, although he was a Centrist. In early March he was officially named Finance Minister, another effort to win the support of the business community. On March 16, after achieving a compromise in secret talks, Hermes introduced a new tax measure in the Reichstag. He was able, for the moment, to secure the cooperation of the major parties.

The economic strains on the government had been intensifying. On February 1 clerical and supervisory employees of the railroad system went on strike. They had good reason. They had been suffering more and more as inflation reduced their real income, while the government, struggling against its deficits and requiring time to make tax adjustments, never made adequate compensation. The strike was the kind of practical political problem to which Wirth's abilities were admirably suited, and he brought it to an end by February 8. Requiring a pay increase, the settlement encouraged similar strikes by other governmental employees, who also had eroded incomes to protest. In a Reichstag speech on February 9 Wirth covered his concessions by harsh criticism of the railroad strike. It was only words. The point was, as he said, "This could

---

[11] Büro des Reichspräsidenten: Wirtschafts- und Finanzkonferenz in Genua, DZA, no. 687.

gravely endanger our dealings in foreign policy just when we are struggling the hardest."[12]

The inflation, temporarily held back by the Cannes arrangement, was getting worse again. The mark fell from the level of 200 to the dollar, where it had hovered since December. By March 1 it took 230 marks to purchase a dollar. On March 14 the evening edition of the *Vossische Zeitung* carried the headline, "DOLLAR 275 MARK." On March 22 the mark reached 304.5.

The mark was reacting to the Reparation Commission note of the day before. The note of March 21,[13] while granting the provisional moratorium, had demanded, among other things, that the government overturn its new tax law—now at its second reading—and increase taxes by 60 billion paper marks. It set a deadline of May 31, when the tax measure and a series of economic reforms had to be in effect. At that date the moratorium would be confirmed or withdrawn. As far as the taxes were concerned, this meant another billion gold marks at the March exchange rate, a 50-percent rise. It called into question all of Finance Minister Hermes' labors for the tax compromise. Even such supporters of the fulfillment policy as the Socialist *Vorwärts* and the Democratic *Berliner Tageblatt* wanted to reject the note out of hand. The government met all day on April 24 to discuss a reply. At a cabinet council in the afternoon, Rathenau, reviewing the reparation problem at great length, also favored rejection. He said reassuringly that the approach of the Genoa Conference would prevent the commission from taking drastic action. Wirth, even more acutely responsive to public opinion, said he would counterattack with a patriotic speech in the Reichstag, and President Ebert picked up the idea: "The Chancellor's speech will have to show firmness with a patriotic undertone."[14] Wirth made that kind of a speech on March 28.[15] Rathenau followed him the next day, giving the strongest speech of his political career, but nevertheless moderating Wirth's demagogic negatives.[16] The

---

[12] *Vossische Zeitung*, February 10 (A.M.).

[13] Copy in Ausführung, BA, R43I/25.

[14] Kabinettsprotokolle, BA, R43I/1375.

[15] *Stenographische Berichte*, 354: 6613–22; also in Wirth, *Reden während der Kanzlerschaft*, pp. 309–35.

[16] *Stenographische Berichte*, 354: 6651–57; also in Rathenau, *Gesammelte Reden*, pp. 375–97. The Berlin correspondent of *The Times* noted (March 30) the distinction between Wirth's emotional outbursts, meant for German public opinion, and Rathenau's diplomatic restraint, concerned with the Allied reaction and attempting to keep communications with the commission intact.

government then drafted its reply, which debated the wisdom of the commission's demands. The reply arrived only on April 10, the day the Genoa Conference opened. Rathenau had been right. The Allied leaders, concentrating on the conference, kept the commission from doing anything for the moment. Carl Bergmann, single-mindedly pursuing the objective of satisfying the commission as an expert on reparations, felt that "the government had barricaded itself in a position of harsh rejection. . . . The two leading exponents of the fulfillment policy, Rathenau and Wirth, had become spokesmen of open defiance. . . ."[17] From his secondary position with its limited responsibilities, he failed to recognize the other claims on Wirth and Rathenau. There was more to German foreign policy than fulfillment.

As Foreign Minister, Rathenau had to withdraw from direct responsibility for reparations, and by late March, Finance Minister Hermes had assumed it. A man of dedication, integrity, and administrative imagination, Hermes combined several years of foreign experience as an agricultural expert in a Rome-based organization with distinguished service in the Weimar government. Hermes had conceived and organized the republic's Food Supply and Agriculture Ministry, the Kaiser's imperial government having depended on the agriculture ministries of the states. Firmly and fluently, Hermes took up negotiations with the Reparation Commission. Rathenau addressed himself to the complex demands of Genoa, with particular attention to Soviet Russia.

The history of German-Soviet relations was labyrinthine.[18] The Brest-Litovsk Treaty of March, 1918, which had torn away a great

[17] Bergmann, *Der Weg der Reparationen*, p. 155. Bergmann had resigned as a State Secretary in the Finance Ministry in the fall of 1921 to join a bank, but returned temporarily to government service as an expert. This was in January, in time to assist in the Cannes negotiations.

[18] There is an enormous literature on the subject and on the Treaty of Rapallo. Studies I found useful included: Fritz René Allemann, "Rapallo: Mythos und Wirklichkeit," *Der Monat* 14 (1962): 5–12; Edward Hallett Carr, *German-Soviet Relations between the Two World Wars* (1951), *The Bolshevik Revolution 1917–1923*, vol. 3: *Soviet Russia and the World* (1953), and "Radek's 'Political Salon' in Berlin 1919," *Soviet Studies* 3 (1951–1952): 411–30; Francis L. Carsten, *Reichswehr und Politik 1918–1933* (1964); Gordon A. Craig, "Three Republican Statesmen: Rathenau, Stresemann, Brüning," in *From Bismarck to Adenauer: Aspects of German Statecraft* (1958); Gerald Freund, *Unholy Alliance* (1957); Herbert Helbig, *Die Träger der Rapallo-Politik* (1958); George F. Kennan, "Rapallo," in *Russia and the West under Lenin and Stalin* (1961); Eric C. Kollman, "Walther Rathenau and German Foreign Policy: Thoughts and Actions," *Journal of Modern History* 24 (1952): 127–42; Wilhelm Orth, *Walther*

stretch of Russian territory, had been invalidated at Versailles, but it had remained a confusing factor and an irritation. Another irritation was the murder of the German Ambassador to Soviet Russia, Count Wilhelm von Mirbach, on July 6, 1918, by five Social Revolutionaries. (Karl Helfferich was the next, and the last, Imperial Ambassador. He arrived at the end of July, but disagreeing with his government's policy and finding himself in danger, returned to Germany after ten days.) In the summer of 1920, as Soviet armies wheeled through Poland in the direction of Germany, Foreign Minister Simons called for the resumption of relations. He was supported by most of the nation's political opinion, including that of the Right. As an argument of potential friendship he announced that Germany would not allow the transit of munitions to Poland. The defeat of the Soviet forces before the end of the summer removed the urgency, however, and many difficulties intervened. Nevertheless the Germans and Russians were moving closer to each other under the effects of general circumstances and Allied postwar policy. The rationale had been articulated in an article in Maximilian Harden's publication, *Die Zukunft,* back in December, 1919. The writer was Karl Radek, special Soviet emissary to Germany and the future editor of *Pravda.* At the time Radek was being held in detention for having aided the Spartacists. He argued that Germany and Russia needed each other against the Entente. On his return to Russia Radek continued to urge cooperation, and Lenin told the All-Russian Congress of Soviets in December, 1920, that the Versailles Treaty set conditions for Germany "which do not permit her to exist." He predicted that Germany "would be forced to ally herself with Russia."[19] Behind Lenin's comments was the knowledge that Germany had already begun to work closely with Soviet Russia on substantive programs.

The cooperation between Germany and Soviet Russia dealt with two general areas, matters of daily necessity and the greater ambi-

---

Rathenau und der Geist von Rapallo (1962); A. J. P. Taylor, *The Origins of the Second World War* (1962).

Other works consulted included: Gustav Hilger, *Wir und der Kreml: Deutschsowjetische Beziehungen 1918–1941* (1956); Friedrich von Rabenau, *Seeckt: Aus seinem Leben 1918–1936* (1940).

Ernst Laubach's *Die Politik der Kabinette Wirth 1921–1922* (1968) gives much detail on the Wirth government's foreign policy. Kessler, himself present at Genoa as a member of the German delegation, writes from his own experience in the Rathenau biography.

[19] Quoted in Carr, *German-Soviet Relations,* p. 40.

tions of *Realpolitik*. The first area covered the surviving commercial relations, questions of property and claims, and prisoner exchange. Much of this work had been carried out by two dedicated specialists. One was Moritz Schlesinger, a Jewish Social Democrat and a former army sergeant who had been running a camp for Russian prisoners near Berlin. The other was Gustav Hilger, a German businessman who had spent most of his life in Russia and who then managed a welfare office in Moscow for German prisoners. The office, established in April, 1920, and officially attached to the German Finance Ministry, was actually headed by Schlesinger. Shuttling between Berlin and Moscow, Schlesinger used his position to assist Germany's foreign policy aims in the East. Much of this was done under the general direction of Wirth, Finance Minister since March, 1920. Many years later, after the Nazi power seizure, Wirth was trying to prove his patriotism, and he sent a memorandum dated September 2, 1933, to the government. Referring to rapprochement with Russia, he wrote: "I claim the honor of having inaugurated this policy with General von Seeckt and Ago von Maltzan." The objective, he said, was "to find a spot where I could break through the iron ring of Versailles."[20] This was the *Realpolitik*, as carried out by all the leaders of the Weimar Republic responsible for foreign policy.

Beginning in the spring of 1920, Wirth, Seeckt, and Maltzan initiated a wide range of actions in association with Soviet Russia. Wirth had just become Finance Minister, Seeckt had just taken command of the Reichswehr, and the ambitious aristocrat Maltzan had recently become head of the Russian desk in the Foreign Ministry. One early action was the negotiation of the German-Russian agreement of April 19, 1920, which provided for the establishment of prisoner-exchange offices. In the winter of 1920–21 Seeckt organized *Sondergruppe R*, a Reichswehr office responsible for managing German military operations in Russia. Wirth gave it 150 million paper marks (worth about $1 million at the time) when he organized his second cabinet in the fall of 1921, the first of many payments hidden in the budget.[21] About then, also, Wirth's Finance Ministry formed the *GEFU*, a cover organization which later built up the Soviet munitions industry while producing shells,

[20] Quoted in Laubach, *Die Politik der Kabinette Wirth*, p. 113.
[21] Freund, *Unholy Alliance*, p. 97.

aircraft, and tanks for Germany.[22] Implementation was slow on all the projects because of the postwar problems of both countries.

In the fall of 1921, with Wirth's second cabinet, the German-Soviet joint activities became more intense. Two opponents of cooperation were dropped, Foreign Minister Rosen and Gustav Behrendt, head of the Foreign Ministry's Eastern Department. Maltzan, promoted by Wirth to Behrendt's position, could act freely. Meanwhile, Russia was becoming friendlier under the effects of the New Economic Policy, begun in the spring. During the last days of 1921 Rathenau took the time from his busy efforts for reparation relief to meet with Wirth and Seeckt on Russian policy. According to Seeckt's biographer, Rathenau agreed with this statement of Seeckt's about German objectives: "Germany must build up its strength at home and then wait to strike at the right moment."[23] A month later Rathenau was Foreign Minister and responsible for negotiations with the Russians.

Rathenau's distinguished talents for sympathy and ambiguity were useful in the negotiations. His own unorthodox views made him open-minded to the Soviet experiment. In early 1919 he had told Kessler that Bolshevism "was a magnificent system, to which the future would probably belong. . . ." But his sense of reality gave him pause: "During the day, when he saw our workers and office people he was no Bolshevik at all, or not yet. . . ." As for Russia: "The present Russian Bolshevism is like a magnificent play being put on out in the provinces by a shabby third-rate troupe."[24] In 1919, also, Rathenau had twice visited the imprisoned Karl Radek, the second time accompanied by Felix Deutsch, the AEG general director and husband of Lili Deutsch. Rathenau crossed his legs, called himself a "constructive socialist," and, in the course of giving an hour's lecture on the world situation, suggested sending German technicians to Russia.[25] His vague ideas had led, however, to a plan

---

[22] *Gesellschaft zur Förderung gewerblicher Unternehmungen.* Details in Carsten, *Reichswehr und Politik*, pp. 150 and 254–59; Rabenau, *Seeckt*, pp. 310–12, and Carr, *German-Soviet Relations*, pp. 59–62.

[23] Rabenau, *Seeckt*, p. 310.

[24] Kessler, *Tagebücher*, p. 131. This was the moment (see chap. III) when Kessler thought Rathenau was used up.

[25] Carr, *German-Soviet Relations*, pp. 19–20. Radek saw Rathenau as a "great abstract intelligence, an absence of any intuition, and a morbid vanity" (p. 19). Rathenau later described Radek to D'Abernon: "He is, of course, clever and witty, but very dirty. The real type of low Jew-boy" (quoted in the latter's *Versailles to Rapallo*, p. 279, entry of February 2, 1922).

which aroused Soviet suspicions. This was the international project for reconstructing Russia which Rathenau had discussed with Lloyd George in London at the end of 1921. It was given the form of an economic consortium, and officially announced in a British government statement on February 21, 1922.[26] Before that time, however, the Soviets had a good idea of its general character. The Economic Consortium was imagined as an international body with a senior membership that included Britain, France, Italy, Belgium, Japan, and the United States. Of course the United States had not been consulted. Germany, in a subordinate role, would do most of the work, contributing her expertise to the work in Russia. She would receive her reward in the profits produced by the enterprise, although half would be passed to the Reparation Commission as German reparation payments. Despite the humiliation and profit-sacrifice, this feature attracted Rathenau as a way of demonstrating German good will. It was, furthermore, a construction of a kind he liked, claiming to do several things at once. The word "profits," however, was enough to put off the Soviets totally, while the British statement insisted on the maintenance of "economic principles . . . essential to the development and even existence of private enterprise." To the Soviets the Economic Consortium was simply an instrument to exploit the proletarian homeland for the benefit of international capitalism. Rathenau, persisting, debated the excellences of the idea with Radek, who was back in Berlin, at meetings in late January. Rathenau was still a private citizen, and the meetings, with the industrialists Deutsch, Stinnes, and Wiedfeldt participating, had to do with the vague subject of economic cooperation between German business and the Soviet government. Stinnes, incidentally, supported Rathenau on the Economic Consortium. He also thought it was the only way of achieving German-Russian cooperation without angering the Allies.[27] Radek was not convinced.

Radek, meanwhile, was pursuing a simple idea. Immediately upon his arrival in Berlin he had begun to work with Ago von Maltzan. By January 22, 1922, Maltzan could show Wirth the first draft of what would become the Treaty of Rapallo.[28] At the second

---

[26] Copy in Büro des Reichsministers: Genua, PA, AA, vol. 1, January 1–April 8, 1922.

[27] Minutes of meetings on January 25 and 30, Politische Abteilung IV: Deutsch-russischer Vertrag von 16.4.22, PA, AA, vol. 1.

[28] Laubach, *Die Politik der Kabinette Wirth*, p. 186, according to a memorandum of Maltzan of that date.

meeting with the industrialists, on January 30, Radek made it clear that Russia looked on the Economic Consortium as a threat. He used a counterthreat himself, mentioning Article 116 of the Versailles Treaty, which specifically reserved Russian claims for reparations from Germany. Radek was insisting that Soviet Russia would press its claims under Article 116, if she could not work out an arrangement with Germany. On the other hand an arrangement between the two countries would repudiate the claims, and this was the case with the treaty draft he had written with Maltzan. Article 116 remained a powerful factor in Soviet and Allied diplomacy. Rathenau himself, during his first weeks in the Foreign Ministry, still held to the consortium idea. He refused to admit that the article worried him when he spoke to the Foreign Affairs Committee of the Reichstag on February 21.[29] He preferred to keep Allied good will, even at the cost of seeing France and England conclude agreements with the Soviets themselves—and he was aware that negotiations to that end were being held. The Allies could also deal in threats; their reparation policy, with a temporary relief arrangement that might be withdrawn, remained a pressing danger. Meanwhile, on February 16, Maltzan and Radek had produced a second draft of the proposed treaty.[30]

The Russians wanted an agreement. Their Genoa delegation, headed by Foreign Minister Georgi Chicherin and Deputy Foreign Minister Maxim Litvinov, arrived in Berlin on April 1. On that day Radek and Maltzan had drawn up their third draft, which was very nearly in the final form the treaty would take. On Monday, April 3, Wirth and Rathenau received the delegation and resolved most of the differences with Soviet Russia. But, as Chicherin reported, Rathenau "spoke wonderfully in a pleasant baritone voice, but endlessly." Rathenau mentioned "some misunderstanding or other." It was a diplomatic way of rejecting the agreement. Rathenau tried to reassure Chicherin about the Economic Consortium and, at least, agreed to make any German initiative in that direction dependent on Soviet approval. That very nearly destroyed the consortium idea, which was becoming less and less substantial daily. But, as Chicherin reported, "he showed himself to be essentially negative

---

29 Laubach, *Die Politik der Kabinette Wirth*, pp. 187–88.
30 *Ibid.*, pp. 189–90.

in spite of the wealth of expressions of friendship."[31] The Russians went on to Genoa.

The opening speeches on Monday, April 10, expressed the immense vacuity of the conference. Except for Chicherin the speakers matched each other in noncommittal commonplaces. Lloyd George did not dare make any promises. Poincaré gave his opinion of the conference itself by refusing to attend. Chicherin, confronting the obvious hypocrisies of the capitalist powers, could play the reckless idealist without danger. He demanded universal disarmament and, as proof of sincerity, offered to disband the Red Army. Louis Barthou, Poincaré's lieutenant and chief of the French delegation, was maneuvered into protesting against peace on earth. Lloyd George humorously and feelingly claimed a fondness for peace, too, but argued that the conference would accomplish nothing if it attempted everything. While he skilfully removed the embarrassment, the conference failed to produce anything positive.

The next day Lloyd George sent the conference off on a direction irrelevant to its announced objectives. At the meeting of the Political Commission he submitted the London Memorandum as a basis for proceeding. The memorandum was a statement of Allied claims which had been drawn up at the end of March. It repeated the old demand that Soviet Russia recognize the tsarist debts, but it also affirmed Russia's right to claim reparations from Germany under Article 116. Lloyd George's meaning was clear. He was not serious about the international program to reconstruct Russia: the Economic Consortium vanished. He was serious about making an old-fashioned bargain with Russia.

The bargaining began. The Russians requested a postponement to study the proposal. On Wednesday, April 12, they began conferring with the Prime Minister in the Villa de Albertis, his residence in Genoa. For the rest of the week rumors were the most important news. On Thursday an editorial in *The Times* complained that "Genoa has become a stage for the Bolsheviks" and on Friday its correspondent was reporting a "strange iridescence" in Genoa. All the hopefulness was gone. The conference had become an occasion for negotiating dangerously with the Soviets.

---

[31] Quoted in *Neue Zürcher Zeitung*, April 11, 1964, in a review of Soviet diplomatic documents on the Treaty of Rapallo.

Rathenau was under tremendous pressure. He had to stand by passively while the British and the Russians engaged in mysterious initiatives. The dangers represented by Article 116 expanded. On Thursday, April 13, he tried unsuccessfully to reach Lloyd George three times, twice by note and once by telephone.[32] Lloyd George was unavailable to the Germans. Carl Bergmann, in Genoa also, was still single-mindedly negotiating for reparation relief, his amiable French opposite number encouraging him to believe that Poincaré would approve concessions.[33] Maltzan was advancing his Russian treaty with his own single-mindedness, as a memorandum he wrote on these events indicates.[34] Rathenau's communications of that intense week describe the important realities of the conference with an accuracy which all subsequent historical research confirms. He was melancholy, but the facts justified it. In a fifteen-page letter to President Ebert he said that, while Germany's finances were moving unchecked toward disaster, French and British public opinion would prevent any real reparation relief. On the other hand, "the Russian matter holds out more dangers than opportunities for us."[35]

This was the situation that drove Rathenau to act. One important guide to action, although a negative one, was the role of an Italian diplomat, Amedeo Giannini, a financial expert and secretary to his country's Foreign Minister. Almost a half-century of scholarship has failed completely to explain the sense of what Giannini did. It is a fact that the Italian cabinet, the last feeble parliamentary government before Mussolini, had desperate motivation for winning Britain's favor.[36] In any case, Lloyd George was using Giannini to

[32] Kessler, *Rathenau*, p. 336.

[33] *Der Weg der Reparationen*, pp. 159–64. The French official was Jacques Seydoux, Deputy Director of Commercial Relations in the Quai d'Orsay.

[34] The memorandum, entitled, "Last steps in the signing of the German-Russian Treaty," is in Büro des Reichsministers: Genua, Rapallo-Vertrag, PA, AA, vol. 1, April 10–September 2, 1922. It has a day-to-day account from April 11 to 17. Kessler in *Rathenau* (pp. 326–51) covers much of the same material, drawing from his own experience but also from the memorandum itself and other information deriving from Maltzan. Many other accounts confirm the essential details as recounted here, including Laubach (*Die Politik der Kabinette Wirth*, pp. 190–208), who has investigated the major German archives. I found additional confirmation in documents of the British government in the PRO.

[35] Büro des Reichsministers: Collection entitled "Genua," NA, 1734/3398/738344–58.

[36] Maurice Hankey, British cabinet secretary, reported to the cabinet on February 10—two months before Genoa—that Giannini, then in London, had ap-

deal with the Germans. Refusing to see them while he devoted himself to the Soviets, he passed on selected information to them through Giannini. Lloyd George was trying to avoid the danger that blank silence would drive the Germans into rash action. It might be better to tell them something, even if it were unpleasant. Furthermore, if the Germans were prepared for the actual conclusion of a British-Soviet agreement, they would be less likely to make difficulties when it was announced. Of course Giannini's reports to the Germans could have the opposite effect, and Lloyd George was confusing his own people as well. John Gregory, his Russian expert, was enraged to find himself excluded from the negotiations in favor of another Russian expert favored by the Prime Minister. The favored expert was a former War Office official named Edward F. Wise, to Gregory "the infamous Wise." On Friday, April 14, Gregory was sufficiently misinformed to report that the Russians "were really out for settlement," while Chicherin was writing that his talk with Lloyd George confirmed the impossibility of any settlement.[37] On Friday, also, Giannini intervened mysteriously and radically. According to Maltzan's memorandum, the Italian saw Wirth at 11 P.M. and reported in circumstantial detail that the Russians and the British were close to agreeing.[38] Giannini told Wirth that the Russians were willing to make some compensation for tsarist war debts and nationalization of foreign property, although on a long-term basis. It was frightening news. Wirth took Giannini to Rathenau, who said that Article 116 was a particular threat to Germany and that she would be obliged to make her own arrangements with Russia. When Giannini left, Rathenau told Maltzan to call the Soviet delegation. It was almost midnight.

The rumors were very bad the next day, Saturday. The Russians were said to be close to an agreement with the Allies. During the

---

proached him to inquire about British views on Genoa and to offer his cooperation. Lloyd George thereupon said that he wanted to keep the Italians "closely informed" (Cabinet Conclusions, PRO, CAB 23/29).

[37] Gregory's letter to his superior in the Foreign Office (Lampson), April 14 (Thursday), Foreign Office 371, PRO, item 8187N3704; Chicherin's report to Moscow quoted in article in *Neue Zürcher Zeitung*, April 11, 1964 (mentioned above), which itself quotes directly from diplomatic documents published by the Soviet Union. E. F. Wise had negotiated a trade agreement with Russia on March 16, 1921, the first Soviet trade agreement with a capitalist power.

[38] Kessler describes this episode at some length in *Rathenau*, pp. 337–39.

forenoon Maltzan saw two members of the Russian delegation, arranging the meeting in a public place so that the British would know about it, he later claimed. In the afternoon he spoke with Wise and told him about the meeting. He also emphasized German fears about Article 116, as he had done in interviews with John Gregory on Tuesday and Wednesday. Wise was noncommittal about Lloyd George's plans. He said, however, that the Prime Minister knew the German situation but "saw no way to bring about an alleviation." Wise also indicated that the British-Russian talks were going well and that they would continue on Easter Monday. Wise thus seemed to be confirming what Giannini had said the evening before and what the rumors were repeating. The German delegation went to bed unhappy that evening.

An hour or so later, about 1:15 A.M. on Easter Sunday, a member of the Russian delegation called Maltzan. He asked if the German delegation would come to Rapallo at 11 A.M. The German delegation held its famous "Pyjama" Conference. By now the decision had been made: Germany would sign the treaty. It seemed as if circumstances and not the active judgment of any person—not Rathenau, not Wirth, not both together—had made the decision. At that point the decision had simply become inevitable. There was only one question, whether the British should be informed. Rathenau said he wanted to tell Lloyd George. Wirth and Maltzan, the latter threatening to resign, dissuaded him. It was the last difficulty which Rathenau, sensitively aware of the other demands on German foreign policy, put in the way of the treaty. In Rapallo shortly before noon, Rathenau spent two hours discussing the draft with Chicherin. He then went off to visit a friend in Portofino while Maltzan and Litvinov cleared up the details. At 7 P.M. he returned to sign the treaty.

The Treaty of Rapallo itself was a simple document of six articles.[39] It provided for the mutual repudiation of claims for war costs and damages. Russia gave up any possible claims under Article 116, while Germany renounced claims arising from the nationalization of Germany property in Russia, unless Russia made concessions on this point to a third power. In general, either party granted the other most-favored-nation treatment and promised to

[39] Copy in Büro des Reichsministers: Genua, Rapallo-Vertrag, PA, AA, vol. 1.

cooperate economically. They would immediately reestablish diplomatic and consular relations. E. H. Carr, in a classic of understatement wrote: "The fact of signature was more important than the formal contents."[40]

Among the exhausted fictions of Genoa the Treaty of Rapallo was a shocking reality. The fictions required a burst of moral indignation. "The excitement was indescribable and took on ... grotesque forms," Kessler wrote. "The French delegation loudly packed its bags in the Hotel Savoy."[41] From Paris, Wilhelm Meyer, the German Ambassador, reported: "The news of the ... treaty struck here like lightning."[42] The military was alerted throughout France. Kessler found that Lloyd George "raged picturesquely, but not very convincingly."[43] Kessler thought that the treaty was not at all unwelcome to the British Prime Minister as a counterforce to French power. In any case, Lloyd George quickly quieted down. After failing to get the Germans to repudiate it at a meeting on April 19, the first time he actually saw them in Genoa,[44] he worked amicably with them for the rest of the conference. Indeed, in the first week in May, he used Rathenau and Wirth as intermediaries in a vain effort to get a Soviet concession on the tsarist debts.[45] It was one way of admitting that the Germans had gotten their hands on firm substance.

Many illusions remained. The conference continued for more than a month after the signing of the Treaty of Rapallo. For Rathenau it meant lost time. He could do little besides play the game of international representation. At the final session of the conference, on May 19, he had another opportunity to put Germany's case before an unhearing world. Speaking in slow, impeccable French, he repeated the wretched old truths about the destructive

[40] *Bolshevik Revolution*, 3: 375.
[41] *Rathenau*, p. 346.
[42] Telegram to Auswärtiges Amt, Berlin, April 18, copy in Büro des Reichsministers: Collection entitled "Genua," NA, 1734/3398/738406.
[43] *Rathenau*, p. 346.
[44] Report by Gregory to Foreign Office in telegram, April 20, Foreign Office 371, PRO, item 8187N3745. Gregory faithfully recorded the moral indignation: "The German delegates either did not, or pretended not to realize, how dishonorable it was to conclude behind the back of the conference, a treaty on the very questions with which the conference was dealing and Prime Minister found considerable difficulty in bringing this home to them." Rathenau's "manner throughout was intractable."
[45] Laubach, *Die Politik der Kabinette Wirth*, p. 219.

effects of reparations and war debts, and reviewed, once again, the irony in the creditors' policies which refused to permit the debtors to earn the revenues to pay their debts. Without apology, he defended Rapallo as a bridge between Russia and the world. He won hopeful applause when he finished by quoting Petrarch in Italian: "I go through the world and call, 'Peace, Peace, Peace!'"[46]

Superficial history sees a contradiction in Rathenau's actions. He went to Genoa as the spokesman for Germany's western orientation and left as an agent of an eastern *Realpolitik*. The change, however, was a matter of emphasis, depending on the tactical needs of day-to-day survival. Rathenau was no more inconsistent than the German frontier. "There was no choice between East and West . . . as there cannot be for any German Foreign Minister who tries to serve the interests of his country."[47]

Rathenau has been roundly criticized for Rapallo, but most comments betray embarrassment. Some have substituted indignation for argument, imputing a peculiar villainy and cynicism to the agreement. A few German expressions at the time, demanding only advantages and unhappy about the drawbacks, approved the principle and objected to the details. On April 27 *Die Weltbühne*, the organ of left-wing Democrats, while admitting that "the contents of the treaty are splendid," sharply attacked the timing. It could not suggest a moment that would have been more propitious. Bergmann thought that Rapallo destroyed the chance of a reparation settlement, but he was ignoring the whole weight of French public opinion and Poincaré's leadership. He had a secondary argument, relevant to the logic of Article 116. He said that the article was a hollow threat, that the idea of Russian reparations was too insane to be considered, and that the British and Russians could never have come to an agreement. He was probably right, but Rathenau had a better sense of the real effects of unrealities. It would have

[46] Speech in *Gesammelte Reden*, pp. 398–403. He got the idea for the quotation from Legation Councilor Kurt Riezler in a letter of April 27, and thanked him gracefully on May 2: "You have made me very happy with the choice of the beautiful citation. . . . It is indeed the theme of all the Conference's initiatives, but the first violins are so loud that they drown out the warm cello" (Riezler's letter and carbon of Rathenau's in Büro des Reichsministers: Persönliche Angelegenheiten des Ministers PA, AA, vol. 9).

[47] Freund, *Unholy Alliance*, p. 244. He was discussing Stresemann, but his logic includes the other Foreign Ministers of the Weimar period—and of our own time. Walter Scheel is within that tradition.

been quite possible for the artful Lloyd George and the no less subtle Soviets to have flourished a piece of paper that claimed to be an agreement and was not, destroying German government and finances before it was evaluated. In any case a German arrangement with the Soviets had more value than that of merely preventing an Allied agreement with them. A German-Soviet agreement meant a substantial increase in strength for both nations, while Germany had absolutely nothing to gain by obliging the Allies. Bergmann was more concerned with justifying his own actions than with doing justice to all the important factors. At the other extreme, Maltzan thought Rathenau too timorous and argued that the treaty should have been signed in Berlin. Such an act, however, would have brought too heavy a condemnation upon Germany for destroying Genoa before the conference had a chance to organize international cooperation. It was more prudent to let the Allies try to fulfill their promises, or, as was demonstrated, play so obvious a Machiavellian game with the Russians that Germany would be free—or forced— to try to save herself. When all the irrelevancies were removed, the choice was simple—the sacrifice of worthless and temporary good will for long-term advantage resulting from an increase in German power. Rathenau was the first to recognize that the long-run advantage was no defense against short-run disaster. In a letter to a friend on May 5 he wrote: "The chance to carry out a positive foreign policy through Rapallo . . . seems to me to be slight." Nevertheless, "there was no sense in a feeble and cringing policy. . . . We shall do better to advance our interests aggressively and tenaciously."[48]

It would be useless to regret that the Treaty of Rapallo, representing the pursuit of national interests, should have had so much effect on history, while the Genoa Conference, claiming to further international cooperation, had so little.

While in Genoa Rathenau had been distractedly trying to help in negotiations with the Reparation Commission. These concerned two objectives. One was negative. Germany still had to resolve the problem of the May 31 deadline, when the commission would or would not confirm the moratorium provisionally granted on March

[48] Hans von Raumer, Büro des Reichsministers: Persönliche Angelegenheiten des Ministers, PA, AA, vol. 11.

21. The commission remained officially angry over the intransigence shown by Wirth and Rathenau in March and Wirth's disobliging note of April 7. Rathenau agreed that Andreas Hermes be dispatched to Paris to attempt to appease it. During the first week in May Rathenau spoke with the American Ambassador to Italy, who happened to be in Genoa, asking him to press the Americans on the commission toward favorable action on the deadline.[49] He was also talking about reparations with Lloyd George. Although the Prime Minister had gotten over his anger about Rapallo, there was little he felt he could do.[50] If this was all essentially negative, Rathenau was trying to assist positive action. He was working with the more sympathetic members of the Reparation Commission to interest international bankers in lending money to Germany, but he was well aware of the odds against success. In his May 5 letter he wrote: "We are facing extraordinarily difficult and critical negotiations, and we shall have to thank our Creator if we get through this Scylla-and-Charybdis voyage without damage." When Rathenau returned to Berlin in the latter part of May, he had to deal with an acute crisis in the German government caused by the Hermes negotiations and the problem of the deadline.

[49] Letter of Rathenau to Auswärtiges Amt State Secretary von Haniel, May 6, in *ibid*.

[50] Also mentioned in the letter to Raumer, Büro des Reichsministers: Persönliche Angelegenheiten des Ministers, PA, AA, vol. 11.

CHAPTER VIII

Dealing with
the Reparation Commission

For a year the Reparation Commission acted as the chief agent of the Allied will in Germany. The period began in January, 1922, when the commission, meeting in Cannes, was permitted to announce the preliminary decision to grant Germany temporary reparation relief. It ended when French and Belgian troops occupied the Ruhr the following January. Throughout 1921 the Allied leaders had frankly accepted the responsibility for enforcing the Versailles Treaty. The Genoa Conference, in the spring of 1922, might have meant resuming this style of European leadership. Instead, the conference increased the Reparation Commission's importance by officially excluding reparations from its agenda. During a whole year "horrible and girning . . . sentencing and spurning," the commission was "connoisseur of all transgression"[1] for Germany.

Originally created because of Allied divisions, the commission won its central position in 1922 because of the new character of these problems. Poincaré's rise to the premiership meant that the divisions had become much deeper. Besides disagreeing on reparations, France, supporting the Turks, and Great Britain, supporting the Greeks, were competing for power in the Middle East. If the

---

[1] Canto V of Dante's *Inferno* in the translation of Dorothy C. Sayers.

Allied leaders did not propose to let it happen, their rivalry might nevertheless pass on to others the power to make the great decisions on Germany and reparations. There was always the danger that they would postpone a decision so long that the delay itself would constitute one. This was the Reparation Commission's opportunity.

The character of the commission's authority can be suggested by an episode occurring at a British cabinet meeting. John Bradbury, as Britain's chief representative on the commission, defied Prime Minister and cabinet. The cabinet was discussing reparation policy on May 23, 1922, and Lloyd George asked Bradbury to confer with a cabinet member about a note to France.[2] Bradbury objected that the issue "might come before him in his judicial capacity on the Reparation Commission." At that, according to the record, "the Lord Chancellor [Lord Birkenhead—F. E. Smith] resented the language and attitude taken up by Sir John Bradbury toward the Cabinet." In the end, Lloyd George having reacted with great forbearance, Birkenhead had to accept a compromise formula that narrowed British sovereignty. Bradbury agreed to "listen to the views of the Solicitor-General . . . and derive any advantage he could from them, while expressing no definite or definitive view of his own." Bradbury would not have insisted upon his formal powers if some substance were not behind them.

For Germany the commission was all the more dangerous because of the period's conventional economic thinking. Although the Allies knew that reparations were a great burden, doctrinaire economics persisted in placing great emphasis on the balancing of budgets. Germany, with her huge deficits, must be in a state of sin. She was undeserving of mercy until she made a sincere effort to correct matters, and the commission was her judge.

In the first half of 1922 the commission represented both an overwhelming threat and a small hope for Germany. The threat, of course, grew out of the discharge of its responsibility for collecting reparations; it might demand so much that she would go bankrupt immediately. In their inconsistent way, however, the Allied governments were admitting that their old enemy needed help, and they charged the commission with arranging that as well. Help would take the form of a loan that might permit real stabilization.

[2] Cabinet Conclusions, PRO, CAB 23/30.

This was the hope. The commission manipulated both threat and hope actively.

The threat was given its precise form by the character of the relief temporarily granted in January. If Germany failed to fulfill a series of conditions, it would be withdrawn. The Allies, however, were tacitly admitting that this relief was not enough, that Germany was still being required to pay too much in reparations. A loan might give her the necessary supplement of aid.

The Allies articulated the idea officially in March, reviving the objective that Rathenau had vainly pursued in London toward the end of 1921. The British had learned to appreciate the loan idea under the impact of German distress upon their own economy. A conference of Allied Finance Ministers had been held in Paris to deal with various reparation matters. The conference communiqué, drafted on March 11, recommended that the Reparation Commission help arrange a loan for Germany.[3] It had been the proposal of Sir Robert Horne, the Chancellor of the Exchequer. Then, on April 4, the commission passed a resolution calling for a committee of experts to explore the question. The commission wanted more than experts; it wanted men with money. It persuaded the banker J. Pierpont Morgan to help, and organized a group called the Loan Committee around him. This was an unofficial but thrilling connection to the United States and its immense resources.

The Reparation Commission, manipulating threat and promise, could torture Germany in a very precise way. The situation had been fixed into a rhythm of demand and response reaching climaxes on three dates. When Wirth and Rathenau went to Genoa in April they had already withstood the first two climaxes—those of January 13 and March 21. On the first date the commission had drawn up the arrangement providing for temporary payments every ten days. Its note of March 21 thereupon granted the provisional moratorium, which required payments of 720 million gold marks in cash and 1,450 million gold marks in goods in 1922, while setting conditions which had to be fulfilled by May 31. The penalty for failing to

[3] Specific purpose of the conference was to allocate future reparation payments among the Allies, arrange for compensation for military occupation costs, etc. The Ministers also set certain limits to the moribund Wiesbaden Agreement. The loan proposal, which was an afterthought, had more life than anything else the conference decided.

comply would be the loss of the provisional moratorium and a return to the terms of the London Payments Plan. Even though the German leaders did not think the commission would be so harsh, they knew that it could drive the country into bankruptcy with much milder sanctions. The May 31 deadline was suspended over the heads of Wirth and Rathenau as they were conducting their Genoa negotiations.

The total of the conditions was formidable. Besides demanding the tax increase of 60 billion paper marks, the commission ordered Germany to increase future taxes in proportion to the loss in value of the mark, raise an internal loan equal to the budget deficit (including the reparation costs), permit the Committee of Guarantees, the commission's agency charged with assuring German compliance, to place officials at the various levels of the tax administration and see to it that the promised taxes were collected, submit a plan by April 30 for preventing capital flight, and pass a law giving autonomy to the Reichsbank by May 31. The commission really wanted a fraction of all that. Bradbury had been the note's principal author, and the German reaction had grieved him. He told Bergmann that he had been "obliged to use a harsh tone to get some concrete concessions" from the French. "He . . . had hoped that the German government would understand the situation and give the note the appropriate reception."[4] Bradbury was hinting that the promise was as important as the performance.

The workings of German domestic politics had defeated the commission's purpose, obliging Wirth and Rathenau to make their intransigent speeches of March 28 and 29. As they anticipated, the convocation of the Genoa Conference inhibited the commission's response, but it had no such restraint after Rapallo. Wirth tergiversated all that he could. On May 3 he sent a telegram to the commission's president, Louis Dubois, in which he regretted his failure to answer its notes of the past six weeks.[5] The German government had been busy in Genoa and he was sending Bergmann the next day to give more details, Wirth explained. Moreover, Finance Minister Hermes would go to Paris the following week for extended talks. The Chancellor would be grateful if the commission would

[4] Bergmann's telegram from Paris to Rathenau and Hermes, April 5, Ausführung, BA, R43I/26.
[5] Copy (in French) as sent to Ebert by Rathenau to inform him of Wirth's action, Ausführung, BA, R43I/28.

postpone discussing the important questions until then. On May 13 Hermes arrived in Paris.

Before his Paris trip Hermes had been active in Genoa and Berlin —and in a manner that caused Wirth some unpleasantness. At a cabinet meeting in Genoa on April 18 Hermes had objected to the Rapallo Treaty: "It is more important . . . to create the right atmosphere for settling the reparation issues than to make a treaty that will have unpredictable results for Germany."[6] Then, back in Berlin, Hermes opposed the Wirth-Rathenau policy direction in talks with leaders of the important parties. Edgar von Haniel, State Secretary in the Foreign Ministry, passed this information on to Rathenau and urged him to return to the capital to clear up the "*diskrepanz*."[7] Rathenau could not leave Genoa, but Hermes got little support beyond that of the Socialist Vice-Chancellor, Gustav Bauer. It was just enough to bend government policy into a slightly different direction. Bauer, a labor leader, had been an uninspired Chancellor in 1919 and early 1920, and a generally disregarded member of the Wirth government. Remaining in Berlin, he took advantage of the situation to attempt to increase his influence. Bauer had supported the Hermes mission to Paris.

The commission handled Hermes roughly. Louis Dubois, whom he saw on his first evening, was cold and rigid.[8] Three days later Dubois told Bergmann, who was describing Germany's situation: "You cannot convince me, and if you could, I could not convince public opinion in France."[9] John Bradbury was more encouraging, but for a price. On May 20, Lloyd George, returning from Genoa, stopped off in Paris and added his persuasions to those of the British delegate. The two men convinced Hermes that only substantial concessions would get the moratorium confirmed at the end of the month and provide the conditions for a loan. Hermes, in a report of that day to his government, defended the concessions he had made. He argued that the tax proposals embodying them need not be introduced into the Reichstag until the fall.[10] In response to the commission demand for 60 billion paper marks of new taxes,

[6] Reichskanzlei: Genua, BA, R43I/2451.

[7] Letter of May 1, Büro des Reichsministers: Persönliche Angelegenheiten des Ministers, PA, AA, vol. 11.

[8] Report of Hermes to Ebert, Wirth, and Rathenau, May 15, Ausführung, BA, R43I/28.

[9] Report of Hermes, May 17, *ibid.*, R43I/28.

[10] *Ibid.*, R43I/28.

Hermes agreed to a tax increase of 30 billion paper marks and a forced loan of 40 billion paper marks. Both the original tax plan and the tax-cum-forced loan were more imaginary than real, and the difference between the two represented additional fantasy. Yet as a statement of intent, however insincere, the plan would have certain effects in domestic politics. The government would have to discard the laboriously achieved tax program and persuade the political parties to agree to a new allocation of greater sacrifices. The sacrifices might be only paper sacrifices—tax increases wiped out by inflation—but no one could be sure, and meanwhile the parties would struggle ferociously to protect the interest groups they represented. Still in Paris, Hermes sent a deputy, *Ministerial-direktor* von Brandt, to Berlin to defend his action. At a cabinet meeting on the morning of Monday, May 22,[11] three days after the end of the Genoa Conference, Wirth listened to von Brandt explain how unhappy the Reparation Commission had been about Germany's earlier failure to give satisfaction. Unhappy himself, Wirth refused to believe in the need for such great concessions. He accused the absent Hermes of presenting the cabinet with a *fait accompli*. Rathenau, also distressed, wondered if the government might not be obliged to repudiate the Hermes agreement. Wirth continued to talk. Reacting with more and more heat, he went on to make a number of negative and irrelevant comments. He argued that the idea of going to Paris had originated with Hermes. He seemed to be trying to dissociate himself from his own responsibility as the head of the government. It did not make sense: Wirth had approved the trip and indeed could not have avoided sending Hermes. Helplessly, Wirth remarked that "two completely unconnected governments had been going their own directions." He threatened to resign.

It was a governmental crisis. Bauer defended Hermes and himself redundantly, and then went over to the counterattack: Wirth and Rathenau "had been making policy on their own" in Genoa. The lines were drawn, Wirth-Rathenau against Bauer-Hermes.

The crisis lasted for five days—from Monday, May 22, to Saturday, May 27—in a form acute enough to halt all important decision-making. It was nevertheless not a true crisis and it was rather

[11] Kabinettsprotokolle, BA, R43I/1376.

mad. Bauer and Hermes were presenting themselves as truer ful-fillers than Wirth and Rathenau, the authors of the fulfillment policy, but the chief figures gave the impression that they expected nothing to change. Moreover, the Socialist Bauer, committed to labor, and the Centrist Hermes, oriented to agriculture and business, had little in common. Before the first cabinet meeting of May 22 was over—there were two meetings that day—Rathenau had moved away from his negative position. While remaining personally close to Wirth, he agreed with the thinking of Bauer and Hermes. He convinced the cabinet that it would be dangerous to quarrel with the Reparation Commission. At the second meeting on May 22, beginning at 6 P.M., Wirth was silent and Bauer was aggressively unpleasant: "If the Genoa delegation has such an enormous success in its pocket, then we could perhaps go so far as to reject the agree-ment." Rathenau coolly returned: "The delegation . . . has no such guarantee. We shall have to accept the agreement because it is more bearable than an acute crisis."[12] More talking in cabinet meet-ings twice a day and in meetings with party leaders; the return of Hermes on May 25; and a restrained debate between Hermes and Wirth—all led back to Rathenau's conclusion of the evening of May 22. On Tuesday, May 23, Rathenau masterfully got the cabinet to suspend its sense of reality.[13] Again supporting the Hermes concessions, he suggested that the government try to avoid new taxes—as if the new taxes were not essential to the concessions! He soothed Wirth. The passage in the cabinet minutes, in indirect paraphrases, reads: "[Rathenau] is under obligation to him per-sonally and politically, and he understands his position, but he begs him to continue to serve his country. . . ." Supported by President Ebert and the other leaders, Rathenau had the last word at the Saturday cabinet meeting, when he said that the Hermes agreement had to be accepted essentially as it stood. The minutes conclude: "Upon this the difference of opinion within the cabinet was re-solved."[14]

The arguments for the agreement had been too strong. On the one hand the Reparation Commission could cause the economy to collapse by withdrawing the provisional moratorium on the May

[12] *Ibid.*, R43I/1376.
[13] *Ibid.*, R43I/1376.
[14] *Ibid.*, R43I/1376.

31 deadline. On the other hand, the Loan Committee was coming into being—J. P. Morgan having arrived in London on May 20—and it would begin meeting officially on June 1. The Reparation Commission's power to punish or reward was overwhelming.

Wirth's conduct was a classic exercise in the Weimar Republic's game of responsibility. Throughout its history, the republic's leaders had been forced to accept sacrifices and to admit to defeats—the Armistice, the Versailles Treaty, and now, the fulfillment policy. Wirth had borne the burden for a year, and he was human enough to have found it unbearable for a moment. He had only recently gotten through the exhausting negotiations for the tax compromise. Now he would have to return to the Reichstag and demand much more. It was an appalling prospect even if he did not have to begin the struggle until next September. Wirth was, however, too resilient to break down, and Rathenau's understanding of the man and the politics helped to provide a saving formula.

The thinking and actions of the British government—the Germans simply could not resist the British—argue for the tactical wisdom of the Hermes agreement. At a meeting during the German government's week of crisis—on May 23—the British cabinet agreed that Germany had to make substantial concessions.[15] Bradbury and D'Abernon had been brought back to London for a review of the situation, the sense of which, as summarized by Arthur Balfour, was: "Germany ought to be pulled up but on the snaffle and not the curb." Balfour added drily: "The misfortune was that we had an ally who at one and the same time wanted a Germany rich enough to pay indemnities, and also a Germany that was ruined." Great Britain might try to keep the contradiction from being fatal to Germany, but her government would not extend itself too far. It was indicative of the situation that Germany no longer enjoyed Churchill's sympathy. In an access of nationalistic resentment he remarked that she could not very well complain of her burden while Great Britain, with unemployment at two million, had to pay a far greater sum to the United States. Lloyd George was willing to face the eventuality that Germany would suffer "a terrific collapse." He went on to mention Herbert Asquith's idea of canceling reparations completely. While it was entirely reasonable in

15 Cabinet Conclusions, PRO, CAB 28/30.

his opinion, it was out of the question because of the British war debts owed the United States: "The position would be quite different if the United States were to forgive us our debts as we forgive those of our debtors." The cabinet comforted itself with the hope, but only the hope, that the loan was possible and would save the situation.

The German government, even if it could not read the minutes of British cabinet meetings, had a good sense of what Great Britain wanted. British opinion had been a factor in Wirth's return to reason. Having accepted the Hermes agreement at the cabinet meeting on May 27, Wirth despatched a note to the Reparation Commission the next day. Accompanying the note was a budget plan for the new fiscal year (April 1, 1922, to March 31, 1923).[16] Together, note and budget plan had the character of the German government's official response to the commission's note of March 21 and the various demands contained in it—as modified and elucidated by the Hermes agreement. Wirth tried to qualify everything he was granting. He insisted, first, that his concessions were contingent on a foreign loan. Having established that point, he promised to hold the floating debt to the level of March 31, 1922, cooperate with the Committee of Guarantees to permit the financial supervision of the country—provided there was no violation of national sovereignty, introduce a law to prevent capital flight, and assure the autonomy of the Reichsbank. Wirth's budget began with an original figure of 115.5 billion paper marks as an estimate of tax revenues, to be increased by 39.2 billion paper marks of new taxes, plus supplementary receipts of 40 billion paper marks through the forced loan. This produced 194.7 billion paper marks in total government revenues—equivalent to nearly 3 billion gold marks at the May rate. With expenditures at 123.9 billion paper marks, there would be a surplus of 70.8 billion paper marks—about 1 billion gold marks—for reparations. The surplus depended on a number of eminently remote possibilities: stabilization of the German economy, control of steadily increasing government expenditures, willingness of the interest groups to accept extraordinary burdens, and the

[16] Note and budget are reprinted in a report by Rathenau and Hermes entitled *Nachtrag zu dem Weissbuch, "Aktenstücke zur Reparationsfrage von Mai 1921 bis März 1922"* (hereafter cited as *Nachtrag*), in Ausführung, BA, R43I/29. Also reprinted in the *Nachtrag* are major communications between Germany and the Reparation Commission from April 13 to June 10.

elimination of such negative factors as an annual deficit equivalent to a third of a billion gold marks in the railroad system and the postal services. The Reparation Commission officially believed almost all that Wirth claimed. Obliged, however, to demonstrate that Germany could not make a complete fool of it, the commission refused to accept Wirth's surrender immediately. It demanded that the 40-billion forced loan be collected not in the fiscal year, but by the end of the calendar year 1922. Another note of Wirth's, on May 30, made that promise, too, and on the deadline the next day the commission confirmed the moratorium.

In Paris, on June 1, the Loan Committee held its first formal meeting—and began with discouragement. Germany was in its desperate situation because the reparation loss had destroyed financial stability. The Reparation Commission had just now confirmed relief in reparations, but in a way that actually meant a continuing deficit. Nothing had been changed in Germany's economic position. John Bradbury was hoping to arrive at a general arrangement that could lead to a resolution of the whole reparation problem. Since such an arrangement would include war debts as well, it made an assumption about the American position which nothing justified except Bradbury's stubborn will. Rathenau judged the situation somewhat more objectively. Certain that Bradbury was unrealistic, he wanted a small loan—some 4 billion gold marks —that might relieve Germany through 1923. On May 7 Rathenau described his conception in a cable to Otto Wiedfeldt, whom he had assigned to Washington a few weeks earlier as Germany's first postwar Ambassador. He hoped that Wiedfeldt would communicate the idea to Morgan before the banker came to Europe. Rathenau explained: "The English conception of dealing with the whole reparation problem [has] very little prospect of success."[17] Wiedfeldt did not get the opportunity to see Morgan, but it made no difference. Enormous problems encumbered any loan that would be substantial enough to give real relief. The problems were forcefully present at the Loan Committee's first meeting.[18]

Morgan put the issue simply and absolutely: Germany had to have a reduction in reparations before any one would risk lending her money. Jean Sergent, a financial expert representing France on

[17] Büro des Reichsministers: Reparationen, PA, AA, vol. 7.
[18] Reports on all the meetings given in telegrams from Bergmann to the government, in Ausführung, BA, R43I/28. Loan Committee report in *Nachtrag* (n. 16).

the Loan Committee, refused to discuss a reduction. The Reparation Commission, he argued, had stipulated that reparations were inviolable when it had drawn up the resolution calling for the Loan Committee. The majority of the Loan Committee then put the question to the Reparation Commission: would it nevertheless consider a loan plan implying a possible change? In the Chamber of Deputies the next day Édouard Herriot, the Radical Socialist leader, was rather feebly advocating more understanding of the German situation. Poincaré interrupted him to say he opposed "dangerous attempts to amputate" French claims. André Tardieu, demanding a harder line toward Germany as usual, balanced off Herriot. Poincaré was again the center of a substantial consensus, and the government won a vote of confidence by 436 to 96.[19] On June 3 Rathenau called in the French Ambassador to press him to use his influence upon his government. How could a telegram from Berlin change Poincaré's policy? Rathenau's actions had almost no effect upon events by this time. On June 3 *Le Temps* got to the point, saying that a reparation solution was dependent on a war-debt solution. The point was American policy.

A small and useless detour wound through the Reparation Commission. On June 7 the majority of the commission gave this reply to the Loan Committee's question: "Nothing should preclude the Committee from examining any one of the conditions."[20] This said that the Loan Committee could consider reducing reparations, but it meant nothing of the sort. Louis Dubois had refused to sign the commission answer, thus destroying the majority affirmative with a French *liberum veto*. If France opposed a decision by the commission, the decision had no force. Carl Bergmann, who was a Loan Committee member, was desperately suggesting a loan of the kind Rathenau had imagined, namely one large enough for real relief but small enough not to mean bringing up the question of a general reparation settlement. But this was false theory: if the loan were large enough to help Germany, it would have reopened the whole reparation issue. The Belgian chief delegate in the commission, Léon Delacroix, was proposing a loan of 1 billion gold marks to cover reparations and clearing debts for one year. It was another illustration of the impossibilities in the situation. Morgan said there was no market for such a loan in the United States, and the French

19 *Le Temps*, June 3.
20 Quoted in Loan Committee report, copy in Ausführung, BA, R43I/29.

and British governments had other objections. On June 9, while awaiting news from the Loan Committee's last meeting that day, Wirth and Rathenau both made speeches in Stuttgart and warned the audience to expect nothing favorable.[21] The Loan Committee agreed that the credit situation was hopeless and submitted a report in that sense the next day. The report criticized France for refusing to permit a rational solution: "The lending public" needed the "assurance that the obligations of Germany . . . [were] within her capacity. . . ." Failing that, the Loan Committee anticipated a "collapse of German finances" and "a social upheaval." The "General Observations" of the report, however, went beyond France. They suggested studying the problem of the "international indebtedness." The point was American policy.

Through the Loan Committee, the Reparation Commission had given Germany another victory in the logic of reparation relief. The committee had expressed an important truth so well that an editorial in *The Times* of June 12 protested: "The bankers have said just a little more than they need have said as a purely financial body." It granted this victory to Germany instead of real help. Within a month Germany would again be begging for relief, and her situation would be so persuasive that she would get it. She would, however, get it under circumstances that compounded within themselves several varieties of disaster. One disaster, the decline of the mark, was arriving swiftly. The mark went from 272 on June 1 to 318 on June 12, and the Wirth government could forget its promises of May 28 and May 30 to the Reparation Commission. By mid-June not even the French were serious about seeing them carried out. Communication between the Reparation Commission and Germany would continue to be vigorous, but it would be irrelevant.

Wirth and Rathenau could do absolutely nothing of consequence. They had to expend their energies defending the government against rightist attacks and the mark against the effects of the Loan Committee failure. The German government had pursued one solution after another at Wiesbaden, Cannes, and Genoa. It had sought a reparation reduction, a moratorium, a loan. Everything was used up.

---

[21] Wirth, *Reden während der Kanzlerschaft*, pp. 365–79; Rathenau, *Gesammelte Reden*, pp. 404–18.

CHAPTER IX

Tendency to
Acts of Violence

The Wirth-Rathenau government still had some small shreds of substance with which to make a verisimilitude of policy after the disappearance of the loan. These were picked over in desultory fashion at the cabinet committee meeting of June 12.[1] Rathenau erected a verbal construction, remarking that Germany was now in a "situation of a two-fold conditional character." He meant that the government's promises of deflationary action had been conditional on the loan, but that the original concessions made by the Reparation Commission in March had themselves been conditional on deflationary action. It was not useful to think in this way. The point, and Rathenau knew it, was that Germany was not going to undertake the promised measures, which would cause immediate disaster, but that she was slipping into disaster without them. Without positive help Germany's finances would collapse, and there was no prospect of help now. Wirth could only say blankly: "In view of the loan failure our domestic and foreign policies must be reexamined." The government decided on action at morning and evening cabinet meetings the next day.[2] The action was feeble and defensive, support for the mark against the damage caused by the bad news, but it was

[1] Minutes in Ausführung, BA, R43I/28.
[2] Kabinettsprotokolle, BA, R43I/1377.

absolutely necessary. As Rathenau put it: "We cannot bear this dollar rate. . . . We must always anticipate the fact that . . . the drop will become catastrophic." He dominated the meetings, which began with a long report by Carl Bergmann that failed to suggest any plan for dealing with the situation. The support action required the expenditure of 60 million gold marks to buy paper marks. Rathenau had to deal with the opposition of Reichsbank President Havenstein, who was taking advantage of the government's past efforts to mollify the Reparation Commission. At the end of May the law making the Reichsbank formally independent had been duly passed. The theory had been that the bank, directed by professionals of finance, would refuse to allow the government to act irresponsibly. No law could give a central bank that much power, but Havenstein's position had been strengthened and he was able to cause temporary difficulties. Rathenau was forced to use all his skill to call him to order and get the money. That accomplished, Rathenau was still faced with the limits to the government's ability to act. No other liquid resources were available, and the reserves of the Reichsbank, whether its president might be cooperative or not, were dangerously low.

Having interposed another brief delay in the process of bankruptcy, Rathenau returned again to the idea of a foreign loan. On June 22 he sent a telegram to the German Ambassador in London, inquiring into the chances of securing Bradbury's help.[3] Actually, Bradbury was sympathetic to the idea, and Basil Blackett, the Treasury reparation expert, was trying to revive the small loan which the Loan Committee had just rejected.[4] The British experts, however, had no command over circumstances, and circumstances were as negative as before. That was as far as the loan initiative went.

Rathenau also had to give his attention to another problem that promised no rewards at all. This was the arrival of the Committee of Guarantees, the Reparation Commission's subcommittee, on June 18. The next day he reported on the visit to the cabinet, but it was Andreas Hermes, still directly responsible for reparations, who drew

[3] Büro des Reichsministers: Reparationen, PA, AA, vol. 7.
[4] Discussed in cabinet committee meeting of June 30 and detailed in a report from the German embassy in London, dated July 1, in Ausführung, BA, R43I/29.

up a program for dealing with the committee.[5] The committee's objective was to set up a financial inspection system, originally demanded in the Reparation Commission's note of March 21, which would prevent Germany from cheating on its promises. Humiliating negotiations—humiliating for either side—ended with a compromise on July 21 providing for limited inspection that violated German sovereignty without giving the Allies any useful information.[6] Rathenau was working on another matter as well, the question of German war guilt. Later, Wirth tried to attribute great importance to it,[7] but he only emphasized its futility. The German government had returned to the old argument. The Allies were using war guilt to justify reparations, and an honest study of war causes would destroy the justification. It was precisely because of their weak case that the Allied governments would never permit— and to this day have never permitted—the matter to be objectively considered. Walter Simons had encountered the Allied reluctance at the London Conference in March, 1921. German finances, moreover, were disintegrating faster than the Allies could think about fundamental questions. On the evening of June 13, after his long day of cabinet meetings, Rathenau made a speech to a private group in which he commented on the publication of German documents relating to the war's origins. He argued that Germany "had never misused [her] power."[8]

On June 19 an official charged with studying public opinion reported to the cabinet. While Commissioner Kuenzer doubted that there would be a putsch of Left or Right, and recommended against taking special precautionary measures, he said: "Of course the increasing inflation is encouraging the tendency to acts of violence."[9]

The actions of the United States, Great Britain, and France at this time confirmed Germany's isolation. A long British cabinet

[5] Kabinettsprotokolle, BA, R43I/1377.

[6] Copy of agreement, Ausführung, BA, R43I/29. It permitted a few inspectors to see financial reports at the top level of the Finance Ministry, but not at various intermediate levels, as the committee had originally demanded. Of course the ministry could control the information shown to the committee's experts. There were discussions about the negotiations and reports on them at cabinet and cabinet-committee meetings throughout these weeks.

[7] In a speech to the Reichstag on June 24, Stenographische Berichte, 354: 8035.

[8] Rathenau, Gesammelte Reden, p. 422.

[9] It was the same meeting at which Rathenau discussed the visit of the Committee of Guarantees, Kabinettsprotokolle, BA, R43I/1377.

meeting on June 16 mentioned all the important international problems.[10] Chancellor of the Exchequer Horne said there was nothing to be gained by delaying payment of war debts. Rather, it would "create fresh difficulties [since] public opinion in America had tended recently to harden on the subject." Poincaré was sending a financial expert to Washington that month to try to get special terms, a fact that Horne reported with some discomfort but no moral indignation. The British were expediting their people to the United States for the same purpose. All the major nations, thus, were pursuing the policy of every-man-for-himself, the Allies among themselves and as a block in relation to Germany. Upon Horne's recommendation the cabinet agreed to make a statement demanding payment by the debtors of Britain so that she could, in turn, make plans for paying the United States. Without any qualification, Horne went on to say that his proposal would result in "increased reluctance on the part of France to make any reparation concessions to Germany." He saw no escape from the end result: "The latter country would go bankrupt and European revival [would be] indefinitely postponed."

It would be impossible to find any coherent pattern in the more violent German responses to the country's situation. Commissioner Kuenzer did not specify any acts as having actually taken place. He forgot to mention one incident that had occurred only a few days previously. The incident illustrated the difficulties of making any sense of the situation. It concerned a political leader, but one who had nothing to do with government policy in 1922. He was Philipp Scheidemann, the Social Democratic colleague of Friedrich Ebert and the man who had called out the republic in the course of the revolutionary overthrow of November 9, 1918. If the Right could hate him for that, he ought to have purchased its tolerance, at least, when he patriotically resigned as Chancellor in May, 1919, rather than accept the Versailles Treaty. On June 4, now in 1922, while Scheidemann was taking a Sunday walk in Cassel, where he was mayor, two men jostled him and splashed prussic acid in his face. Escaping permanent harm, he put his assailants to flight with a pistol. This active defense gave the rightist newspapers an opportunity to condemn him for his tendency to violence. A back-

---

[10] Cabinet Conclusions, PRO, CAB 23/30.

ground of real violence went back to the establishment of the Weimar Republic.

The character of violence during the republic's early years has never been well defined. Judgments about it have been heavily influenced by the thesis advanced in the title of an often-quoted book, *Vier Jahre politischer Mord* (Berlin, 1922), but the contents fail to support the thesis. The author, E. J. Gumbel, was a statistician of distinction, but his other writings show that he was a Marxist and an apologist for the Soviet regime.[11] In his study of political murder he found 376 homicides occurring as a result of political disorder in those four years, but few were political murders by commonly accepted standards. Gumbel had properly included the deaths of Rosa Luxemburg and Karl Liebknecht, Kurt Eisner, Karl Gareis, and Matthias Erzberger. He then listed an indiscriminate collection of summary executions or retaliations. Beastly enough, they could not be called premeditated murder for political ends. Gumbel's calculations were all the more suspect since he attributed only 22 of the cases to the Left and accused the Right of all the rest—a total of 354. The various radical groups, however, had contributed their share to the destruction of life in the Berlin fighting of December, 1918, and January and March, 1919; the anarchist-Communist putsch in Munich in April, 1919; and the rising of the Red Army of the Ruhr in the spring of 1920. It is a fact, furthermore, that the radicals had started these actions. Gumbel's conclusions were clearly influenced by his political orientation, and his book has failed to assist a fair judgment.

The murderous character of rightist thought and action, combined with such tendentious studies by partisans of the Left, has given an impression of much more system and clearer motivation to rightist violence. The Right talked much more political murder than it committed. The Left also talked murder, but never carried out its threats. After Erzberger's assassination the *Hessischer Volksfreund* of Darmstadt speculated on the salutory effects that would result if the "Helfferichs, Ludendorffs, Westarps and Tirpitz's . . .

---

[11] E.g., *Vom Russland der Gegenwart* (1927), which gives a remarkably pretty view of Russia in the winter of 1925–26, when Gumbel was there to prepare Marx's "mathematical notes" for publishing by the Marx-Engels Institute. Also *Vom Fememord zur Reichskanzlei* (1962), which sees Nazism as the inevitable result of Germany's failure to embrace a Marxist solution to its problems.

had made the acquaintance of the lantern post."[12] None of them ever did, although Helfferich had good cause for apprehension. One day late in June, 1922, he received twenty letters threatening his life.[13] Helfferich's relation to the violence illustrates the problems concerning its place in the history of the Weimar Republic. Honorable and sincerely desirous of the best for his country, he refused to appeal to violence. The effect of his political leadership was to encourage it.

Helfferich's career also illustrates the complexity of the problem of the republic's existence. Helfferich came from a background of political liberalism, his father having been a leader in the old Progressive Party. Helfferich himself had been important in the imperial war government, first as State Secretary (i.e., Minister) of Finances, then as State Secretary of the Interior and Vice-Chancellor. He was a man of great ability and overwhelming energy, but his enemies and his association with the defeat combined unfairly to denigrate his accomplishments. Bitter at the ingratitude, he subsequently devoted his ability to attacking the republic. In July, 1919, he began a campaign in the *Kreuz-Zeitung* against Erzberger as a corrupt politician and, as such, the republic's personification.[14] A speech Helfferich gave at the University of Berlin on June 26, 1919, contributed to the murderous formulae in the mythology of the Right: "Our nation collapsed because of a failure of moral force. Let us fight to the death against the dark powers who led our people into this path of shame." He arrived at his man: "Issue and person are simply not to be distinguished in the case of Erzberger."[15] He went on to accuse Erzberger of making private profit out of his political position. The Centrist leader was forced to bring suit for libel. At the trial, extending from January 19 to March 12, 1920, Helfferich could only claim that Erzberger had passed certain persons on to government offices for help, but prejudice and archaic standards of governmental practices produced an odd verdict. Helf-

---

[12] Quoted in Adolf Scheffbuch, *Helfferich: Ein Kämpfer für Deutschlands Grösse* (1934), p. 83.

[13] Scheffbuch, *Helfferich*, pp. 86–88. There was strong motivation in this case; Helfferich was being held responsible for the attack on Rathenau.

[14] Collected in the pamphlet, *Fort mit Erzberger* (1919), which also includes Erzberger's replies. These were originally published in the *Deutsche Allgemeine Zeitung*. Erzberger, who understood this style of conflict, was no gentler with Helfferich. He unfairly accused Helfferich of mishandling the nation's war finances: "the most irresponsible of all Finance Ministers"—quoted on p. 24.

[15] Scheffbuch, *Helfferich*, pp. 67, 69.

ferich was found guilty of libel and ordered to pay a nominal fine. Erzberger, however, was held to be guilty of impropriety, perjury, and mixing business and politics. While the trial was going on, in January, a discharged ensign shot and lightly wounded Erzberger, explaining: "Erzberger was a borer-from-within, working against Germany's interests."[16] The verdict drove Erzberger out of public life and, incidentally, gave Joseph Wirth, who had been close to Erzberger, his great opportunity. It also left a cloud of killing connotations above Erzberger's head, and he was more efficiently shot in October, 1921. Helfferich had destroyed an important leader of the republic and seriously damaged the republic itself. Nevertheless he had a compulsion to be constructive that led him repeatedly to deny his principles and help the government. After supporting it during the time of the London Ultimatum, he would later conceive of the plan for a sound currency introduced in 1923. The Helfferich plan provided the domestic financial strategy that led the country out of the great inflation. In 1921 and 1922 Helfferich represented a potential of valuable assistance and a present danger to the republic and its leaders.[17]

Helfferich, having begun as a critic of the republic, went on to condemn its policy of fulfillment as one more betrayal of the true national interest. The figure of Rathenau provided him with a new personification for the wretched government. Perhaps the Erzberger tragedy restrained him. He did not take advantage of the opportunity, and refused to attack Rathenau personally. He preferred to deal directly with the issues and, with his undoubted competence as a financial man, to attempt to show that he could solve the problems. He never brought any suggestion of anti-Semitism into his criticism. Indeed, he helped combat the anti-Semites among the Nationalists so effectively that they resigned from the party before the end of 1922.[18] But Helfferich's criticism, fair or not, provided a base for other, less controlled, less responsible persons and groups.

The wilder man, unlike Helfferich, preferred to personify fulfillment. Rathenau suited them excellently. The choice, however, was not always clear, and the Right had more hatred than could be ex-

---

[16] Quoted in Gumbel, *Vier Jahre politischer Mord*, p. 70.

[17] The question of whether he might have ended as a thorough supporter of the republic remains unanswered. He was killed in a train accident in Switzerland on April 23, 1924.

[18] Lewis Hertzman, *DNVP: Right-Wing Opposition in the Weimar Republic, 1918–1924* (1963), pp. 143–48.

hausted upon one man. The *Vossische Zeitung* called Scheidemann "the best hated man after Erzberger."[19] On June 13, a week after the Scheidemann assault, the Karlsruhe *Volksfreund* expressed the fear that Wirth would be assassinated.[20] Rathenau was still the best candidate for murder. Long before he became identified with an unpopular policy he had been able to inspire blinding anger. There was the episode at the upper-class luncheon during the war when the guests competed with each other in denouncing him for evils they knew he had not wrought. He was an intellectualizing Jew and disgustingly wealthy. Disgustingly wealthy, he was urging the nation to greater sacrifices. People found many reasons—old and new —to hate Rathenau.

German resentment about policies and persons, however, was not as great as selected and unexamined facts could suggest. It was true that the nation was angry and unhappy. The anti-Semites were active. In early 1922 a shabby racist publisher railed in a pamphlet: "Our Chancellor, blindly helping the drive toward Jewish world control, switches us onto the right track. Germany has its Jewish foreign minister. . . . The nomination is a bald provocation of the German people."[21] The *Völkischer Beobachter*, the Nazi organ, was directing its early journalistic violences against the Wirth government. The headline of one article read: "The Resurrected from Marx to Rathenau."[22] The sum of all these attacks was rather modest. Few Germans were willing to reduce their thinking to the level of psychotic commonplaces, while those who did had many other concerns. The German Right, sane or mad, was too confused to know very well what it was against, since it really did not know what it wanted. The blows it delivered against half-perceived enemy shapes were scattered and uncertain. A dissertation studying fulfillment and German public opinion was unable to show any great weight or consistency in the attacks on the fulfillment policy, the fulfillment policy and Rathenau, the fulfillment policy and the Wirth government, or the fulfillment policy and the Weimar Republic.[23]

[19] June 6 (A.M.).

[20] Clipping in Reichskanzlei: Personal-Akten, Prof. Dr. Joseph Wirth, BA, R43I/3631.

[21] Theodor E. Fritsch [F. Roderich-Stolheim], *Anti-Rathenau* (1921), p. 1.

[22] On May 14, 1921. The article called the government "the same old coalition team which Germany can thank for revolution, armistice, and peace treaty" (clipping in Ausführung, BA, R43I/19).

[23] Gerhard Zwoch, "Die Erfüllungs- und Verständigungspolitik der Weimarer Republik und die deutsche öffentliche Meining" (dissertation, 1950).

TENDENCY TO VIOLENCE 167

In 1922 many signs were pointing to violence—futile, mindless, and perverse violence. The perversity was articulated very precisely in a hate verse threatening Scheidemann, Wirth,—and Rathenau. It mocked Scheidemann with the famous phrase he had used when he resigned as Chancellor: "What hand would not wither that gave itself and us up to these chains?"[24] The verse ran: "Scheidemann with his withered hand,/ Traitor and fat cat—to the wall!" His patriotic action was one more reason to destroy the man. As for the present Chancellor: "Give it to Wirth—but hard." The verse then repeated an older couplet about Rathenau that went back to 1921: "Knock off Walther Rathenau,/ The god-damned Jew pig."[25] The reasons for hating Rathenau had been dulled by his political action in 1922. He had withdrawn from direct fulfillment responsibility after the Cannes Conference. His Reichstag speech of March 29 had been well received by the Right because of its eloquent criticism of Allied demands. The dispute within the government at the end of May, moreover, had marked Andreas Hermes as more conciliatory to Germany's oppressors. The Treaty of Rapallo, reasonably interpreted, was an even more forceful argument for Rathenau's loyalty to the fatherland. Nearly all right-wing opinion agreed with him that the treaty's assistance to bolshevism was incidental to the great strengthening it meant in Germany's international position. All this was too logical.

German society had been trained to look for a scapegoat. The racism of the latter part of the nineteenth century had tried to find someone to blame for the discomforts of progress. The need was all the greater afterward, when the country was experiencing real pain. In 1919 Rathenau himself described the general tendency: "We understand logic of this sort: 'It's the fault of the police, the rationing system, the Prussians, the Jews, the English, the priests, the capitalists.' " He concluded: "Long before the educated classes have become capable of making sensible verdicts, the utterly incompetent masses of the rawest youth . . . will be turned loose and handed the job of hanging judges."[26]

[24] Quoted in *Vossische Zeitung*, May 13, 1919 (A.M.).

[25] Quoted by the Karlsruhe *Volksfreund* article, above. Rathenau had a newspaper clipping of an earlier version of the verse. The recent killing of Gareis was celebrated in this, while Rathenau and Wirth were suggested as the next victims. Rathenau sent the clipping to his racist correspondent, Wilhelm Schwaner, in a letter of June 26, 1921 (in Rathenau-Nachlass, BA).

[26] *Die neue Gesellschaft* (1919), pp. 7, 25.

In April, 1922, a boy of 17 got the idea of killing Rathenau and mentioned it to a 25-year-old former Free Corps officer named Erwin Kern.[27] A blond Nordic of the type that Rathenau found so attractive, Kern was attached to Captain Ehrhardt's Organisation Consul. Kern shouldered aside the adolescent and took the leadership in the conspiracy. All of the nearly twenty plotters were either secondary-school students or men of Kern's age. According to one of them, Kern had made these statements: Rathenau was a dangerous leftist carrying out a "policy of fulfillment [that was] treason committed against the German people [and] would inevitably lead to the destruction of the German nation"; Rathenau became a minister by giving President Ebert a 24-hour ultimatum; Rathenau was an exponent of creeping Bolshevism and had married his sister to Karl Radek to bind the alliance with Russian bolshevism; Rathenau was one of the 300 Elders of Zion who were trying to control the world; and Germany needed a civil war between Right and Left to clear out the corruption.[28] Neither the trial of the surviving assassins—Kern had been killed—nor the other sources of information suggest that more responsible thoughts or persons were behind the conspiracy.

Rathenau had been repeatedly warned. Shortly after he became Foreign Minister, according to Lili Deutsch, a priest was told a story of a murder plot in the confessional. He reported it to Wirth after getting permission from the Papal Nuncio. Wirth, "his teeth chattering," informed Rathenau, and Rathenau let him assign a guard. Rathenau, however, repeatedly sent the men away.[29] A few months earlier, on September 17, 1921, he wrote to a young woman friend: "Don't worry about my life. If an honorable life is to end,

[27] According to the trial of the Rathenau assassins, held in Leipzig, October 3–14, 1922. Minutes of the (probably) most important testimony in the pamphlet by Karl Brammer, *Das politische Ergebnis des Rathenau-Prozesses* (1922). Analysis in Gumbel, *Vier Jahre politischer Mord*, pp. 71–72. Two of the conspirators published memoirs about the plot. One of them, Ernst-Werner Techow, appears to be telling the truth more often than not, from comparison with the minutes, in *"Gemeiner Mörder?!" Das Rathenau-Attentat* (1934). The other conspirator, the Free Corps chronicler and screenwriter Ernst von Salomon, obviously used his facile talent for fiction in his account in *The Outlaws* (1931), pp. 179–85 and 239–42.

[28] This was the testimony of Techow, in Brammer, *Das politische Ergebnis*, pp. 25–26; quotation, p. 25.

[29] Kessler, *Tagebücher*, p. 555. The Nuncio was Eugenio Pacelli, the future Pius XII.

then it happens not arbitrarily, but because that life has found its conclusion."[30] It was the same self-conscious valedictory note that he had sounded during the war. A member of the British embassy visited him in the Grunewald in June, 1922, and mentioned that he had been questioned by a plainclothesman. Rathenau thereupon made a telephone call complaining that his guests were being disturbed. No police were visible when the Englishman left.[31] Lili Deutsch, interpeting one aspect of Rathenau, said: "He could not endure to have people . . . continuously keeping him under guard and spying on him."[32] Lord d'Abernon wrote in his diary on May 10, 1922, while in Genoa: "Rathenau has to face the undying hatred of the Right." D'Abernon added, innocently capturing Rathenau's truly morbid vanity: "But he has often hold me he is sure to be assassinated."[33]

In the latter part of June, while renewing his efforts to get reparation relief, and while supporting the action to keep the mark from collapsing entirely, Rathenau carried out the less important but no less demanding duties of the public man. He was in the Reichstag on Wednesday, June 21, to answer interpellations about incidents involving the French in the occupied Rhineland and Saar. Among those speaking were Gustav Stresemann and Wilhelm Marx, the latter a Centrist leader and future Chancellor. Stresemann and Marx were not trying to embarrass the government. Indeed the subjects indicated cooperation between the deputies and Minister, so that Rathenau might protest against what all Germans agreed were injustices committed by the French. It was another moment in the conventional quarrel between the occupiers and the humiliatingly occupied. Rathenau's politically indignant statement[34] was well received, eliciting expressions of approval from the Right—"Hear, hear!" The Right applauded when he finished.

On Friday, June 23, Rathenau was lending his services to the industry of the Rhine and Westphalia in negotiating an adjustment in deliveries of reparation coal.[35] The point was to satisfy the Allies on

[30] Rathenau, *Ein preussischer Europäer*, p. 401.

[31] Kessler, *Tagebücher*, p. 617.

[32] *Ibid.*, p. 555.

[33] *Versailles to Rapallo*, p. 323.

[34] *Stenographische Berichte*, 355: 7941–45; also in *Gesammelte Reden*, pp. 423–37.

[35] According to an account by U.S. Ambassador Houghton, quoted in D'Abernon, *Diary of an Ambassador: Rapallo to Dawes 1922–1924* (1930), entry of

their coal demands without causing domestic shortages that would force German blast furnaces to shut down. Rathenau met with Hugo Stinnes, Fritz Thyssen, and other industrialists in rooms in the Reichstag at 6 P.M. While they were talking, Karl Helfferich, in the Reichstag's great hall, launched into a speech of an hour and a half that challenged every important aspect of the government's policy.[36] Reported to Rathenau, the speech caused him some distress and delayed his arrival at the American embassy, where he had been invited to dinner. Helfferich, referring to Rathenau's protest of Wednesday, accused him of failing properly to stand up to the French: "*Bei Gott*, that is pretty weak stuff." Helfferich went on to a general criticism of fulfillment. The occasion had been provided by enabling legislation, before the Reichstag at this moment, for two agreements deriving from Rathenau's Wiesbaden Agreement. No one, surely not Helfferich, believed in the reality of these arrangements, but they provided a political target. "The Calvary of fulfillment . . . has brought us the frightful devaluation of the German currency," he said. "It has crushed our middle class, dragged countless persons and whole families into the depths of poverty, driven countless others into despair and suicide." Helfferich raised his pitch: "It has handed great chunks of our own resources over to foreigners. It has shaken our economic and social order to the foundations!"[37] Accusing the government of permitting Germany's sovereignty to be violated, Helfferich said that its members "should be brought up before the Supreme Court."[38] The speech was unfair enough. He was implying treason, but then he was only implying it. As Lord d'Abernon commented, the speech was "not of an exceptionally violent character."[39] Helfferich was often attacked as harshly and unfairly, and, indeed, that happened in the course of the speech itself, a Communist calling him "Bankruptcy Minister" and "war criminal."[40] Helfferich had begun on the defensive, impelled once again to try to justify his wartime services. Nor was the speech an attack on Rathenau. It dealt him a glancing blow on the

---

June 28, pp. 46–48. Houghton got some of the facts from Hugo Stinnes, who himself dictated a memorandum about the events in question on July 4, 1922. This latter is quoted in Gert von Klass, *Hugo Stinnes* (1958), pp. 282–91.

[36] *Stenographische Berichte*, 355: 7988–8001.
[37] *Ibid.*, 355: 7792.
[38] *Ibid.*, 355: 7797.
[39] *Rapallo to Dawes*, p. 53.
[40] *Stenographische Berichte*, 355: 8001.

Rhineland-Saar matter and passed on to other things. When Helfferich reached the subject of fulfillment he mentioned Wirth and not Rathenau, discussing it as a policy of the whole government. He was also saying things about the disastrous economic effects of reparations with which anybody in the government would agree. After the irresponsibly argued negatives, furthermore, he actually tried to suggest a positive policy. Of course, his ideas were useless: the government should refuse to buy dollars when the mark had declined beyond a certain point (a Social Democrat, who interrupted to ask, "And then what happens?" went unanswered) and appeal once again to England and America.[41] Helfferich had been restrained by his own sense of responsibility. He had treated Erzberger much worse.

No one thought the Reichstag session was important. The debate was diffuse. Helfferich had introduced at least three other subjects, and other speakers brought up still more. A Communist speaker drove out nearly all the deputies with a conventional denunciation of everything middle class; only a half-dozen were left when he had finished.[42] The *Vossische Zeitung* reported the debate in detail, but on the fourth page. A Democrat defended fellow-Democrat Rathenau only casually, obviously because he had not felt that the reference to him was an important part of Helfferich's remarks. The Democrat went on with gentle humor to suggest that Helfferich was making use of "an exaggerated expressionism or Dadaism" to characterize conditions.[43] It was indicative of the government's division of responsibility that Hermes and not Rathenau made the rebuttal to Helfferich.[44] Thereupon the Reichstag quietly passed the enabling act for the useless reparation agreement, and, at 9:04 P.M., adjourned.

At the embassy dinner[45] Rathenau undertook one more action on reparations and had another confrontation with Hugo Stinnes. Rathenau had gotten himself invited to discuss the coal problem, and after going through it with the American Ambassador, Alanson B. Houghton, he suggested that Stinnes be called. The Ambassador thought that Rathenau wanted to see Stinnes not for the coal prob-

[41] *Ibid.*, 355: 8000–8001.
[42] According to article in *Vossische Zeitung*, June 24 (A.M.).
[43] He was Adolf Korell, *Stenographische Berichte*, 355: 8014.
[44] *Ibid.*, 355: 8019–21.
[45] The dinner was in honor of James A. Logan, the U.S. deputy representative on the Reparation Commission.

lem, which was only an excuse, but so that he could attempt to come to some sort of understanding with him on reparation policy in general. In any case, Rathenau asked Stinnes, according to the industrialist's recollection, what he now thought about reparations. Consistent with his style, Stinnes launched into aggressive criticism. He thought government policy was mistaken, although, like Helfferich and all the other critics, he had no good ideas himself. Nevertheless, Houghton thought that Stinnes was willing, on principle, to cooperate with Rathenau. The two men had so much to say that they did not separate when they left the embassy at 1 A.M. They went to the Hotel Esplanade, one of the Stinnes properties and his residence in Berlin, and continued talking there until about 4 A.M. According to Stinnes, the interchange ended amicably but vaguely. Rathenau departed for his office about 10:45 A.M. that Saturday, June 24, slightly later than usual because of his later retiring hour. He left behind a few notes on a desk pad, two dozen key words, some abbreviated, under the heading, "General Overview of Policy." The first word was "unfulfillable."[46]

On that day, one of the first days of summer, Rathenau's automobile had its top down. It was overtaken about a half-mile from his villa, still on Königsallee in the Grunewald, by another open automobile. A Berlin construction worker noticed two young men in "spanking new" leather jackets and caps in the back seat of the car.[47] They were Erwin Kern and his friend Hermann Fischer, also a young former officer. The driver was a still younger man. When their vehicle was a half-length ahead, it forced Rathenau's automobile to the side, and Kern calmly shot Rathenau with a submachine gun. A moment later Fischer threw a hand grenade, the force of the explosion lifting Rathenau from his seat. The conspirators' vehicle then accelerated and disappeared.

A nurse who happened to be nearby climbed into Rathenau's automobile, and found him unconscious and presumably dead. A few minutes later, after the unharmed chauffeur had driven the vehicle back to the villa, the doctor arrived and examined the body. He found that Rathenau had been shot five times. The jaw and backbone had been shattered.

[46] "*Gesamtrahmen d. Pol.*" and "*unerfüllbar*," in Rathenau, *Politische Briefe* (1929), p. 343.
[47] His account, along with others, in the *Vossische Zeitung*, June 25 (Sunday).

In 1899 Rathenau had published a story in biblical style that told of a prophet who restored the sanity of the king but aroused the anger of the people. It was said that "he yearns for the staff and diadem." The story went on: "The people called out, 'the prophet is mad.' And they seized him, dragged him before the gates, and stoned him."[48]

The police, finding an informant among the conspirators, ran Kern and Fischer to ground in a small town near Cassel on July 17. They killed Kern in an exchange of gunfire. They said that Fischer killed himself after shouting: "Hurrah for Captain Ehrhardt!"[49]

The mark went from 332 to 355 to the dollar on the assassination day.

The nation expressed itself incoherently. On Sunday, workers marched in the western districts of Berlin, and a crowd of some 200,000 listened to speakers in the Schlossplatz in the city center making conventional attacks on the Right. At noon on Tuesday, June 27, on the occasion of a 24-hour funeral holiday, another great demonstration took place in Berlin, as a million workers marched heavily. A half-dozen other cities had parades of more than 100,000 workers. There was a great tramping of boots and shoes, and a respectful listening to overstrained commonplaces.

The funeral service began in the Reichstag after Joseph Wirth led Mathilde Rathenau, "her face looking as if it had been chiselled of stone," into the emperor's box.[50] The orchestra played the Coriolanus Overture, and at the end, the funeral march for Siegfried from *Götterdämmerung*. The cortege, with an honor guard and under the rolling of drums, went through the Brandenburg Gate and on to the Rathenau family plot. Kessler remembered that Ferdinand Lassalle, the brilliant and vain socialist leader of the mid-nineteenth century, and a Jew, had dreamed of entering Berlin through the arch as President of a German republic.

In the Reichstag on Sunday, two days before, Wirth had tried to discover a usable meaning in the event.[51] He began and ended with a denunciation of the Right. He quoted a Nationalist who had

---

[48] "The Voice of the People," in *Gesammelte Schriften*, 4: 313–14.
[49] *Vossische Zeitung*, July 18 (P.M.).
[50] Kessler, *Tagebücher*, p. 326.
[51] *Stenographische Berichte*, 355: 8055–56. He had also spoken on Saturday, pp. 8034–35.

charged the government with being the agent of French policy and turned to the Nationalists: "Doesn't the blush of shame rise in your faces?" He failed to mention Helfferich, whom some persons had accused of inspiring the assassination. Kessler had written in his diary on the assassination day: "Helfferich is the murderer, the real one, the responsible one."[52] Kessler was too completely the aesthete to be sound in his instincts. If Helfferich had his responsibility, only an arbitrary judgment would exclude the countless others who bore more or less guilt, or neglect all the other contributing causes. Wirth's tribute to Rathenau was manfully moving, the expression of honest friendship and professional esteem. Wirth ended, according to the minutes of the Reichstag: "There (pointing to the right) is the enemy—pouring his poison into the wounds of his nation. There is the enemy—and no one can have any doubt about it— the enemy is on the Right!" It was the best Wirth could do, but it was not good enough. Kessler wrote in his diary the day before: "A new chapter of German history begins with this assassination—" But then he went on: "—or should begin."[53] It did not.

The assassination produced no suggestion of a crisis. On June 25 Georg Bernhard wrote not unfeelingly about Rathenau: "He would use a simile and believe he had produced a proof." Rathenau had, after all, represented a policy that every German detested; and the policy had lost touch with reality. The nation could not be made to mourn. On June 24 Bernhard had written: "The republic itself is in danger," but his *Vossische Zeitung* was entirely calm by the next day. There had been no danger. The Right did not have the remotest idea of a putsch at the time, and the marching workers were making an unnecessary gesture. Most responsible Germans remained loyal to the republic at the moment for lack of something better. When the ghost of danger would be gone, they would have to go on living in a worn world where the best efforts seemed always to fail. In losing Rathenau the government had lost the promise of a solution to its crushing problems, but only a few moments before the promise was shown conclusively to be empty.

[52] *Tagebücher*, p. 322. Kessler also thought that the "Reichstag should be adjourned and accounts should be settled with murderers like Helfferich." The best republicans of the Weimar Republic were sometimes shocked out of their republicanism.
[53] P. 324.

CHAPTER X

Conclusions to the Logic
of Reparations and Fulfillment

Very quickly it seemed as if Rathenau had never been Foreign Minister. Fulfillment halted. It was not repudiated; it simply was not there. For a time Germany would proceed without a definable policy.

Fulfillment as Rathenau had conceived it, however, would later be revived under another name. Moreover, he had contributed perdurable elements to the composition of twentieth-century Germany and Europe.

A brief survey of events for a few months after Rathenau's murder will show the immediate aftereffects of the ideas he represented. With that established, another view will use the present day as starting point and extend over the whole period of the Weimar Republic. Together, both views should suggest Rathenau's importance in the republic's life and death, and in the world's progress from one great war to the next.

The assassination had shocked many persons in the Allied countries into thinking more clearly. France refused to admit it, but the international business community knew very well that Germany could not pay reparations much longer without going bankrupt. Economists might dispute whether it would occur in a month, six months, or x months. No one could responsibly deny that it would happen if Germany received no help. There was no prospect of help.

175

The general operating deficit, at an annual rate of 3 billion gold marks, remained huge.[1] The mark traced a luminous declining curve: 401 to the dollar on July 1, a week after the assassination, 670 by the end of the month, 1,725 by the end of August. The trading on the currency exchanges destroyed the sense of the budget in the course of any one day, reducing the scoldings of the Reparation Commission about budgetary virtue to repetitive absurdities. Germany now felt she had demonstrated her good will to the point of proving that fulfillment was indeed impossible. On June 30, with the mark at 374—a day before it broke through 400—Wirth told a cabinet committee meeting: "We will have to cut down on the payments. We will give the collapse of the mark as our argument."[2]

The British, as the cabinet meeting of June 16 showed,[3] had given up on reparations. After Rathenau's death, John Bradbury and Basil Blackett, in a talk with a member of the German embassy in London, said they wanted to see a moratorium on cash payments at least until 1924,[4] but their government could not ask the British people to make sacrifices for the Germans. In France Poincaré's position rested on the premise that he would get some sort of concrete satisfaction out of Germany. He was not obliged to act immediately, however, and British reluctance was restraining him.

Germany resumed her unhappy interchange of arguments with the Reparation Commission and the Allied governments. On July 12 Wirth sent a note saying that Germany would pay the next installment of 50 million gold marks, due in three days, as one more proof of good will. He then formally requested a moratorium through 1924.[5] The commission members referred the question to their home governments, who found themselves in total disagreement. The commission's answer was delayed for a month and a half. Wirth, meanwhile, attempted to deal directly with Poincaré about reducing the clearing payments—compensation to Allied private citizens (see Chapter II)—but the Premier held to his legal rights.[6] Germany could only wait.

[1] Germany, Statistisches Amt, *Wirtschaft und Statistik* (1924), vol. 9 of bound monthly bulletin, p. 276, table.

[2] Ausführung, BA, R43I/29.

[3] Cabinet Conclusions, PRO, CAB 23/30. Mentioned in chap. IX.

[4] Discussed at the German cabinet meeting of June 30, see n. 2 above. The diplomat was Albert Dufour-Feronce, a German despite the name.

[5] Copy in Ausführung, BA, R43I/29.

[6] Copies of Wirth notes of July 14 and 31, and Poincaré note of July 26 in Ausführung, BA, R43I/29 and 30.

Britain and France debated. The Balfour Note of August 1 put the British position forcefully. The sense of the note had been discussed at the important cabinet meeting of June 16, when the British government decided it could no longer delay in acceding to the American demand for debt payment. Britain regretfully explained to her debtors—France was first among them—that the United States was forcing her to turn around and require payment from them. Britain urged America and France to reflect once again on the wisdom of demanding money for war debts in the one case, reparations in the other.[7] The note was partially a move to put the onus on the United States and, to a lesser extent, on France. It was meant also to gain an advantage over Poincaré, due to come to London for the Allied conference on reparations of August 7–14.[8] The British were asking Poincaré to relent on German reparations, although the Americans were remaining obdurate about the French debt. It was not fair. On August 7, at the opening of the conference, Poincaré told Lloyd George: "France is at her last gasp. . . ." He argued that American and British policy were driving France into bankruptcy. His solution was reparations-as-usual, or "the occupation and exploitation of the Ruhr. . . ." He threatened: "If we have to do it alone . . . we will not hesitate."[9] Against this, Lloyd George contended that Germany did not have the money and that an occupation would not magically create it.[10] The Prime Minister told a cabinet meeting three days later: "There might be a great change in French public opinion if M. Poincaré . . . occupied the Ruhr at great expense and produced nothing for the French exchequer except quantities of useless paper."[11] On August 14 the participants admitted they could not resolve their disagreement and adjourned the conference sine die.

The next reparation installment, 50 million gold marks, was due the following day. Germany was still waiting for an answer to Wirth's moratorium request of July 12. Her finances were so bad that she let the day go by without paying. She also stopped clearing payments on August 17. Poincaré, controlling three of the five votes

[7] Balfour Note in *The Times* and world press, August 2; also in Moulton and Pasvolsky, *War Debts and World Prosperity*, pp. 112–13.

[8] Minutes in France, Ministère des affaires étrangères, *Documents relatifs aux réparations* (1924), 2: 9–101.

[9] *Ibid.*, 2: 14; Poincaré's statement, pp. 10–17.

[10] *Ibid.*, 2: 19–30.

[11] Cabinet Conclusions, PRO, CAB 23/30.

on the Reparation Commission,[12] could have got the commission to declare Germany in default. Feeling, however, that it was not yet entirely safe to do anything so important, he found a way of postponing action without humiliating himself. Louis Dubois, the French commission president, was under great pressure from the other representatives to agree to a plan that was called a compromise. It was not a compromise; it was a deception. The commission would accept German treasury notes for the rest of 1922 although the notes were backed neither by Reichsbank gold nor other negotiable reserves. The notes were worthless. As usual in such circumstances, Dubois sought Poincaré's guidance, but the Premier had become unavailable. Correctly interpreting this, the commission president approved the plan. On September 1, a day after the commission announced its decision, Poincaré wrote a recriminating letter that drove Dubois to resign.[13] Poincaré had felt obliged to make a concession without appearing to do so. Using the privilege of the leader, he had transferred the blame to a lesser figure. The Reparation Commission's statement of August 31, in the form of a reply to Wirth's moratorium request, was an exercise in Aesopian language. It scolded Germany for economic frivolity, formally rejected the request—and granted it by accepting the unbacked treasury notes.[14] Germany had her relief. It did little good.

Since Wirth had accepted the London Payments Plan, Germany had paid in cash reparations an initial 1 billion gold marks in 1921 and 450 million gold marks in 1922 (of the 720 million originally ordered under the provisional moratorium of March 21, 1922), plus 615 million gold marks in clearing payments.[15] All during 1921 she had shipped coal and a few other varieties of goods worth about 400 million gold marks.[16] The provisional moratorium pro-

----

[12] Besides the original one vote for France, there was the extra vote of the commission president, who was French, while Belgium was obliged to support France.

[13] Episode recounted in Jean Leyrette, "The Foreign Policy of Poincaré: France and Great Britain in Relation with the German Problem 1919–1924" (dissertation, 1955), pp. 130–35.

[14] Copy in Ausführung, BA, R43I/30.

[15] Bergmann, Der Weg der Reparationen, p. 186.

[16] I determined this figure by first taking the value credited Germany for the coal, in Gradl, Die Reparations-Sachleistungen von Versailles, p. 106, table. This value was calculated on the German domestic price of coal, which was about half of the international price (see chap. VI, n. 2). To the coal figure I add a few millions for the other goods.

vided for deliveries in kind of 1,450 million gold marks in 1922, and Germany had continued making these deliveries after she stopped cash payments. During 1922, in sum, she shipped 695.6 million gold marks worth; the Allies refused to take more—France, for example, accepted only 20 percent of the 950 million gold marks in goods to which she was entitled.[17] The total of all these cash and value transfers was not enormous—about 3 billion gold marks in a year and one-half—but it contributed substantially to the increases in the general operating deficit at a time when stability required reducing that deficit.

On November 12 a lead article by Georg Bernhard in the *Vossische Zeitung* said that the Wirth cabinet was "used up." Wirth had been maneuvering skillfully and desperately. The Reparation Commission, which had been in Berlin for nearly two weeks, had just returned to Paris. Now under the presidency of Louis Barthou, Poincaré's close associate, it ignored Wirth's pleas for mercy and, in a note of November 6, quite reasonably refused to believe his promises to undertake real financial reforms.[18] Wirth had just persuaded a committee of experts that included John Maynard Keynes to come to Berlin. The committee submitted a report on November 7.[19] Wirth had hoped that it would give him a usable recommendation, but although it called for relief, the committee said that Germany must initiate action by using its gold reserve to stabilize the economy. The decision was hardly consistent with Keynes' views before or after, and Wirth had good reason to believe that the relief plan would cause bankruptcy before the relief could take effect. The gold reserve was the last barrier to the world financial community's ultimate loss of faith in Germany. During all of 1922, despite the bitter need in the country, the government and the Reichsbank defended the reserve so well that it dropped by only 40.2 million gold marks, going from 995 to 954.8 million gold marks.[20] Wirth the political man refused to let the dangerous report defeat him. Apprised of its contents in advance, he convinced

[17] Weill-Raynal, *Les réparations allemandes*, 2: 304, table.
[18] Copy of note, minutes of meetings of Reparation Commission with Wirth, etc., in Ausführung, BA, R43I/32.
[19] Copy in *ibid.*, R43I/32. Other signatories included the bankers R. H. Brand of Britain, Jeremiah W. Jenks of the United States, and Gustav Cassel of Sweden.
[20] Germany, Kriegslastenkommission, *Deutschlands Wirtschaft, Währung u. Finanzen* (1924), p. 64, table.

two other experts, besides one of those who signed the original advice, to make still another recommendation on the same day. This called for relief without making any embarrassing suggestions about opening up the gold reserve.[21] Wirth let the first recommendation remain in the files and sent the second to the Reparation Commission on November 8.[22] Then, on November 14, he sent the commission another plan for financial reform to justify help.[23] There was no real hope. Poincaré, giving precise orders to the new president of the Reparation Commission, was preparing a new movement, and German promises were irrelevant to it. An immediate answer, however, would have been irrelevant to Wirth himself. On the evening of November 14, 1922, at about 10 P.M., Wirth resigned.

For more than a month Wirth had been trying to broaden the government, a recurrent project in the history of the Weimar Republic. The objective was to share the terrible responsibility with more elements in German society, most particularly with the business community. Rathenau's period in office had suggested—but only suggested—business support, and now he was dead. The plan, in its political specifics, meant bringing the People's Party into the government. At a meeting on November 14, however, the Social Democrats rejected the idea. They feared for the eight-hour day, which business was then attacking as uneconomic.[24] Once more the Germans could not agree on a division of the sacrifices. Domestically as well as internationally, the Wirth leadership was used up.

The new Chancellor was Wilhelm Cuno, managing director of the Hamburg-America Line. Never in his life had Cuno been more than a figurehead. That made little difference. The Social Democrats, preferring to avoid the responsibility for the while, refused to enter the government, and Germany found herself under the leadership of businessmen who talked budget-balancing in the midst

[21] Copy in Ausführung, BA, R43I/32. It was Brand who also signed this recommendation; the others were the bankers Gerard Vissering of The Netherlands and Leopold Dubois of Switzerland.

[22] According to the covering letter to the commission. The letter used the second recommendation as support for another argument for relief, in *ibid.*, R43I/32.

[23] Copy in *ibid.*, R43I/32. This time he sent the first recommendation as well.

[24] Gustav Bauer, Wirth's Social Democratic Vice-Chancellor, tried to explain it at a cabinet meeting at 9:30 P.M., November 14. The minutes end: "The Chancellor thereupon left to present himself to the President of the Reich" (Kabinettsprotokolle, BA, R43I/1381).

of bankruptcy proceedings. Whatever the competence of Cuno and his associates, the Allies held the initiative.

At last Poincaré had to act. In London, at the failed conference in August, he had clearly stated what he wanted: "productive pledges" (*gages productifs*). These were the German mines and forests, which would yield a steady income to an Allied occupation while the loss of that income would persuade Germany to resume the honest payment of reparations.[25] Impeccably and exclusively political, Poincaré's reasoning had no relation to economics. The occupation would, after all, produce only goods, and not the cash which the Premier had claimed he would get. Actually, Germany was continuing to send goods into France and the other Allied countries, and only asked to send more. French public opinion, however, would no longer wait for satisfaction, even if the satisfaction had to be metaphysical. A final conference in London with the British Prime Minister, now Bonar Law, on January 2 to 4, 1923, produced a final disagreement, as Poincaré rejected a British plan for a four-year moratorium. On January 11 French and Belgian troops began the Ruhr occupation. The British said it was illegal.

The occupation was a thorough disaster. All the participating Allies got a total of perhaps 1.1 billion gold marks in goods out of it,[26] but such figures take on an insane meaning beside the losses which the various governments could calculate and did not, and the incalculable losses. The economic disorders, playing back on France, severely strained her finances and caused the franc to fall abruptly. Germany herself responded with a burst of unity and carried through an effective, if painful, policy of passive resistance, enlivened with strikes and the operations of revived Free Corps units. One estimate put the German loss during the occupation at 3.5 billion gold marks,[27] but, again, this makes little sense against the immeasurable suffering and damage. It was the time of the great German inflation, when laundry baskets were needed to carry the payrolls of small shops, and when employees rushed from the pay windows to buy what they needed before the prices changed too

[25] Ministère des affaires étrangères, *Documents ralatifs aux réparations*, 2: 10–17.
[26] Gradl, *Die Reparations-Sachleistungen von Versailles*, p. 53.
[27] Albert Schwartz, *Die Weimarer Republik* (1958), p. 103.

much. The mark was at 7,260 to the dollar at the beginning of 1923. At the end of January it had reached 49,000. The government once more made use of its gold reserve and rolled the mark back to 20,975 at the end of March by purchases on the currency exchanges. But then the final fall began: 74,750 on June 1; 160,000 on July 1; 1,100,000 on August 1; 242 million on October 1; and 4.2 trillion on November 20, when the old mark was withdrawn in favor of a new currency, the *Rentenmark*. The middle classes lost their last savings and sense of security. Hitler, battening on the disorders and anger, became a real force. He attempted the Beer Hall Putsch on November 8–9.

The Ruhr occupation resolved a great deal. It established the conditions for the first real international economic cooperation since the war, an order of things that lasted for the rest of the decade. The sobered French were willing to admit more of the economic and political truth. They admitted that blind force would give them neither real reparations, nor real security. Poincaré fell after the election of May, 1924, to be succeeded by the conciliatory Édouard Herriot, accompanied by the conciliatory Briand. The Americans admitted more of the truth about their world responsibilities. It was not a great deal, but it was enough to make them reduce their demands and help a little. The result was the Dawes Plan, a new and bearable reparation settlement. Germany could stabilize her currency and economy, and enjoy five or six good years, as could most of the world.

The politics of fulfillment dominated the political life of the Weimar Republic until its breakup. Gustav Stresemann, Foreign Minister from August 14, 1923, to his death on October 3, 1929, worked out the policy called *Verständigung*. The word could be translated as "accommodation." The policy was another approximation of fulfillment in what had become a somewhat different context. During these years, as Germany shared in the world's recovery from the war's dislocations, Stresemann had to strain all his political skill to satisfy both Allies and his increasingly irritable countrymen. He negotiated the Locarno Treaties in October, 1925, which guaranteed Germany's western frontiers and eased relations with France; balanced that on April 24, 1926, by negotiating the Berlin Treaty with Soviet Russia as an extension of the Rapallo Treaty; and balanced that by taking Germany into the League of Nations on September 10, 1926. He won the Nobel Peace Prize along with Aristide Briand and died in the month of the great stock market crash. Stresemann had been negotiating the change from the Dawes Plan to the Young Plan during the last year of his life. The first plan, which had begun with a loan and a virtual moratorium, was calling for payments of 2.5 billion *Reichsmarks*[28] annually by 1928–29, and Stresemann had wanted to reduce the payments and get the Allied troops out of the Rhineland. According to the Young Plan, which went into force in May, 1930, Germany had to pay 1.9 billion Reichsmarks annually, while the occupation of the Rhineland was ended. Before then the Young Plan had provided the occasion for vicious chauvinistic responses to Allied exactions. The Nazis, joining with the Nationalists, won a new respectability through the anti-Young Plan campaign, a brilliant propaganda effort to persuade Germany to reject the plan. While it failed of that purpose, it had great destructive effect on the Weimar Republic. After that, the government of Heinrich Brüning, Chancellor from March 30, 1930, to May 30, 1932, was crushed under the weight of reparations and the World Depression. The need for a reparation moratorium had determined Brüning's economic policies. Early in 1930 he told the Reichstag that Germany must balance her budget and foreign trade so that no one "could attribute to her a lack of good will . . ." as she sought relief.[29] Pursuing this policy, Brüning achieved an extraordinary technical success. Through three rigorous wage-and-price reductions he brought costs down. He also restricted imports sharply. From 1929 to 1932 he reduced imports from 13.4 billion to 4.7 billion Reichsmarks, producing a trade surplus of more than a billion Reichsmarks in 1932; although, as other nations retaliated, German exports fell from 13.5 billion to 5.7 billion Reichsmarks between 1929 and 1932.[30] Brüning's plan worked: The Lausanne Conference of June–July, 1932, reduced German reparations to a nominal sum. Brüning, however, was out of office. His economic policy, combined with all the other effects of the Depression, had caused an increase in unemployment to about

[28] The Reichsmark replaced the Rentenmark in 1924; it had the same value.
[29] On February 11, before he took office, quoted in Wolfgang J. Helbich, *Die Reparationen in der Ära Brüning* (1962), p. 30.
[30] Walther G. Hoffmann, *Das Wachstum der deutschen Wirtschaft seit der Mitte des 19. Jahrhunderts* (1965), pp. 520–21, table.

seven million—one-third of the work force—by February, 1932. The unemployment and despair gave Hitler the last materials he needed for gaining power. The politics of reparations had ended.

When it was over, what did Germany pay in reparations? All figures are untrustworthy, but it does not matter. Étienne Weill-Raynal, author of the three-volume study of German reparations mentioned in these pages, calculated that Germany paid a total of 22.9 billion marks (gold marks, Rentenmarks, and Reichsmarks added together indiscriminately) in reparations from the beginning to the end.[31] The figure compounds innumerable questionable calculations about valuation of goods and interest payments, among others. It does not credit Germany with many transfers of wealth, including the mines of the Saar, and public works and steel mills in Lorraine. It ignores such factors as the malformations in the German economy, and the costs—and the trauma—of the Ruhr occupation. It can, however, begin to suggest part of the meaning. Compared with the 22.9 billion, foreign creditors and investors sent the equivalent of 25.5 billion marks into Germany from 1924 to 1930. This was the source of the money which Germany used to pay reparations under the Dawes and Young Plans.[32] Before that time, Germany got foreigners to help pay reparations by innocently selling them marks or mark credits. From the Armistice until the inflation in 1923, speculators bought 7.6 to 8.7 billion gold marks worth of the paper mark values.[33] They were risking their money in the expectation of an earlier German recovery, and this money had helped the Germany of Rathenau survive. Later, Hitler's government defaulted on all the loans that could not be recalled, while also blocking the investments. Thus, admitting all the approximations and those factors not translatable into financial statistics, one can still say that by and large American and Allied creditors and investors paid German reparations. It was only reasonable: Germany did not have the money and they had. The Dawes Plan,

[31] *Les réparations allemandes*, 3: 769–71. His figures: 10.5 billion marks before the Dawes Plan, 7.6 billion under the Dawes Plan, and 3.7 billion under the Young Plan, plus 1.1 billion as correction. This also includes the mark (gold mark, Rentenmark, Reichsmark, as the case may be) value of deliveries in kind.

[32] According to the Layton Report (Walter Layton was a British banker), submitted to the London Conference of 1931, quoted in Gustav Stolper, *Deutsche Wirtschaft seit 1870* (1964), p. 116.

[33] According to an economic study for the Dawes Plan, cited in Constantino Bresciani-Turroni, *The Economics of Inflation* (1937), p. 252.

which had made things bearable, helped construct this payment mechanism. Of course, it had not solved the transfer problem; Germany was never permitted to develop trade surpluses that would have given her the excess funds to finance real payments. In fact, Germany's trade balance was passive. She simply lacked the money, but she had to pay it. She solved the problem by paying interest rates of up to 9 percent, double those of other countries.[34] This solution worked on the principle of the classic swindle, which attracts victims by offering returns greater than those of a sound business. The disproportionate returns bring in new waves of investors, whose money, and not the profits, is used to finance the large payments to the original investors. Eventually something creates a doubt, new investors are frightened away, the old ones try to sell out, and the operation collapses. This is what happened to Germany during the Depression and Brüning's chancellorship. Reparations meant an incalculable loss to everybody.

The reparation question was never an economic question. Keynes understood this well. Indeed, he made a temerarious leap into the arena of political judgment, offering advice to the politician Lloyd George. In June, 1919, Keynes resigned as Treasury representative at the Peace Conference to write his *Economic Consequences of the Peace*. He would not continue to help with the peace which would produce "that final civil war between the forces of Reaction and the despairing convulsions of Revolution, before which the horrors of the late German war will fade into nothing. . . ."[35] Two years later, in his *Revision of the Treaty*, he conceded "a plausible defense," at least, for Lloyd George's "terrifying statesmanship."[36] Keynes recognized the argument that "public passions and public ignorance play a part in the world." He granted that "the Peace of Versailles was the best momentary settlement which the demands of the mob and the characters of the chief actors conjoined to permit. . . ." Keynes had not quite said that Lloyd George had been right and he himself wrong about the politics of the peace in 1919, but the admission was there to be deciphered in his verbal arrangements. In 1921, in any case, Keynes submitted proposals to alter the Versailles Treaty: "My concluding proposals assume that this element of

[34] Karl Erich Born, *Die deutsche Bankenkrise 1931* (1967), p. 16.
[35] P. 268.
[36] P. 1; the introduction is dated December, 1921.

make-believe has ceased to be politically necessary."[37] Keynes was only assuming; he had produced no proof that the element of make-believe had really disappeared. Lloyd George still knew better. Public passions, at least in France and the United States, prevented the kind of sensible revision Keynes wanted. Whatever honor his economics won for him, Keynes never demonstrated that he could compete in political judgment with Lloyd George.

Many economists have remarked upon the connection between the peace of 1919 and the economic collapse beginning in 1929. None, however, has fully developed the subject. Keynes, who could claim prophetic force for what he wrote in 1919, preferred to study other causes in his *General Theory*, published in 1936. Was the Depression not one of the greatest of the consequences of the peace? The economist Lionel Robbins has written: "The financial convulsions of the Great Depression were, in part at least, the product of the system of international borrowing and lending. . . ."[38] The thought might be profitably pursued much further, with particular attention to the borrowing and lending caused by reparations and the Dawes Plan.

In view of all this, what alternatives did Rathenau have? All the reparation payment plans had their inherent difficulties. No one can argue credibly that Rathenau and Wirth missed the opportunity for a less destructive mode of paying reparations and satisfying the Allies. Beyond such details, one might argue that it would have been better for them to have declared incompetency. They might conceivably have let the Allies accept the immediate consequences of their demands and occupy the whole country. But no national leadership gives up even a tortured sovereignty for none at all. Moreover, the German government reasonably feared the loss of the Rhineland to French-encouraged separatism, as well as other territorial losses to Poland in the East. It would have been politically impossible. Another kind of advice was given by an economist of our generation in a study of the Versailles Treaty. He argued that the Wirth-Rathenau government should have carried through radical financial measures to show the Allies the unlimited extent of its good will. The Germans should have stabilized the currency,

[37] *Ibid.*, pp. 2, 7.
[38] Introduction to Bresciani-Turroni, *Economics of Inflation*, p. 5.

whatever the risks of a depression. "It seems very improbable that [the Allies] would have let Germany go the deflationary road straight up to the door of hell, that is to say, up to radical-revolutionary destruction of the republic," the economist wrote.[39] To this one must say that in the first place Lloyd George believed that Great Britain would indeed have to stand by while Germany suffered, as he put it, her "terrific collapse."[40] In the second place, the author is accurately describing what happened ten years later. Most criticism of Rathenau has concentrated on the unquestionably negative effects of his policy while failing to offer any firm alternative. This was the case with Helfferich and the other Nationalists, who went on and on about Germany's humiliation without suggesting anything to end the humiliation. Then there were alternatives that vanished upon examination. The fiercer rightists wanted to fight, but they had neither troops nor weapons to throw against the Allied armies. Arthur Rosenberg, a distinguished historian of the Weimar Republic and a man of the Left, was reasoning in the same way when he said that Germany missed her chance to do something in 1919: "Germany should at that time have laid stress upon her desire for an understanding with France, but at the same time have refused to do anything that could not be reconciled with a fair interpretation of the Peace Treaty."[41] Just how could she have refused? The advice was as useless to Rathenau and his successors as it would have been to the leaders of the prostrate Germany of the spring of 1919. Few persons have taken any of the alternatives seriously, except the authors themselves.

Fulfillment, as the major factor in all government policy in the Weimar period, thrust an engine of deceit into the hands of the German people. They had to operate it. Fulfillment was impossible, at least by normal standards. Any effort to live with it meant the production of all manner of falsehoods. The lies soaked into all those issues that are normally fought out among the interest groups. If the class war was not entirely an honest issue, fulfillment reduced the amount of truth in it. Workers and employers might think they were struggling against each other over wages and hours, but they

---

[39] Erich Wüest, in *Der Vertrag von Versailles im Licht und Schatten der Kritik: Die Kontroverse um seine wirtschaftlichen Auswirkungen* (1962), p. 206.

[40] Cabinet meeting, May 23, 1922, Cabinet Conclusions, PRO, CAB 23/30.

[41] *A History of the Weimar Republic* (1936), p. 154.

were really trying to save themselves from the foreigners, chiefly the Americans. The fact that a worker's family was suffering from malnutrition was not due, or not so much due, to the selfishness of the German capitalists, who controlled the situation even less than they thought, but to the international obtuseness, however forgivable it might have been, of the ordinary American citizen. The deceptions were no less destructive for all the innocence of their origins.

The lying was ubiquitous. If the Germans were lying to each other, they were also turning their deceptions upon the foreigners, and the outside world was lying to itself and back at the Germans. Of course the Wiesbaden Agreement did not work; it was not meant to work. Of course Americans and other foreigners paid reparations in the end. Similarly, the Reparation Commission never thought that Germany should listen to its lessons in financial responsibility. The commission knew they would bankrupt her overnight. If her policy was a concentrate of deceptions, Germany was part of a world in which big lies were normal currency. The international fictions and distortions appeared in the form of the unadjusted trade deficits and surpluses, the American farming depression in the midst of prosperity, chronic British unemployment, financial manipulation by the French government, economic war among the successor states of Central and Eastern Europe, the fumbling rejection of what Soviet Russia and international communism represented, the futile peacemaking by the League of Nations, and all the disguised expressions of self-destructive nationalism. In this ocean of mendacity, as Rathenau knew, the fulfillment policy had to mean evading fulfillment as much as possible. Later, Brüning fulfilled only too well.

This was the situation in which Rathenau had been obliged to act. How well or badly had he dealt with it?

Any account of the 1921–22 period shows what Rathenau's services meant in Germany's day-to-day survival. Even before he took office he had raised a screen of ideas that became the fulfillment policy. He carried it out as Reconstruction Minister, expert extraordinary, and Foreign Minister. His negotiation and manipulation of the Wiesbaden Agreement, his diplomacy in London and Cannes, his ability to keep a balance between fulfillment and the demands of power politics—Rapallo!: these were the indestructible evidences of his effectiveness. But it was a short-term success.

The need to survive drove the government to take certain actions that inevitably resulted in long-range evils. To Germany fulfillment meant unjust sacrifice, and the association of fulfillment with responsible parliamentary government harmed that government. Alan Bullock wrote in his biography of Hitler: "All events were on the side of the extremists."[42] Bullock made the point that Hitler attracted his first important crowds to protest the Allied reparation demands of early 1921. The bitter necessity of fulfillment had given him his initial strength as well as the final force to capture the power. Without Rathenau the career of Nazism would have been significantly different.

The subject is not exhausted when it is admitted that Rathenau's ideas and actions led to disaster in the long run. The Weimar Republic was much more than an antechamber to the Nazi period. It was the forcing bed of a creativity that has enormously enriched the twentieth century. Its products can only be hastily catalogued here: the Bauhaus, with its revolutionary union of the beautiful and the practical; the paintings of Kandinsky, Klee, Kokoschka, Grosz, and Feininger, most of them associated with the Bauhaus; the music of Schönberg, who came to Berlin from Vienna, and the other great innovators; the work of Einstein; the theater of Bertolt Brecht, which got its violent truth from the evils of the time; the writings of Thomas Mann, Heidegger, Tillich, and of Max Weber, who died too early; and the vital journalism, publishing industry, and cinema. All this coexisted with the republic's murderous potentials. The good and evil cannot be separated, and Rathenau was a part of it all.

Beyond Weimar and Nazi Germany, beyond the good and evil, contemporary Germany lives in a new long run, as measured from Rathenau's era. From this newer vantage point, what other judgments can be made of Rathenau?

It cannot be denied that Rathenau's influence helped improve German politics. After World War II, the West German government could take up the parliamentary mode so smoothly because men

[42] *Hitler: A Study in Tyranny* (1952), p. 77.

like Rathenau had given it so much vigor in the twenties. The national leadership has been trying more or less honestly to build on the irreducible values which Rathenau had defended and enhanced. The world lives easily with this bland Germany. If it might feel some regret, it has no right to complain that the new Germany has accomplished very little in the area of culture that can be compared with the legacy of Weimar Germany. The mediocre can be a relief after so much tragedy.

We move insensibly past the point in time when Germany was a leading nation. If we are American, we should appreciate the irony in the fulfillment logic that reduced her to second rank. For American policy, insisting on the impossible payment of war debts and refusing to accept the country's responsibilities, accomplished that effect while driving Europe and the world into disaster. Now the United States accepts its responsibilities and risks disaster in newer forms.

Bibliography

MAJOR ARCHIVES

BA	Bundesarchiv, Coblenz
DZA	Deutsches Zentralarchiv, Potsdam
NA	National Archives, Washington
PA, AA	Politisches Archiv, Auswärtiges Amt, Bonn
PRO	Public Record Office, London

PRIMARY SOURCES

Archives

I. Bundesarchiv

Reichskanzlei

Ausführung des Friedensvertrags, June, 1919–January, 1923
England, 1920–26
Interfraktioneller Ausschuss, 1921–22
Kabinettsprotokolle, 1920–22
Personal-Akten, Prof. Dr. Joseph Wirth
Socialisierung, Allgemeines, 1919–20
Wiederaufbau der Feindgebiete, 1919–22
International Conferences:
  Brüssel
  Genf
  Genua

Spa, Allgemeines
Spa, Finanzen
Spa, Heer
Spa, Kolonialfragen
Spa, Wirtschaftliches

Finanzministerium
Ausführung des Friedensvertrags, 1919–23

Wiederaufbauministerium
Äusserungen u. Vorschläge zur Lösung der Reparationsfrage
Beiratssitzungen, 1920–21
Londoner Ultimatum vom Mai 1921
Pressestimmen über Rm. für Wiederaufbau, 1920–21
Reparationen, Allgemeines
Reparationsverhandlungen mit Frankreich, 1921–22
Stand der Aufbauarbeiten in Frankreich u. Belgien
Statistiken

Nachlässe
Prince Bernhard W. von Bülow, Maximilian Harden, Erich Koch-Weser, Karl Legien, Wichard von Moellendorff, Walther Rathenau, Arnold Rechberg, Paul Silverberg, Wilhelm Solf, Rudolf Wissell

II. Deutsches Zentralarchiv

Büro des Reichspräsidenten
Politische Abteilung, Ausführung des Friedensvertrags, March, 1919–March, 1924
Wirtschafts- und Finanzkonferenz in Genua

Reichskanzlei
Anrufung der Vermittlung des Präsidenten der Vereinigten Staaten
International Conferences:
Finanzkonferenz, 1920 (Brussels)
Brüsseler Finanzkonferenz (Beiakten)
Konferenz der Allierten in London, March, 1921
Spa-Konferenz

Wiederaufbauministerium
Deutsche Leistungen beim Wiederaufbau Ostpreussens, 1921–23
(1,800 volumes of material on details of Ministry administration, a few of which were sampled)

Wirtschaftsministerium
Geldwerterfassung der Industrie, 1921
Vorläufiger Reichswirtschaftsrat (Minutes), 1920

Reichswirtschaftsrat II
  Reparationsausschuss (Minutes), June 1, 1921–October 4, 1922
  Unterausschuss zur Sozialisierungsfrage, October 11, 1920–April 25, 1922

Sozialisierungskommission
  (Minutes), April 17, 1920–March 10, 1922

III. Politisches Archiv, Auswärtiges Amt
  Büro des Reichsministers
    Reparationen
    Persönliche Angelegenheiten des Ministers, January 1, 1922–July 7, 1922
    International Conferences:
      Cannes, December 23, 1921–March 2, 1922
      Genua, January–May, 1922
      Genua, Rapallo-Vertrag, April 10–September 2, 1922
      Spa, Allgemeines, April 22–September 11, 1920
      Spa, Kohlenfrage, July 7, 1920–January 20, 1921
      Spa, Deutsche Sitzungsprotokolle
      Spa, Sitzungsprotokolle der Allierten

  Politische Abteilung IV
    Deutsch-russischer Vertrag vom 16.4.22

IV. National Archives (microfilmed records of Auswärtiges Amt)
  Büro des Reichsministers
    Collection Entitled "Genua"
    Collection Entitled "Reparationsfrage"

  Presseabteilung
    Collection Entitled "Deutschland"

V. Public Record Office
  Cabinet
    Conclusions of the Meetings of the Cabinet, 1921–22
    Cabinet Papers, vols. 36, 40, 41
    War Cabinet, Finance Committee, Memoranda, September 20, 1919–December 5, 1921
    War Cabinet, Finance Committee, Minutes, July 24, 1919–July 31, 1922

  Foreign Office
    Foreign Office [Documents] 371, 1921–22

Other Archives and Source Collections

Hauptarchiv Berlin-Dahlem
  Eugen Schiffer-Nachlass
Historische Kommission zu Berlin
  Rudolf Wissell-Nachlass
Beaverbrook Library, London
  Private Papers of David Lloyd George
Leo Baeck Institute, New York
  Rathenau Correspondence with Constantin Brunner
Personal files, Günter Milich, Generalbevollmächtigter, Allgemeine Elektricitäts-Gesellschaft, Berlin
  Press clippings of comments on Rathenau

Documents

Agence interalliée des réparations. *Rapport final aux gouvernements membres.* Bruxelles, 1961.
Calmette, Gaston, ed. *Recueil de documents sur l'histoire de la question des réparations.* Paris: Costes, 1924.
Commission des réparations. *Rapport sur les travaux de la Commission des réparations de 1920 a 1922,* vol. 2. Paris: Felix Alcan, 1923.
Deutsches Industrie-Institut, Frankfurt. *Sondersammlung zur industriellen Verbandsgeschichte.* Veröffentlichungen des Reichsverbands der deutschen Industrie, vol. 17. Munich, 1921.
Documents on British Foreign Policy 1919–1939, 1st ser., vols. 8, 15, 16. London, 1958–68.
France. *Assemblée nationale: Annales: Chambre des députés.* Paris, 1921–22.
————. Ministère des affaires étrangères. *Documents diplomatiques. Demande de moratorium du gouvernement allemand à la Commission des réparations. Conférence de Londres. Conférence de Paris.* Paris, 1923.
————. Ministère des affaires étrangères. *Documents relatifs aux réparations,* vols. 1, 2. Paris, 1922–24.
Germany. Kriegslastenkommission. *Deutschlands Wirtschaft, Währung u. Finanzen.* Berlin: Zentralverlag, 1924.
————. *Reichstag: Stenographische Berichte.* Berlin, 1921–22.
————. *Sammlung von Aktenstücken über die Verhandlungen auf der Konferenz zu London vom. 1. März bis 7 März 1921* (pamphlet). Berlin, 1921.
————. Statistisches Amt. *Statistik des deutschen Reiches: Der auswärtige Handel in den Jahren 1920, 1921, und 1922,* vol. 310. Berlin, 1924.
————. Statistisches Amt. *Germany's Economic and Financial Situation: An Exhibit of After-Effects of the World War.* Berlin: Zentralverlag, 1923.

————. Statistisches Amt. *Wirtschaft und Statistik*, vol. 9. Berlin, 1924.

————. *Stenographische Berichte über die Verhandlungen des vorläufigen Reichswirtschaftsrats*, vols. 1, 2 (minutes of each meeting as bound by Humboldt-Universität Library, East Berlin), 1920–23.

Great Britain. Foreign Office. *Treaty of Peace between the Allied and Associated Powers and Germany*. London, 1919.

League of Nations. *International Statistical Year-Book 1926*. Geneva, 1927.

————. *Memorandum on Balance of Payments and Foreign Trade Balances 1910–24*, vols. 1, 2. Geneva, 1925.

————. *Memorandum on Public Finance 1921–22*. Geneva, 1923.

————. *Monthly Bulletin of Statistics, 1920–22*. Geneva, 1923.

————. Secretariat: Economic, Financial and Transit Department. *Industrialization and Foreign Trade*. New York, 1945.

A Rathenau Bibliography

By Rathenau

A brief listing of his major and most characteristic writings. The following editions have been selected because of their inclusiveness or convenience.

Briefe. 2 vols. Dresden: Carl Reissner, 1926.

Briefe: Neue Folge. Dresden: Carl Reissner, 1928.

Briefe. 3 vols. Dresden: Carl Reissner, 1930. (Comprising all of the contents of the above editions and a few other letters.)

Briefe an eine Liebende. Dresden: Carl Reissner, 1931.

Gesammelte Reden. Berlin: S. Fischer, 1924.

Gesammelte Schriften. 5 vols. Berlin: S. Fischer, 1918.

————. 6 vols. Berlin: S. Fischer, 1925–29. (A reprinting of the first 5 volumes of the 1918 edition, plus vol. 6: *Schriften aus Kriegs- und Nachkriegszeit.*)

Impressionen. Leipzig: S. Hirzel, 1902.

Nachgelassene Schriften. 2 vols. Berlin: S. Fischer, 1928.

Die neue Gesellschaft. Berlin: S. Fischer, 1919.

Der neue Staat. Berlin: S. Fischer, 1922.

Politische Briefe. Dresden: Carl Reissner, 1929.

Ein preussischer Europäer: Briefe. Edited by Margarete von Eynern. Berlin: Käthe Vogt, 1955. (The more important letters, most of them concerned with politics.)

Reflexionen. Leipzig: S. Hirzel, 1908.

Schriften. Edited by Golo Mann. Berlin: Berlin-Verlag, 1965.

Schriften und Reden: Auswahl und Nachwort. Edited by Hans W. Richter. Frankfurt: S. Fischer, 1964.

Tagebuch 1907–1922. Berlin: Reichsdruckerei, 1930.

————. Edited by Hartmut Pogge-von Strandmann. Düsseldorf: Droste, 1967. (A new publication, with notes on persons and issues.)

About Rathenau

Böttcher, Helmuth M. *Walther Rathenau*. Bonn: Athenäum, 1958.

Federn-Kohlhaas, Etta. *Walther Rathenau: Sein Leben und Wirken*. 2nd expanded ed. Dresden: Carl Reissner, 1928.

Gottlieb, Ernst. *Walther Rathenau—Bibliographie*. Berlin: S. Fischer, 1929. (A comprehensive listing of writings by and about Rathenau until 1929, ranging from major works to newspaper and periodical items.)

Joll, James. *Three Intellectuals in Politics*. New York: Pantheon, 1960.

Kerr, Alfred. *Walther Rathenau*. Amsterdam: Querido, 1935.

Kessler, Harry. *Walther Rathenau: Sein Leben und sein Werk*. Berlin: Klemm, 1928.

————. *Walther Rathenau: His Life and Work*. London: Heinemann, 1929.

————. *Walther Rathenau: Sein Leben und sein Werk*, with reminiscence, "Erinnerung an Walther Rathenau," by Hans Fürstenberg. Wiesbaden: Rheinische Verlags-Anstalt. 1963[?], 1st ed. 1928.

Kollmann, Eric C. "Walther Rathenau and German Foreign Policy: Thoughts and Actions," *Journal of Modern History* 24 (1952): 127–42.

Ludwig, Emil. *Leaders of Europe*. London: Nicolson and Watson, 1934.

Marck, Siegfried. "Rathenau als Denker." *Logos* 11 (1922–23): 181–90.

Möllers, Elisabeth. "Walther Rathenau: Eine publizistische Persönlichkeit." Dissertation, Universität zu München, 1952.

Musil, Robert. *Der Mann ohne Eigenschaften*. Hamburg: Rowohlt, 1952.

Orth, Wilhelm. *Walther Rathenau und der Geist von Rapallo*. (East) Berlin: Buchverlag Der Morgen, 1962.

GENERAL SECONDARY SOURCES

Books, Pamphlets, Articles

Albertin, Lothar. "Die Verantwortung der liberalen Parteien für das Scheitern der grossen Koalition im Herbst 1921." *Historische Zeitschrift* 205 (1967): 566–627.

Allemann, Fritz René. "Rapallo: Mythos und Wirklichkeit." *Der Monat* 14 (1962): 5–12.

Allen, Henry T. *The Rhineland Occupation*. Indianapolis: Bobbs-Merrill, 1927.

Allgemeine Elektricitäts-Gesellschaft. *50 Jahre AEG: Als Manuskript Gedruckt*. Berlin: AEG, 1956, 1st ed., 1933[?]

Bach, Otto. *Rudolf Wissell*. Berlin: Arani, 1959.

Baker, Ray Stannard. *Woodrow Wilson and World Settlement*. New York: Doubleday, Page, 1922.

Baruch, Bernard M. *The Making of the Reparation and Economic Sections of the Treaty*. New York and London: Harper & Brothers, 1920.

Baumont, Maurice. *La faillite de la paix*. Paris: Presses universitaires de France, 1946.

Bechtel, Heinrich. *Wirtschaftsgeschichte Deutschlands im 19. und 20. Jahrhundert.* Munich: Callwey, 1956.

Bergmann, Carl. *Der Weg der Reparationen.* Frankfurt: Frankfurter Societäts-Druckerei, 1926.

Binion, Rudolph. *Defeated Leaders: The Political Fate of Caillaux, Jouvenel, and Tardieu.* New York: Columbia University Press, 1960.

Birdsall, Paul. *Versailles Twenty Years After.* New York: Reynal & Hitchcock, 1941.

Bonn, M. J. *So Macht Man Geschichte.* Munich: Paul List, 1953.

————. *Wandering Scholar.* New York: John Day, 1948.

Born, Karl Erich. *Die deutsche Bankenkrise 1931.* Munich: Piper, 1967.

Borsky, G. *The Greatest Swindle in the World: The Story of German Reparations.* London: New Europe, 1942.

Bowen, Ralph Henry. *German Theories of the Corporative State.* New York: McGraw-Hill, 1947.

Bracher, Karl Dietrich. *Die Auflösung der Weimarer Republik.* Villingen: Ring, 1959, 1st ed., 1955.

Brammer, Karl. *Das politische Ergebnis des Rathenau-Prozesses* (pamphlet). Berlin: Verlag für Sozialwissenschaft, 1922[?]

Braun, Otto. *Von Weimar zu Hitler.* New York: Europa, 1940.

Brecht, Arnold. *Aus nächster Nähe.* Stuttgart: Deutsche Verlags-Anstalt, 1966.

Brecht, Bertolt. *Gesammelte Werke in acht Bänden,* vol. 1. Frankfurt: Suhrkamp, 1967.

Bresciani-Turroni, Constantino. *The Economics of Inflation.* London: Allen & Unwin, 1937.

Brinckmeyer, Hermann. *Die Rathenaus.* Munich: Wieland, 1922.

Brook, Warner F. *Social and Economic History of Germany 1888–1938.* London: Oxford University Press, 1938.

Brunet, René. *L'opinion publique et les partis politiques en France entre l'armistice et la paix* (pamphlet). Paris: Paix des Peuples, n.d.

Buchheim, Karl. *Die Weimarer Republik.* Munich: Kösel, 1960.

Bullock, Alan. *Hitler: A Study in Tyranny.* London: Oldhams, 1952.

Bülow, Bernhard von. *Denkwürdigkeiten,* vols. 2, 3. Berlin: Ullstein, 1930–31.

Burnett, Philip M. *Reparation at the Paris Peace Conference.* 2 vols. New York: Columbia University Press, 1940.

Burnham, James. *The Managerial Revolution.* New York: John Day, 1941.

Calmette, Germain. *Les dettes interalliées.* Paris: Costes, 1926.

Cameron, Elizabeth R. *Prologue to Appeasement: A Study of French Foreign Policy.* Washington: American Council on Public Affairs, 1942.

Campbell, F. Gregory. "The Struggle for Upper Silesia," *Journal of Modern History* 42 (1970): 361–85.

Carr, Edward Hallett. *The Bolshevik Revolution 1917–1923.* Vol. 3: *Soviet Russia and the World.* London: Macmillan & Co., 1953.

————. *German-Soviet Relations between the Two World Wars*. Baltimore: Johns Hopkins Press, 1951.

————. "Radek's 'Political Salon' in Berlin 1919." *Soviet Studies* 3 (1951– 52): 411–30.

Carré, Wilhelm. *Weltanschauung und Presse: Eine soziologische Untersuchung*. Leipzig: Hirschfeld, 1931.

Carsten, Francis L. *Reichswehr und Politik 1918–1933*. Cologne-Berlin: Kiepenheuer u. Witsch, 1964.

Castillon, Richard. *Les réparations allemandes: Deux expériences 1919– 1932, 1945–1952*. Paris: Presses universitaires de France, 1953.

Clark, R. T. *The Fall of the German Republic*. New York: Russell & Russell, 1964.

Craig, Gordon A. *From Bismarck to Adenauer: Aspects of German Statecraft*. Baltimore. Johns Hopkins Press, 1958.

————, and Gilbert, Felix, eds. *The Diplomats*. Princeton, N.J.: Princeton University Press, 1953.

Cron, Hermann. "Die Organisation der Kriegswirtschaft im Kriege 1914– 1918 und ihre Überleitung in die Friedensverhältnisse sowie Wertung ihrer Akten." Unpublished manuscript, bound by Deutsches Zentralarchiv, Potsdam, 1942.

Czernin, Ferdinand. *Versailles 1919*. New York: G. P. Putnam's Sons, 1964.

D'Abernon, Viscount Edgar Vincent. *The Diary of an Ambassador: Rapallo to Dawes 1922–1924*. New York: Doubleday, Doran, 1930.

————. *The Diary of an Ambassador: Versailles to Rapallo 1920–1922*. New York: Doubleday, Doran, 1929.

Denais, Joseph. *Nos finances et l'indemnité allemande* (pamphlet). Paris: Albin Michel, 1919.

Dubois, Louis. *Dettes de guerre et réparations* (pamphlet). Paris: Union des intérêts économiques. January, 1929.

Elster, Karl. *Von der Mark zur Reichsmark*. Jena: G. Fischer, 1928.

Epstein, Klaus. *Matthias Erzberger and the Dilemma of German Democracy*. Princeton, N.J.: Princeton University Press, 1959.

Erkelenz, Anton, ed. *Zehn Jahre deutsche Republik*. Berlin: Sieben Stäbe, 1928.

Euler, Heinrich. *Die Aussenpolitik der Weimarer Republik 1918–1923*. Aschaffenburg: Pattloch, 1957.

Eyck, Erich. *A History of the Weimar Republic*. 2 vols. Translated by Harlan P. Hanson and Robert G. L. Waite. Cambridge, Mass.: Harvard University Press, 1962–63.

Feldman, Gerald D. "The Social and Economic Policies of German Big Business, 1918–1929." *American Historical Review* 75 (1969): 47–55.

Fischer, Rudolf. *Karl Helfferich*. Berlin: Historisch-Politischer Verlag, 1932.

François-Poncet, André. *De Versailles à Potsdam*. Paris: Flammarion, 1948.

Freund, Gerald. *Unholy Alliance*. New York: Harcourt, Brace, 1957.

Friedenburg, Ferdinand. *Die Weimarer Republik.* Hannover-Frankfurt: Norddeutsche Verlagsanstalt, 1957, 1st ed. 1946.

Friedrich, Johannes. *Das internationale Schuldenproblem.* Leipzig: Akademische Verlagsgesellschaft, 1928.

Fritsch, Theodor E. [F. Roderich-Stoltheim] *Anti-Rathenau* (pamphlet). Leipzig: Hammer, 1921.

Fürst, Artur. *Emil Rathenau: Der Mann und sein Werk.* Berlin: Vita, 1915.

Garrigou-La Grange, André. *Le problème des réparations.* Paris: Éditions de la vie universitaire, 1923.

Gay, Peter. *Weimar Culture: The Outsider as Insider.* New York-Evanston, Ill.: Harper & Row, 1968.

Gescher, Dieter B. *Die Vereinigten Staaten von Nordamerika und die Reparationen 1920–1924.* Bonn: Rohrscheid, 1956.

Gessler, Otto. *Reichswehrpolitik in der Weimarer Zeit.* Stuttgart: Deutsche Verlags-Anstalt, 1958.

Goguel, François. *La politique des partis sous la Troisième République.* Vol. 1: *1871–1932.* Paris: Seuil, 1946.

Gradl, Baptist. *Die Reparations-Sachleistungen von Versailles bis zur Bank internationaler Zahlungen.* Berlin: Germania, 1933.

Gropius, Walter. *The New Architecture and the Bauhaus.* London: Faber & Faber, 1935.

Gumbel, E. J. *Vier Jahre politischer Mord.* Berlin: Verlag der neuen Gesellschaft, 1922.

————. *Vom Fememord zur Reichskanzlei.* Heidelberg: Lambert Schneider, 1962.

————. *Vom Russland der Gegenwart.* Berlin: Laubsche Verlagsbuchhandlung, 1927.

Hachenburg, Max. *Lebenserinnerungen eines Rechtsanwalts.* Düsseldorf: Neue Brücke, 1929.

Halperin, S. William. *Germany Tried Democracy.* New York: Cromwell, 1946.

Hannover, Heinrich, and Hannover, Elisabeth. *Politische Justiz 1918–1933.* Frankfurt: Fischer, 1966.

Harris, C. R. S. *Germany's Foreign Indebtedness.* London: Oxford University Press, 1935.

Harrod, R. F. *The Life of John Maynard Keynes.* London: Macmillan & Co., 1951.

Harsin, Paul. *Le problème des réparations: Une expérience de dix ans* (pamphlet). Liège: Liège Printing Co., 1929.

Hauschild, Harry. *Der vorläufige Reichswirtschaftsrat 1920–1926.* Berlin: Mittler, 1926.

Helbich, Wolfgang J. *Die Reparationen in der Ära Brüning.* Berlin: Colloquium-Verlag, 1962.

Helbig, Herbert. *Die Träger der Rapallo-Politik.* Göttingen: Vandenhoeck, 1958.

Helfferich, Karl. *Fort mit Erzberger* (pamphlet). Berlin: Scherl, 1919.

———. *Die Politik der Erfüllung*. Munich-Berlin-Leipzig: Schweitzer, 1922.

Hertzman, Lewis. *DNVP: Right-Wing Opposition in the Weimar Republic, 1918–1924*. Lincoln, Neb.: University of Nebraska Press, 1963.

Hester, James McN. "America and the Weimar Republic." Dissertation, Oxford University, 1955.

Heuss, Theodor. *Erinnerungen 1905–1933*. Tübingen: Wunderlich, 1963.

Hilger, Gustav. *Wir und der Kreml: Deutsch-sowjetische Beziehungen 1918–1941*. Berlin-Frankfurt: Metzger, 1956.

Hirsch, Julius. *Die deutsche Währungsfrage*. Jena: Fischer, 1924.

Hobson, J. A. *The Economics of Reparation*. London: Allen & Unwin, 1921.

Hoefer, Karl. *Oberschlesien in der Aufstandszeit*. Berlin: Mittler, 1938.

Hoffmann, Walther G. *Das Wachstum der deutschen Wirtschaft seit der Mitte des 19. Jahrhunderts*. Berlin: Springer, 1965.

Hofmann, Hanns Hubert. *Der Hitlerputsch*. Munich: Nymphenburger Verlag, 1961.

House, Edward M., and Seymour, Charles, eds. *What Really Happened at Paris*. New York: Scribner's, 1921.

Hunt, Richard N. *German Social Democracy 1918–1933*. New Haven, Conn.: Yale University Press, 1964.

Jenny, Frédéric. *La capacité et les moyens de payement de l'Allemagne* (pamphlet). Paris: Revue politique et parlementaire, 1922.

Jordan, W. M. *Great Britain, France, and the German Problem 1918–1939*. London: Oxford University Press, 1943.

Jouhaux, Léon. *Notre politique des réparations* (pamphlet). Paris: Confédération général du travail, 1923.

Kaeckenbeeck, Georges S. *The International Experience of Upper Silesia*. London: Oxford University Press, 1942.

Kennan, George F. *Russia and the West under Lenin and Stalin*. London: Hutchinson, 1961.

Kessler, Harry. *Gesichter und Zeiten: Erinnerungen*. Berlin: S. Fischer, 1962.

———. *Tagebücher 1918–1937*. Frankfurt: Insel, 1961.

Keynes, John Maynard. *The Economic Consequences of the Peace*. New York: Harcourt, Brace & Howe, 1920.

———. *Essays in Biography*. London: Macmillan & Co., 1933.

———. *Essays in Persuasion*. New York: Harcourt, Brace, 1932.

———. "The Experts Reports, 1: The Dawes Report," and "The Experts Reports, 2: The McKenna Report." *The Nation and The Athenaeum* 35 (1924): 40–41 and 76–77.

———. *A Revision of the Treaty*. New York: Harcourt, Brace, 1922.

———; Ohlin, Bertil; and Rueff, Jacques. "The German Transfer Problem" and debate on subject. *Economic Journal* 39 (1929): 1–7, 172–82, and 388–408.

Kimmich, Christoph M. *The Free City: Danzig and German Foreign Policy 1919–1934*. New Haven, Conn.: Yale University Press, 1968.

Kindleberger, Charles P. *International Economics.* 3rd ed. Homewood, Ill.: Irwin, 1963.

Klass, Gert von. *Hugo Stinnes.* Tübingen: Wunderlich, 1958.

Klemperer, Klemens von. *Germany's New Conservatism.* Princeton, N.J.: Princeton University Press, 1957.

Laubach, Ernst. "Die Politik der Kabinette Wirth 1921–1922" (with an appendix containing press comment on the major issues). Dissertation, Philipps-Universität, Marburg, 1966.

————. *Die Politik der Kabinette Wirth 1921–1922.* Historische Studien, vol. 402. Lübeck-Hamburg: Matthiesen, 1968. (The published version of the above dissertation, without the press opinion appendix.)

Laufenberger, Henry. *Comment l'Allemagne paiera-t-elle?* (pamphlet). Paris: Documents Jeune Patron, 1946.

Launay, Louis. *M. Loucheur* (pamphlet). St. Cloud: Éditions de Bourse et République, 1925.

Lescure, Jean. *Le Problème des réparations.* Paris: Plon, 1922.

Lewis, William A. *Economic Survey 1919–1939.* London: Allen & Unwin, 1949.

Leyrette, Jean. "The Foreign Policy of Poincaré: France and Great Britain in Relation with the German Problem 1919–1924." Dissertation, Oxford University, 1955.

Liebe, Werner. *Die Deutschnationale Volkspartei 1918–1924.* Düsseldorf: Droste, 1956.

Lloyd George, David. *Memoirs of the Peace Conference,* vol. 2. New Haven, Conn.: Yale University Press, 1939.

————. *The Truth about Reparations and War Debts.* New York: Doubleday, Doran, 1932.

Loewenberg, Peter Jacob. "Walther Rathenau and German Society." Dissertation, University of California, Berkeley, 1966.

Louis Loucheur 1872–1931. St. Paul, Minn.: Les Moulineaux, 1931.

Luckau, Alma. *The German Delegation at the Paris Peace Conference.* New York: Columbia University Press, 1941.

Lüke, Rolf E. *Von der Stabilisierung zur Krise.* Basel-Zurich: Polygraphischer Verlag, 1958.

Lumm, Karl von. *Karl Helfferich als Währungspolitiker und Gelehrter.* Leipzig: Hirschfeld, 1926.

Lütge, Friedrich. *Deutsche Sozial- und Wirtschaftsgeschichte.* Berlin-Heidelberg-New York: Springer, 1966.

McFaydean, Andrew. *Reparation Reviewed.* London: Benn, 1930.

Mangoldt, Ursula von. *Auf der Schwelle zwischen Gestern und Morgen.* Weilheim, Bavaria: Barth, 1963.

Mann, Thomas. *Doctor Faustus.* New York: Alfred E. Knopf, 1960.

Mantoux, Étienne. *The Carthaginian Peace or the Economic Consequences of Mr. Keynes.* London: Oxford University Press, 1946.

Mayer, Arno J. *Political Origins of the New Diplomacy, 1917–1918.* New Haven, Conn.: Yale University Press, 1959.

Meissner, Otto. *Staatssekretär unter Ebert-Hindenburg-Hitler.* Hamburg: Hoffmann u. Campe, 1950.

Mendershausen, Horst. *Two Postwar Recoveries of the German Economy.* Amsterdam: North Holland, 1954.

Mills, John Saxon. *The Genoa Conference.* London: Hutchinson, 1922.

Moellendorff, Wichard von. *Konservativer Sozialismus.* Hamburg: Hanseatische Verlagsanstalt, 1932.

Moeller van den Bruck, Artur. *Das dritte Reich.* Hamburg: Hanseatische Verlagsanstalt, 1931.

Mohler, Armin. *Die konservative Revolution in Deutschland 1918–1932.* Stuttgart: F. Vorwerk, 1950.

Mommsen, Wilhelm, and Franz, Günther. *Die deutschen Parteiprogramme 1918–1930.* Leipzig-Berlin: Teubner, 1931.

Morsey, Rudolf. *Die deutsche Zentrumspartei 1917–1923.* Düsseldorf: Droste, 1966.

Mosse, George L. *The Crisis of German Ideology.* New York: Grosset & Dunlop, 1964.

Moulton, Harold G., and Pasvolsky, Leo. *War Debts and World Prosperity.* Washington: Brookings Institution, 1932.

Neumann, Gustav A. *Rathenaus Reparationspolitik.* Leipzig: Helion, 1930.

Nicolson, Harold. *Curzon: The Last Phase.* London: Constable, 1937.

———. *Peacemaking 1919.* London: Constable, 1933.

Noël, Pierre. *L'Allemagne et les réparations.* Paris: Payot, 1924.

Noske, Gustav. *Von Kiel bis Kapp.* Berlin: Verlag für Politik u. Wirtschaft. 1920.

Owen, Frank. *Tempestuous Journey: Lloyd George—His Life and Times.* London: Hutchinson, 1954.

Preller, Ludwig. *Sozialpolitik in der Weimarer Republik.* Stuttgart: Mittebach, 1949.

Prest, A. R. "National Income of the United Kingdom 1876–1946." *Economic Journal* 58 (1948): 31–62.

Rabenau, Friedrich von. *Seeckt: Aus seinem Leben 1918–1936.* Leipzig: Hase u. Koehler, 1940.

Rasmuss, Hainer. *Die Januarkämpfe 1919 in Berlin* (pamphlet). Berlin: Verlag des Ministeriums für nationale Verteidigung, n.d.

Reichardt, Fritz. *Andreas Hermes.* Neuwied am Rhein: Raiffeisendruckerei, 1953.

Reichert, Jakob. *Rathenaus Reparationspolitik.* Berlin: Scherl, 1922.

Roesler, Konrad. *Die Finanzpolitik des deutschen Reiches im ersten Weltkrieg.* Berlin: Duncker u. Humblot, 1967.

Ronde, Hans. *Von Versailles bis Lausanne.* Stuttgart-Cologne: Kohlhammer, 1950.

Rosen, Friedrich. *Aus einem diplomatischen Wanderleben,* vols. 3–4. Wiesbaden: Limes, 1959.

Rosenbaum, Kurt. *Community of Fate: German-Soviet Diplomatic Relations 1922–1928.* Syracuse, N.Y.: Syracuse University Press, 1965.

Rosenberg, Arthur. *A History of the Weimar Republic.* London: Methuen, 1936.

Salewski, Michael. *Entwaffnung und Militärkontrolle in Deutschland 1919–1927.* Munich: R. Oldenbourg, 1966.

Salin, Edgar. *Das Reparationsproblem.* 2 vols. Berlin: Reimar Hobbing, 1928.

Salomon, Ernst von. *Answers of Ernst von Salomon (Fragebogen).* London: Putnam, 1954, 1st ed. 1951.

————. *Nahe Geschichte.* Berlin: Rowohlt, 1936.

————. *The Outlaws.* London: Jonathan Cape, 1931.

————. *Das Reich im Werden* (pamphlet). Frankfurt: Moritz Diesterweg, 1938.

Sauvy, Alfred. *Histoire économique de la France entre les deux guerres.* 2 vols. Paris: Fayard, 1965–67.

Schacht, Hjalmar. *My First 76 Years.* London: Allan Wingate, 1955.

Scheffbuch, Adolf. *Helfferich: Ein Kämpfer für Deutschlands Grösse.* Stuttgart: Belfer, 1934.

Scheidemann, Philipp. *Memoiren eines Sozialdemokraten.* 2 vols. Dresden: Reissner, 1928.

Schiff, Viktor. *So War Es in Versailles.* Berlin: Dietz-Nachfolger, 1929.

Schmid, Royal J. *Versailles and the Ruhr: Seedbed of World War II.* The Hague: Martinius Nijhoff, 1968.

Schulz, Gerhard. *Zwischen Demokratie und Diktatur,* vol. 1. Berlin: Walter de Gruyter, 1963.

Schwab, Maurice. *La question de la Ruhr* (pamphlet). Nantes: Imprimeries du Commerce, 1923.

Schwartz, Albert. *Die Weimarer Republik.* Konstanz: Athenaion, 1958.

Seymour, Charles. *Woodrow Wilson and the World War.* New Haven, Conn.: Yale University Press, 1921.

Simon, Hugo F. *Reparation und Wiederaufbau.* Berlin: Heymanns, 1925.

Simonds, Frank H. *How Europe Made Peace without America.* New York: Doubleday, Page, 1927.

Sontheimer, Kurt. *Antidemokratisches Denken in der Weimarer Republik.* Munich: Nymphenburger Verlagshandlung, 1962.

Spengler, Oswald. *Preussentum und Sozialismus.* Munich: C. H. Beck, 1920.

Steinbömer, Gustav. *Herren und Narren der Welt.* Munich: Paul List, 1954.

Stern, Fritz. *The Politics of Cultural Despair.* Berkeley: University of California Press, 1961.

Stern, Howard. "The Organisation Consul." *Journal of Modern History* 35 (1961): 20–32.

Stolper, Gustav. *Deutsche Wirtschaft seit 1870.* Brought up to date by Karl Hauser and Knut Borchardt. Tübingen: Mohr, 1964.

Stresemann, Gustav. *His Diaries, Letters, and Papers,* vol. 1. Edited by Eric Sutton. London: Macmillan & Co., 1935.

————. *Vermächtnis: Der Nachlass in drei Banden,* vol. 1. Edited by Henry Bernhard. Berlin: Ullstein, 1932.

Studenski, Paul. *The Income of Nations.* New York: New York University Press, 1958.

Suarez, Georges. *Briand: Sa vie—son oeuvre.* Vol. 5: *L'artisan de la paix 1918–1923.* Paris: Plon, 1941.

Tardieu, André. *The Truth about the Treaty.* Indianapolis: Bobbs-Merrill, 1921.

Taylor, A. J. P. *The Origins of the Second World War.* New York: Atheneum, 1962.

Techow, Ernst-Werner. *"Gemeiner Mörder?!" Das Rathenau-Attentat.* Leipzig: Verlag für nationale Literatur u. Geschichte, 1934.

Temperley, H. W. V., ed. *A History of the Peace Conference of Paris.* 6 vols. London: Oxford University Press, 1920–24.

Tschuppik, Karl. *Ludendorff: The Tragedy of a Military Mind.* Boston-New York: Houghton Mifflin, 1932.

Turner, Henry Ashby. *Stresemann and the Politics of the Weimar Republic.* Princeton, N.J.: Princeton University Press, 1963.

Vergé, Armand. *La bataille des réparations 1919–1924.* Paris: Dunod, 1924.

Vermeil, Edmond. *Doctrinaires de la révolution allemande.* Paris: Sorlot, 1918.

Waite, Robert G. L. *Vanguard of Nazism: The Free Corps Movement in Postwar Germany 1918–23.* Cambridge, Mass.: Harvard University Press, 1952.

Weill-Raynal, Étienne. *Les réparations allemandes et la France.* 3 vols. Paris: Nouvelles éditions latines, 1938–47.

Wheeler-Bennett, John W. *The Nemesis of Power.* New York: St. Martin's Press, 1954.

————. *Wooden Titan.* New York: Morrow, 1936.

————. *The Wreck of Reparations.* New York: Morrow, 1933.

————, and Latimer, Hugh. *Information on the Reparation Settlement.* London: Allen & Unwin, 1930.

Wirth, Joseph. *Reden während der Kanzlerschaft.* Berlin: Germania, 1925.

Wolff, Theodor. *Through Two Decades.* London: Heinemann, 1936.

Woytinsky, W. S. *Die Welt in Zahlen,* vol. 1. Berlin: R. Mosse, 1925.

————, and Woytinsky, E. S. *World Commerce and Government.* New York: Twentieth Century Fund, 1955.

Wüest, Erich. *Der Vertrag von Versailles im Licht und Schatten der Kritik: Die Kontroverse um seine wirtschaftlichen Auswirkungen.* Zurich: Europa, 1962.

Zimmerman, Ludwig. *Deutsche Aussenpolitik in der Ära der Weimarer Republik.* Göttingen: Musterschmidt, 1958.

Zsigmond, Laslo. *Zur deutschen Frage 1918–1923.* Translated by P. Félix. Budapest: Akadémiai Kiado, 1964.

Zwoch, Gerhard. "Die Erfüllungs- und Verständigungspolitik der Weimarer Republik und die deutsche öffentliche Meinung." Dissertation, Christian-Albrechts-Universität zu Kiel, 1950.

Press

Newspapers

Vorwärts, Berlin, 1921–22
Vossische Zeitung, Berlin, 1921–22

The Times, London, 1921–22

Le Figaro, Paris, 1921–22
Le Temps, Paris, 1921–22

Periodicals

Deutsche Rundschau, Berlin, 1921–22
Simplicissimus, Munich, 1918–22
Sozialistische Monatshefte, Berlin, 1918–22

Revue des deux mondes, Paris, 1920–22

Index

THE JOHNS HOPKINS PRESS

Designed by Arlene J. Sheer

Composed in Times Roman text and display by Monotype Composition Company

Printed on 60 lb. Perkins and Squire, R by Universal Lithographers, Inc.

Bound in Riverside Linen by L. H. Jenkins, Inc.

DATE DUE

NO 8'82			